Damned Old Crank

A Self-Portrait of E.W. Scripps

Jerry Clemens Photo

E. W. Scripps on his yacht the "Kemah" off Singapore in 1924, two years before his death.

Damned Old Crank

A Self-Portrait of E. W. Scripps
Drawn from his Unpublished Writings

EDITED BY
CHARLES R. McCABE

GREENWOOD PRESS, PUBLISHERS
WESTPORT, CONNECTICUT

Originally published in 1951
by Harper & Brothers Publishers, New York

Reprinted with the permission
of Harper & Row, Publishers, New York

First Greenwood Reprinting 1971

Library of Congress Catalogue Card Number 77-156209

SBN 8371-6159-2

Printed in the United States of America

CONTENTS

INTRODUCTORY NOTE vii

I. *A Damned Old Crank* 1
II. *Independence for a Penny* 13
III. *The Laziest Boy in the County* 28
IV. *The Value of Being a Nuisance* 41
V. *I Buck My Big Brother* 58
VI. *Bad Habits, I: Wicked Women, etc.* 71
VII. *Bad Habits, II: Alcohol, Nicotine, etc.* 85
VIII. *Some Outlandish Rules for Making Money* 94
IX. *I Kill Henry Chisholm* 113
X. *Shooting Irons and the Blair Eye* 124
XI. *My Toughest Customer: Myself* 129
XII. *Undialectical Materialism* 135
XIII. *"Whatever Is, Is Wrong"* 142
XIV. *I Hire Some Christians* 153
XV. *Marriage Is Work* 164
XVI. *Letter to a Young Editor* 170
XVII. *The High Cost of Ignorance* 180
XVIII. *I Break with Jim Scripps* 188
XIX. *I Buck the A. P.* 198
XX. *I Buck the Advertisers* 210

XXI. *The Case of Roy W. Howard* 217
XXII. *Is Honest Journalism Possible?* 222
XXIII. *Highbrow Scientists and the Ignorant Public* 231
XXIV. *Plain Talk from an Old Journalist* 237
XXV. *Muscles, Mind and Opportunity* 245
XXVI. *Don't Grow Old Gracefully* 252

INTRODUCTORY NOTE

EDWARD WYLLIS SCRIPPS, the thirteenth child of an English immigrant father, was born in 1854 on a Rushville, Illinois, farm and died of apoplexy aboard his yacht, the Ohio, in Monrovia Bay, Liberia, on a hot spring night in 1926, following a dinner which included energetic conversation with his guest, the American consul, and too many cigars. He died distant from friends and family, surrounded only by employees. He was buried at sea.

The broad lineaments of his career are easy to record. E. W. Scripps served a useful apprenticeship in newspaper work under his half brother, James E. Scripps, founder and owner of the Detroit *Evening News.*

Early in life he broke with James E., and created from scratch one of the great news enterprises of the world. At his death he left to his only living son the controlling interest in daily newspapers in fifteen states, the United Press Associations, the Newspaper Enterprise Association (N.E.A.), Acme Newsphotos, United Feature Syndicate, and a proliferation of newspaper mechanical and supply properties. Among the newspapers were the Cleveland *Press,* the Cincinnati *Post,* the Toledo *News-Bee,* the Columbus *Citizen,* the Pittsburgh *Press,* and the San Francisco *News.*

Scripps was the principal founder and supporter of the Scripps Institution of Oceanography at La Jolla, California; the Scripps Foundation for Research in Population Problems, of Miami University, Miami, Ohio; and the Science News Service of Washington, D.C. During his lifetime the Scripps concern never waxed so great as that of either Hearst or Pulitzer; but five years after his death his successors purchased the choicest of the Pulitzer properties, the New York *World*. Since then, his properties have shown, in the main, a healthy and steady growth.

Sound management principles and editorial verve, inherited from the founder, have been largely responsible for this growth. Scripps believed in giving his partners and employees their head (up to a point) so long as he retained fifty-one per cent, or control, of the several enterprises. In return for his fifty-one per cent, the concern got his unrelenting editorial integrity and acute, unorthodox business sense.

Scripps was an active newsroom man for only a brief period of his busy life. He became an editorial employee on the Detroit *Evening News* around 1875, and remained tied to an editorial desk (by gossamer, and with two years out for a health-restoring European trip), until 1890. During this year, after a quarrel with James E., he quit on-the-scene newspapering. A combination of misanthropy, raw nerves and family exacerbations drove him as far away from his kind as was possible without loss of his nationality. He built Miramar Ranch on an arid, windswept mesa about sixteen miles from San Diego, in the final southwest corner of the United States. Save for an interval during World War I, when he attempted to resume active editorial direction of the concern in Washington, D.C., he lived in San Diego until 1920. Then he withdrew again, and even farther. That final withdrawal, so like that of the elder Pulitzer, was to a series of yachts where the owner was truly a potentate. The same pressures that had driven him to San Diego, intensified by age and wavering health, drove him to the sea. To the sea, where he could die decently, and proudly, surrounded not by family or friends, but by people on the payroll.

In 1915, at the request of his sister, Miss Ellen Browning Scripps, E. W. made two attempts at autobiography. They are altogether wooden, and were plainly put down out of a sense of duty. Scripps was always much more at home with ideas than with personal narrative. Yet there were times when he felt strongly that his biography should be written and published. He even chose from among his employees one biographer, but later cast him into exterior darkness because his treatment of materials made available to him was "too conventional." His great fear was that a biographer would "select only that material which is creditable to me, and that which is conventionally respectable. . . ." In his will he implied an embargo on the publication of his private papers until his grandchildren were grown.

This time has been reached. It is the feeling of the Scripps grandchildren, shared by the editor, that a useful first-person story can be put together from his unpublished autobiographical writings, his letters and his stream of disquisitions. Scripps felt, as did H. G. Wells, that any autobiographical work should be a research into a life rather than an apology for the subject's actions. That standard, plus the desire to provide an interesting narrative, has guided the editor in handling the mass of unpublished material made available by the Scripps family. To provide a more or less connected narrative the material has been, of necessity, freely edited.

Scripps really "wrote" almost nothing. In his creative period, he dictated everything, and his work shows both the virtues and defects of that method. It is readable and fast-paced. It has great vitality, although it lacks literary "quality." Like Henry James, Scripps on occasion got so wound up in his spoken periods that it is difficult to unravel his meaning. He seldom reviewed or corrected any of his writings. The process, not the result, was interesting. They were something he had to get out of him; that was all. When he was writing at Miramar he told his children, around table, what he was up to, and occasionally would read some of his writings to the family. Less frequently he would reach into an old black steel box where he kept his manuscripts heavily locked and declaim to some of his respected cronies like Clarence Darrow, Judge Ben B. Lindsay, or the young Max Eastman. Mostly, however, his writings were something said to secretaries, when the irritation to his active mind became so great that relief was imperative.

Scripps did not commence serious writing until he was in his early fifties. His description of his youth in the *Self-Portrait* is that of a man already old—very old, in his view. Agonized self-questionings evident in early letters (in the 1870's) to his sisters Annie and Ellen Browning, are lost in the recollection of the older man. As far as can be judged, he did not want them in the face he wished to show to his children and, inferentially, to the public. It may be felt, without at all impugning E. W.'s honesty as an autobiographer, that he was rather less the Roaring Boy of his memory than a lonely, often callow, youth, fighting upstream against a hated humanity. Consider, for instance, his claim that he consumed for many years a gallon of whiskey a day—a claim that finds no support either in the alcoholic studies made since his death, or in the experience of topers. But most men are more revealing in the exaggerations and untruths they tell about themselves than when speaking honestly.

The *Self-Portrait* has confined itself as much as possible to Scripps himself. His relatives and associates enter only when they contribute to the development of his own story. E. W. Scripps fussed a good deal with economics, science and ranching, but of these things there is little here. The *Self-Portrait* is of a newspaperman and newspaper owner, and of his education. Scripps was incapable, by nature and inheritance, of the cultivated ennui of his contemporary Henry Adams, yet the American scene of the late nineteenth and early twentieth centuries forced similarly pessimistic conclusions on both these sharp-eyed observers.

From his "retirement" until his death, E. W. Scripps never relinquished control of his concern, although he turned over its active management to his eldest son, James G., in 1908, and to his youngest son, Robert Paine Scripps, in 1920. He ran the whole show as an absentee landlord, receiving at Miramar brief regular statements of the financial health of his dependencies. He issued occasional incisive ukases to liquidate an unsatisfactory venture, or to sharpen a policy gone dull by inattention, inertia or corruption. Yet his thinking was as far from that of a *rentier* as can be imagined. Lincoln Steffens, in his *Autobiography*, reports a Scripps soliloquy:

> I'm a rich man, and that's dangerous, you know. But it isn't just the money that's the risk; it's the living around with other rich men. They get to thinking all alike, and their money not only talks, their money does their thinking too. I come off here on these wide acres at Miramar to get away from my sort; to get away from the rich. So I don't think like a rich man. I think more like a left labor galoot. . . . They talk about the owner of newspapers holding back his editors. It's the other way with me. I get me boys, bright boys, from the classes that read my papers; I give them the editorship and the management, with a part interest in the property, and, say, in a year or so, as soon as the profits begin to come in, they become conservative and I have to boot them back into their class, and even then—corruption? Yes, but it's they that corrupt me and my papers, those bright boys from off the streets.

To keep the boys straight he aimed bullets at their heads, in the form of letters of advice that were as to-the-point as a police warrant. One of these is included in this volume.

The Scripps will gave majority ownership and complete control of a world-wide newspaper barony to Robert, the only living son of E. W. Scripps. Robert died in 1938 (like his father, on a yacht in the middle of the ocean, distant from the product he sold). Ownership and control then passed to the six children of Robert, where it now resides. Eventually the properties will be divided among the children of these children. Scripps made it clear beyond doubt that, until the expiration of the trust he created, he intended his legatees to accept full and final responsibility for every word that went into a Scripps paper, or over a Scripps wire, or into a Scripps clipsheet. He said to them: "Your business is peddling words to people; but they must be the right words, and not the words of rich men talking to the other rich." He left his grandchildren a huge amorphous body of historical, hortatory and even "inspirational" writing, to insure the continued life of the policies that made his papers rich and respected.

Since the death of the founder there has been a growing tendency on the part of his legatees to hand over control of the words they sell to "those bright boys from off the streets." Today an aggressive management makes policy along lines that would have horrified the founder—"their money does their thinking too." This policy is ratified by a supine and largely indifferent ownership. Such third-generation capitulation to the boys who carry the hod is not unknown in other trust-ridden American business enterprises. It is very nearly customary when receipts run over ten million dollars annually. Its appearance in the Scripps organization has led some employees to the wry observation that the founder ought to be called "Whirling Ed."

All his life E. W. Scripps carried on a kind of guerilla warfare against his advertisers, the men who supplied most of the capital with which to put out his newspapers. More than a quarter century before Marshall Field's *PM* appeared in New York, Scripps was publishing a midget daily in Chicago that refused to carry advertising. For his own reasons, Scripps kept from the public the fact that he backed the paper financially. A staff that included reporter Carl Sandburg kept the *Day Book* on the streets for six years, until World War I killed it. At the time of his death he was planning another ad-less paper. To some of his friends he voiced the hope that he would live long enough to see twenty such Scripps papers published in this country.

Scripps' public fame is almost microscopic, in relation to his size, vitality, and contribution to American journalism. This is pretty much the way he wanted it. He was an extraordinarily articulate man; yet the editor has been unable to find among his papers anything published under his signature in any organ less ephemeral than a daily newspaper. There is precious little of that, even. There exist two biographies by old associates and employees, Gilson Gardner and Negley Cochran. Scripps and what he stood for in journalism, are today almost forgotten by those who once knew, and unknown to thousands of younger men of the present-day working press.

Yet his unpublished utterance was copious. He invented a self-conscious art form he called the "disquisition." A Scripps disquisition might deal with the habits of rattlesnakes, the course and nature of socialism, the kind of edible berries he knew in his Illinois childhood; or it might moot heredity vs. environment, or be a letter to his sons, pregnant with advice. The disquisition was somewhere between an interior monologue and a Manchester *Guardian* leader. It is sometimes autobiographical, sometimes the impaling of an absurdity, sometimes getting an elusive set of disparate facts secured beneath the bell jar of his will. Sometimes it is a questing into the infinite. It is an often contradictory form, because Scripps was trying nothing less ambitious than to find a new way of thinking. His distrust of what he heard and read was limitless. He plainly disliked the way other people figured things out, and thought he could do better. Two real literary enthusiasms were Thorstein Veblen and Count Alfred Korzybski. He liked their agnosticism about formal logic—the neat and ordered marching of major premise into minor premise into conclusion.

Yet, despite Miramar and the yachts and a breastplate of cynicism, he could not rid himself altogether of the disquieting waves of feeling that sweep over the life of reason. The disquisitions have ringing affirmations that William Jennings Bryan could have shouted next to uncertainties Pilatean in character. Often, like the unfortunate Roman colonial administrator, Scripps would not wait for answer.

This gives a schizoid character to his utterance. He had two mutually exclusive bulkheads of sentiment. There was what he wrote his editors and told his children. This was the official credo that was needed to maintain the *élan* of his concern, that good in himself that he wanted to give to the people and the country he shunned. On the other hand, there was the private thing, the quest for straight thinking, that fidelity to what has been given you and what you can put out, that can only be called integrity. His editors and the people of the United States *had* to believe in the voracity of capitalists, the well-deep virtue of the workingman, the abiding economic morality play featuring the Big Bad and the Good Little. But for E. W. Scripps personally it could not be that simple. The cynicisms of a hard-bought culture, the enervations of a busy and largely tragic life, and above all, that hot pursuit of straight thinking, left these cheerful intellectual certainties far behind. The "vigorous" journalist can only see one side of a public question. The good "reporter" is supposed to see two. But there are always some few in the business to whom every question is a many-faceted quartz, never twice the same to the searching eye. Early in the game, Scripps lost the power to write cogent newspaper copy. He found he no longer had the ability to cartoon issues, so essential to the practicing journalist.

The *Self-Portrait*, as a consequence, is filled with alternations of rotund faith and hollow doubt. But the doubt is less credible than the faith, in the long run, since the faith was made public and the doubt kept private. His newspapers were always, in season and out of season, for the laboring man and against the employer. The prevailing system was bad and had to be harried ceaselessly. His baiting of the accepted, the conventionally respectable, was bred in the bone. This despite the private doubt of the author and chief propagator of the policy. "Consistency," Scripps would bellow, "is a crime."

In his own view, E. W. Scripps was clearly an able man, an influential man, even clearly a good man; yet he often chose to portray himself as a bit of a bounder. He could address to imaginary young reporters out of a mood of profound discontent these words:

> If the owner of your paper is a gentleman and your immediate chief is a gentleman, it is probable that you will be working on a newspaper that is to have a short life. . . . Why, journalism is big business, pure and simple.

Yet in 1924, in his final legacy to his son, Robert P., to whom he bequeathed sole personal trusteeship of the Scripps interests, he could say:

> I repeat now what I told you when I first launched you on your career: that I would prefer that you should succeed in being in all things a gentleman, according to the real meaning of the word, than that you should vastly increase the money value of my estate.
>
> Being a gentleman, you cannot fail to devote your whole mind and energy to the service of the plain people, who constitute the vast majority of the people of the United States.

And he repeatedly laid down this trinity of rules for his editors: Do no business except at a profit. Violate none of the Ten Commandments. Always serve the interest of the poor and the working classes.

The writings from which this *Self-Portrait* has been drawn extend from 1906 to 1925. Since Scripps's thinking was so much of a piece during this time it has been seldom found necessary, for the purpose of this narrative, to situate the writings chronologically. When necessary it has been done by placing the year of writing in parentheses.

In the decade before his death, Scripps had several disappointing flirtations with biographers and autobiography. His story would not get itself told the way he wanted it. Yet he was not lacking in ideas about how it should be told. He never ceased to believe there was a good story hidden in his forty years' accumulation of business correspondence, disquisitions, letters to working editors, legal records and autobiographical fragments. (One of the main reasons for the painstaking accumulation was to provide that story.) In 1922 he reviewed the mass of his writings, and his life itself. He found the writings "valuable human documents." Of his life: "I am led to believe there is but very little difference between my life's career and that of the meanest and most ignorant, and that of the wisest and most generous of men. . . ." He desired that anyone who wrote of him should, above all, treat him as an organism, as a whole organism—"primarily psychologically, secondarily what we call morally, and incidentally biologically." He told an aspiring biographer:

> To the physiologist the mouth is no more respectable than the anus. To the biographer the meanest and wickedest deed of his subject is no less characteristic than the loftiest and noblest of his deeds—and no more so.
>
> . . . It is my belief that the true story of such a career as mine (or the true story of any other man whose life work has been mean and lowly, or great and courageous) would if it was universally known, be a great stimulant.
>
> . . . There have been no great or strong personalities that have been formative of my character. There have been no great emergencies that have presented unusual opportunities or great difficulties to overcome. There have been no examples to follow. The man in the case has been neither undereducated nor overeducated, neither well-born nor lowly born. He has been neither brave nor a coward. All his writings prove the mediocrity of his mental equipment. All of the latter that he has obtained has been the result of his own effort—effort directed nowhither and for no purpose. Even the instincts, pride and vanity—call them ambition—have been slight forces.
>
> There are millions of boys and young men in this country today who are no whit less well equipped for accomplishment than your subject. William James says in one of his essays, "Any man can do anything he wants to do if he wants to do it bad enough." That means to say that those men who have not accomplished greatly are not only those who would rather dream than think, but those who would rather loaf than labor.

Introductory Note

For permission to engage in this undertaking the editor is indebted to Mrs. Margaret C. Hawkins, widow of Robert P. Scripps, and to Charles E. Scripps, grandson of E. W. Scripps and chairman of the E. W. Scripps Trust. Even greater is the indebtedness to my wife, Margaret Scripps McCabe, who got the idea in the first place.

C. R. McCabe

Miramar, California
August, 1948

Damned Old Crank

A Self-Portrait of E.W. Scripps

I

A Damned Old Crank

IN 1909 a notorious spiritualist came to San Diego and for several days did a thriving business exchanging guesses for the dollars of the credulous. My oldest son, Jim, was just breaking into business in a serious way, and was pretty anxious just then to find out when a business boom was going to set in again and the revenues of our business increase. He went to consult the faker.

It didn't occur to Jim that on account of his own peculiarly large stature, strength of body and habits of dress, coupled with the fact that he was the son of a man who was locally conspicuous, it would be very easy for him to be "tipped-off" to the faker long before he got from the anteroom to the sanctum.

Jim told me something about the interview, but very little. He did tell me how the faker characterized me, his subject's father. Said the faker, "Your father is a crank. In fact, he is a damned old crank."

There are some truths about a man that he does not like to hear, but there are also some truths about himself which are neither unpleasant nor uninstructive. The word "crank" is used to define the character of a man who does not think and act in exactly the same way as the universality of his fellow men.

Damned Old Crank

I am fully entitled, I feel, to the name of "crank" and I have no fault to find with being called an "old crank." As I am almost universally judged to be peculiar, I am condemned as a crank. I am sorry that I am a crank and I am sorry that I am old, and I am sorry that I am condemned as a crank, because if people lived or acted as I do, I believe the world would be a better world. If all people thought and acted as I do, then I would no longer be a crank, and hence people would not pass such judgment on me.

It is very unfortunate for the world that I am a damned crank. It is unfortunate for me that I am an old crank, and that I am old at all. You see, I am sorry for everybody, including myself.

Wherein am I exposed to the public in the matter of my crankiness? There are some things about me that are visible to everybody who knows me. These are some of them:

I wear a full beard when nearly everybody else shaves clean; to that extent, I am willing to appear like a man, and do not, like my fellows, make myself look like a girl.

I wear long boots, and I wear my pants in my boots, and because they are pants—not "trousers"—I give further evidence of being cranky, since most men who are as rich as I am call their lower garments "trousers." I have several good reasons for wearing boots, and wearing them in the way that I do. One of them is that it is easier to get them on and off. By wearing my boots in this fashion I am entirely free from the pest of fleas. I live in the country and tramp over rough ground and through brush and high grass, and by wearing my boots in this manner, I am saved the annoyance of getting my shoes full of loose dirt, pebbles, and sticky things from the grass and brush. But the main and great reason is that by protecting my ankles and the lower part of my legs from exposure to the cold air I frequently avoid taking cold, and because of this trick of mine I do not suffer half as much from colds as do some men who wear low shoes.

I am also cranky in the matter of the rest of my wearing apparel, as all my life I have been too busy with other things of importance to look after my dress much.

I have another cranky symptom: I am a busy man. I haven't much time to waste, and while I am walking I walk fast to save time. When I am driving horses I drive them on the run, and now in these days of automobiles, I get the biggest, and strongest, and fastest, and most durable—that is to say, the most expensive—machines so that I can get over the ground fast and waste but very little time waiting for my chauffeur to patch up a weak, easily crippled machine.

I never go to church or to the theater, or attend any social functions, nor do I listen to public political speeches, nor do I sit on the bleachers watching other men exercise themselves with baseball and football. I do not hunt or play golf. I am really not interested in any of these affairs and I have not time to be. But I play poker, just like common people do, so that in one respect, at least, I am not a crank. At poker I am an average loser, and therein I am like other people and no crank.

Around the poker table all men are equal in every other respect than the capacity to play the game. The boy and the octogenarian; the millionaire and the adventurer; the gentleman, the rogue; the society king and the bummer (providing the bummer has a roll)—all become adversaries, one against all the others, and there is no distinction between the players other than that of the big and the little stack of chips.

Of course, a game of poker is a game of life. He who knows the world, and especially he who knows the business world, can better determine the character—the mental qualities—of another man at the poker table in an hour, than he can anywhere else in a year.

For a period of about twenty-five years I consumed daily enough whiskey to keep three or four men drunk all the time. I broke the habit when I was in middle age. During the period when I drank about a gallon of whiskey a day, I was seldom actually drunk, in the way that word is actually understood. But then, I was seldom sober either.

Although a highly successful businessman, I have never in my life kept a set of books. I don't know anything about bookkeeping. In fact, I regard the usual bookkeeper and the usual set of books kept by businessmen as an intolerable and unbearable nuisance, and a handicap to business.

I am a crank in another respect: I am a successful businessman and yet I know nothing about anybody else's business but my own. I am a businessman; yet I spend most of my time on my farm or my ranch. I am a businessman, and yet the chief part of my life's energies has been devoted to the thoroughly unbusinesslike practice of library reading. For every hour I have devoted to my business I have devoted at least three hours to literature, and on subjects entirely foreign to my own or any other kind of business. This peculiarity of mine, even if I had no other distinguishing marks, would well entitle me to be called a crank.

One reason why it has been so easy for such an all-around chump as I am to make money has been that I have never yet invested any money in anything that my neighbors and acquaintances didn't judge to be fool ventures. I have had all the advantages of being able to get a good start before imitators began to compete with me.

I have always been a joke and butt for ridicule, and I am today.

Give a man a reputation for being a first-class fool and then even with second- or third- or fourth-rate abilities he will have easy sailing.

The loneliness of my life is great. I am hated by the rich for being a renegade, and I am hated by the poor for being rich. I am not wise enough or learned enough to be an acceptable member in the high-brow club. I have learned too many things to make me a comfortable companion of the man in the field, on the street, and in the shop.

A Damned Old Crank

I sometimes think I do not know the real meaning of the word friendship. Perhaps I have never been able to sense the thing. I have felt a tremendous interest in many individuals. I have admired some of these, and have even respected a few. Yet I think my chief interest in my acquaintances has been that of observing and studying them, in noting the underplay of inheritance and environment in the development of each individual. I have obtained considerable satisfaction in watching the effect of causes. How a certain man of my acquaintance will submit to a certain stimulant is a question I have always been asking myself. Needless to say, I have often attempted to apply this stimulant in order to discover results.

Most rich men like to spend money acquiring reputations for being great lovers of humanity; that is to say philanthropists. They seek fame and notoriety. I am a crank because I don't want the reputation for being good or being wise, or any sort of reputation at all. I have so little respect for humanity that I place small value on the respect or admiration or affection of any human being; in fact, I do not respect myself or make any effort to win or keep my own self-respect. Every wise man will admit that I am perfectly right in the low value I place upon fame; that is to say, the respect, the admiration, the love of anything so wretched as a human being. Nevertheless, it is a fact that these men who coincide with me in judgment on the matter are themselves cranks.

I am one of the few newspapermen who happen to know that this country is populated by ninety-five per cent of plain people, and that the patronage of even plain and poor people is worth more to a newspaper owner than the patronage of the wealthy five per cent. So I have always run my business along the line of least resistance and for the greatest profit, and because I have made money more easily than any other newspaper publisher ever did, and made more than all but a few other publishers, I am odd and cranky.

I am likewise cranky in this. First, above all people, I love my wife;

next I love myself and take care of my own material and spiritual comfort; next in the order of my affections come my children; beyond these I love the whole line of my posterity that will extend generation after generation into the future. Now, I have provided for my wife every comfort and happiness that I think she is capable of enjoying. Personally I possess a home, in fact two homes, that are so nearly what I want that I would not exchange either of them for any other residence. I possess more wealth than I need. Beyond this, I own sufficient property to leave my children wealthy when I die—perhaps too wealthy for their own good. Now, I have provided for wife, self and children; what other motive of affection will move me? The only part of my family that I have not provided for is my unborn posterity.

What can I do for posterity? I can do my best to make the world a better world for them to live in, and particularly to make my country a more enjoyable place for them. Owing to my peculiarly fortunate or unfortunate situation in life there is nothing left for me to do except to work for an unborn posterity. Hence, my occupation is an odd one—and because it is odd I am a crank—yes, a damned old crank. If I wasn't old I would have greater need of my services to make life enjoyable for myself, but being old and nearly done with life there is very little more for me to do for myself.

(It is only too evident from the above that I have one element in my character that is common and is universal—I have vanity! This whole essay is nothing but one long holler of boast, no matter what other virtues it may have in the matters of truthfulness and suggested philosophy.)

There is a story of a wealthy man who had retired from the hurly-burly of the world to a home in the outskirts of a village in the New England mountains. The only occupation of this man was to minister to the welfare of the neighboring community, collectively and individually. His whole life seemed to be one of service.

He was once asked why he never came in contact with the persons he served, why he continued to live alone in his big house on the hill. "Oh," he replied, "I love human beings well enough to die for them. But I do not think I love them enough to live with them."

I often think of this man, this crank. I believe he was a real character. I believe I thoroughly understand his attitude. I cannot truthfully say that I have ever felt a warm glow of pleasure at meeting any man or woman whom I had known in the past or who was, for the time being, on intimate terms with me.

For a long time I have been taking stock of myself, or rather, of my institution. By analysis I discovered that my institution represents 1/10,000 of all the wealth in the United States. By analysis, I have found that I am one of the thousand richest men in the United States.

I have learned the political power, and the something-more-than-political power—let us call it social power—of my institution.

By reason of its good repute and, I venture to say, wise conduct, it has won such a position of power in this country that if there were ninety-nine other men placed as I am—that is to say, holding an equal amount of power—each of these men holding other stations—say, on the bench, or as great political leaders, as scientific men, or what not—with the whole hundred of us acting together we could, and would, rule this country, absolutely.

My conceit has gone so far as to cut this number in half.

This being the case—and I claim it to be the case—I count that I am at least two per cent responsible for all that is good or ill in the management of this great nation.

Having in myself so great a power for good or evil, I have not been able to disabuse my mind, much as I have sought to do so, of the idea that a very grave responsibility is at present resting upon my shoulders, and soon enough is to be resting upon the shoulders of my successor or successors.

I have no right to any of these things that I possess, either wealth or political influence, unless I am both able and anxious to bear full responsibility.

My conceit does not weigh me down oppressively. It causes me no loss of sleep, and perhaps not enough heartburning and anxiety.

(It has been shown that in the recent national election of 1916 when Woodrow Wilson defeated Charles Evans Hughes, my personality, as exhibited through the instrument I had created, had had a greater influence in deciding who should be president than had the combined force of thousands, and even tens of thousands, of other individuals. This being the case, acting as an individual through society, I had placed myself in a position of great power and influence, and even authority, in and over the nation.)

I am morally certain that there are not living today one hundred men in the United States who have built up as large a business institution as my own.

The purpose of the Scripps newspaper institution never was, never should be, and never can be to run newspapers or other businesses for the purpose of making money. The foundation principle of this institution, as far as money goes, has been, is, and must be to make money in order to perform a great and increasingly greater public service.

For thirty years and more I have watched and studied the great and popular newspaper, the immediate and the future effect of its teaching. I believe that few people aside from myself have any idea of the tremendous, the almost invincible power and force of the daily press. I am one of those who believe that at least in America the press rules the country; it rules its politics, its religion, its social practice. I believe that if all the newspaper editors of the United States were of one mind on any one matter on what the public ought to do, and if they had the courage of their convictions, it would only be a question of a short time before the nation as a whole would think as these editors think and do that which these editors think it ought to do.

Yet so great a crank am I that I constantly doubt the assumptions on which my whole life has been built. I sometimes think that I am only one of the blind leading the blind.

By degrees, some years ago, I lost my facility to write matter for my own papers which would attract the attention and the interest of my public.

I had become afflicted with a capacity to see not only both sides, but many sides, of the various questions in which the public was interested. I lost many of my convictions. It became difficult for me to be a partisan of any man or any principle. I never lost my emotional characteristics. My instincts of sympathy were constantly running counter to my reasoning. My instincts prompted me to take one course of action. My reason prompted me to take the reverse attitude. I grew to doubt the correctness of my own reasoning. Logic was no guide to me because logic has to depend, not upon proved facts, but upon hypotheses. And hypotheses are only assumptions, as likely to be wrong as right. Statistics may be used to prove anything. So can logic. But I was a journalist and committed to my calling.

I determined to submit to pure instinct as my guide. I willingly submitted myself to a course guided by instinct.

But I became unable to write effectively for the public on subjects in which the people were interested and this because—well, because, perhaps, I knew too much of the fallibility of my instincts. I became dependent upon others to do the writing for my papers. The success of my journals depended upon the good will of my constituency. Therefore, I deliberately selected men to write for my papers—and to edit them—whose instincts, whose motives, were identical with those that were my own during my youth.

I did not choose as my editors and writers men who had similar knowledge to or more knowledge than myself. I recognized, in fact, that not only is a little knowledge a dangerous thing for a journalist, but a great deal of knowledge is also dangerous. A great deal of knowledge on the part of an editor is not a good thing for the newspaper business!

I admit there was a period of several years during which my mind was greatly confused. During this period I thoroughly suspected myself of being a hypocrite. I felt that perhaps I was only playing the game, and that for a selfish purpose. In time I began to realize that, after all, the duty of a journalist was not so much to be a leader of the people but to be a witness whose duty was to tell the truth, the whole truth and nothing but the truth and leave the people to weigh the evidence and decide for themselves what was right and what was wrong.

I was once a democrat, a believer in democracy. I believed that the best government should be that which depended on the popular vote. In time I began to doubt this. One reason why I am so hopeless and so pessimistic about the practicability of democracy is that my own observations have taught me that it is impossible for any man to be burdened with wealth, office or prestige without losing nearly all sympathy with the proletariat and without losing all of his democracy.

When I was a young man I hated the capitalists as much as ever did a follower of Karl Marx. Later when I discovered I was a capitalist—I discovered I was a millionaire in 1895—I confronted an embarrassing situation. I had to justify myself. The way of my justification was this: I assumed and proved to my own satisfaction that every capitalist had been elected to his position just as much as any political ruler had been elected.

I argued that I and other capitalists had never had any power to compel any man to work for us against his will. Nor had we ever had the power to compel other capitalists, large or small, to place in our keeping, through stocks and bonds, their capital. The money and the labor that the capitalist gathers together to serve his interests is freely and voluntarily offered to him.

The workingman, to whose service I always consider it my duty to devote myself, has, to a large extent by my advice and prompting, organized into a great and powerful army that is using its power to affect politics and industry. The workingman, because he has been a workingman, is necessarily ignorant in matters political and economic. Being ignorant, he is self-confident and knows naught of his power vastly to injure himself as well as all of his fellows in the nation.

While I suppose there are really no capitalists who want to destroy labor, there are many laborers who want to destroy capital, although perhaps the majority of laborers are too indifferent to their own welfare to have any thoughts on the future of capital.

Too many capitalists really wish to, and are striving to, reduce labor to the position of practically dependent slaves. And there are too many capitalists who are unable to comprehend that their own existence depends upon the support of willing labor.

To what extent have I contributed to this class warfare? Have I not, in conjunction with others, overdone things in the matter of inciting labor to organize and unite and become strong? And to what extent have we inspired labor to make unreasonable and impossible demands?

Have I not been really a demagogue? Not in the worst sense of the word. Not for selfish and personal reasons, but through ignorance and thoughtlessness. A *fool* philanthropist may do more harm than the most unprincipled egoist.

But "birds of a feather flock together." Once I was a poor man and hated the capitalists. Now I am a capitalist and I see the other side of the question.

But I am no more sure that my bias today is to be depended upon than I am that my bias of a generation and a half ago was wrong.

I am still blind. I am unfitted to lead.

Can I even depend upon myself to be a fair witness on the stand: one capable of telling the truth, the whole truth and nothing but the truth?

Yet no matter how rich I was, or how doubtful, there was never a time when I told my editors and my sons anything other than: the job of my newspapers is, and must continue to be, to serve the interests of the working class above everything else.

Was there ever such a damned old crank?

II

Independence for a Penny

A PENNY MARKED the turning point in my career.

It was an English penny. One of those big, heavy, copper disks.

Who was I and what was I that a penny should have made so much of me, so much of happiness and misery for me? The answer is simple. I was nobody at all. That is to say, nobody that anybody else would consider anybody.

It was early in the spring of 1878 that the penny began its magic work. Where? At a crossing of Oxford Road in London not more than a few hundred yards from Marble Arch.

I was not quite twenty-four years of age. I was lodging at a small house opposite the house where my grandfather, once publisher of the London *Literary Gazette,* lived. My father and most of my uncles and aunts were born there.

I was a farm boy from the middle lands of the Mississippi Valley, in England as a traveling companion of my brother George, who was fifteen years older than myself. Earlier that year in Detroit George met with a misadventure in one of his erotic pursuits. I found it was going to take some time to close the case, and advised George he had better calculate on staying away from Detroit for six months or a year.

I suggested that he make a trip to England. Through the death of one of his aunts there, he had recently inherited about a thousand pounds. His trip to collect this inheritance would be a plausible enough excuse for his absence from the Detroit *News,* where we were both then employed by my eldest brother James.

George was reluctant about undertaking the trip alone. Finally he proposed that, if I would go along with him, we could have a six months' trip and he would bear all the expenses. That looked good to me, and I accepted the proposition. I turned over my office as city editor to my successor, and arranged for money and traveling expenses, so that, in a few days, we were off for New York, where we took a ship for England.

My brother, like myself, had been a farmer's boy. He laid the foundation of his own fortune as a farmer. He was past thirty-five years of age when James and I induced him to join us in Detroit to go into the newspaper business. On the *News* he had prospered.

As city editor I was not only earning a fair-sized salary but I had established a little business of my own from which I got an income several times larger than my newspaper salary. I was not a poor boy. In fact, I was well enough able to travel on my own hook. But like a great many other men of my race and family I was thrifty. To enjoy this trip abroad at the expense of another was attractive.

Now George was extremely averse to tipping hotel servants, railway porters, cabmen, etc. He knew nothing of the manners and customs of hotels and restaurants. Perhaps he had never given a tip to a hotel servant or a Pullman porter in his life. I doubt if he ever rode on a Pullman car until I joined him to make this trip to Europe. I knew the earnings received by English servants were either small or nil—sometimes, even, the servants paid to get their jobs—and their earnings consisted almost entirely of tips.

No sooner had we arrived at Liverpool than a very embarrassing situation arose. My brother would bargain for and select the hotel rooms (always the cheapest) and it was he who paid the bills. It was he who neglected to tip the boots, the chambermaid, the waiter and the porter. The payment of even moderate tips involved considerable outlay, perhaps not less than twenty or twenty-five per cent of our hotel bills. These I paid covertly. Perhaps because of the very meagerness of the tips that I could afford to pay, the hotel servants would generally waylay us at our departure, making the pretense that something was still due them. I was able to pass through them and look them in the face unashamed, something that I could never do under any other conditions.

There was one class of people that George hated more than any other, and they were the London street sweepers. That was the very class of people that had the biggest pull on my sympathies.

On a certain morning in the very early spring of 1878 my brother and I left our lodgings for a walk toward the City. When we came to Oxford Street we found it covered with mud slush. All over the city where there were street crossings, the sweepers had their stations, and with their coarse brooms swept a path form one side of the street to the other. They kept it pretty clean. Not everyone tipped these street sweepers, but everybody who was somebody did slip them a small tip, probably a penny or halfpenny. And I considered myself somebody.

George was always diffident and backward. In passing through a crowd he would always fall behind to let me elbow a passage through. In fact, wherever we went, instead of walking abreast of me, he would always follow a step or two behind.

It happened that day I did not have any halfpennies in my pocket, but I had a number of pennies and, as I passed a sweeper, I handed him one. My brother observed it. No sooner had we crossed the street than he hurried up to me and commenced to scold me for throwing money away. He thought the penny had come from the common purse, which was really his purse. Then and there, as we were walking along Oxford Road, we had a quarrel. We went into a full discussion of the tipping system. I told him a man who went into a hotel and did not tip the waiters could be compared to a man who employed a servant and defrauded him of his wages.

I was very sore. In the afternoon I broke away from George and returned to my lodgings. I sat in our parlor ruminating that even a few weeks spent in Europe under these conditions would be intolerable. George came back later, and he too was sulky and angry.

I abused him again for his meanness and his stinginess and pointed out to him that it would be impossible for me to continue the trip with him if he continued in his conduct.

"Well, what are you going to do about it. Who's got the money, and how are you going to get home?" he asked, and laughed sardonically.

Then for the first time I told him that I had prepared myself before leaving America for any emergency that might arise, and that I had several hundred dollars of my own sewed up in my vest pocket, quite sufficient to carry me back.

He became a little scared when he saw that I was determined, and that I was not merely threatening him. He had not yet collected his legacy. He had to go some distance from London down to Bristol where he was to present his claim. To make the long trip back alone was more than he could endure.

I even went so far as to tell him that I was a gentleman and proposed to act like a gentleman under all circumstances, and that, as a gentleman, I could not refuse to pay for the services of servants, and to give small alms to the needy. I stated my intention of breaking the trip off right then and there and going home.

When George saw that I was really angry, he immediately began to placate me. He acknowledged his weakness and that it was a weakness, and said it was the result of his early days on the farm, when thrift was necessary.

I told him I was not going to sacrifice my independence for the sole purpose of inheriting the biggest fortune that he could ever hope to make. I told him that unless he agreed to the proposal I would make, I would leave London immediately for home.

In the end George agreed to let me have whatever money I wanted on the trip. He would take my note for the same, and accept payment at some later time. We roughly estimated our expenses of the trip up to the point of our quarrel, and one-half was charged to me and one-half to George. After that, though I was to disburse the money for the two of us, I was to charge him with half of any of our joint expenses. This would leave me free to spend whatever I chose. Thereafter, for the several months that we were together, George made it a point himself to tip, and tip fairly liberally wherever we went, and that out of his own pocket.

But after it all I felt greatly mortified about what had occurred. I have been in London a number of times but I never saw the sun shine more than one or two days. I loathed the town, its fogs, and especially its streets crowded with the poor miserable human beings who constituted probably not less than ninety-eight per cent of the total population. Vice was not only rampant but public. The sights in the public parks of London were horrible. Before I had gone to London I had read Dante's *Inferno*, and there had been nothing in Dante's description of Hell that was more loathsome to me than the sights I could see in London. I wanted to get out of the city.

The evening of the quarrel over the penny, and after our dinner, I went out alone to walk on Brook Street. Brook Street was then, and is now, I suppose, one of the fashionable streets of London. I think it led into Portland Square. I frequently took my after-dinner walk on this street, smoking my cigar. During these walks, and during a great deal of this European trip, I was considering deeply my own case: what goal in life I should seek, what attitude I should take toward society and its conventions, by what road I should arrive at that eminence which I had so long dreamed of.

The London season was on. I found the sidewalk partially blocked. There was a carpet laid down the steps of one of the houses out to the curb. A long string of carriages was parked along the other side of the road, and other carriages were rolling up to the house, discharging their occupants. When the carriage stopped, the footman would swing down from his seat, open the door of the carriage, and stand in respectful attention until the ladies and gentlemen had descended. Then he would close the door, and the coachman would drive off and take his stand at some by-point. The footman would join the little clots of other footmen who stood on both sides of the steps leading up to the house.

I stopped for some time to observe the proceedings. My attention was first fixed entirely upon the men and women who were getting out of the carriages. I studied them as well as I could under the bright lights that extended from the doorway to the curb. As they would climb the steps leading into the house, I could hear the servant receiving them and taking their names. Sometimes I could catch the names. I heard the names of several of the nobility.

As I looked at the house, and at the crowd of carriages, and the incoming stream, I was filled with wonder as to where they could find room to stand, much less sit down. Then I saw that while some were coming, others were going.

I studied the faces of the masters and mistresses of the footmen who were near me and I was struck with the insignificance of most of the men who got out of the carriages. Few of them had fine forms. Many were beyond middle age, and looked just like a lot of other fussy little Englishmen whom I had encountered in the shops and on the streets. But where, oh, where! were the beautiful women—the Ladies this and that, the countesses and marchionesses—that I had read about in storybooks? I did not see a queenly woman among the whole bunch. I saw hardly what could be called a pretty girl. Male and female, old and young, they looked to me a rather measly, scrawny, ornery crowd.

Later I began to give attention to their servants. These footmen that stood around, probably two or three score of them, were generally tall, finely formed, good-looking young Englishmen. It was only when I heard them talk their vulgar cockney, and make vulgar and foul jests, that I could recognize in them the menials that they were.

To my untrained eye—a Western American boy, not yet twenty-four—these men looked like fine fellows. Like gentlemen. I recognized their smart livery and their tall hats and cockades as badges of servitude; but still, they were remarkably well dressed. When I began to compare my own wearing apparel with theirs, I felt a distinct dissatisfaction with myself. When I compared my wearing apparel with that of the guests who were getting out of the carriages, I was even more humiliated. I was wearing a rather loud, light-colored, plaid sack suit with trousers to match. I had on a silk hat. I had a diamond stud in my shirt front. I was wearing yellow doeskin gloves, and I was carrying an ivory-topped cane of switch dimensions. In truth, I was what the English called a perfect "bounder." A young lady cousin of mine told me a few days before that I dressed like, and sometimes acted like, a cad. I became conscious that my own vulgarity was expressed in the curiosity I was showing, both in staring at strange people, and in communing with vulgar menials. But still, uppermost in my mind was this question: Were all of the servants fine, big-looking men, and all of the masters and mistresses either mangy, or scrawny, or ugly, or little, or sometimes all of these things together?

Finally, I got by the crowd and continued my walk. Long that night did I walk; past midnight, and well toward morning. I was thinking. I thought that I did not want to be a great man, if the price of greatness was going to be such a scandalous disfigurement of my physical person which would put me on an equality with these men getting out of the carriages. I thought that perhaps these men and women were what they appeared to be because of the lives they had to live as a result of the positions they held in the social world, or because of the lives that had been led by their fathers and mothers, and grandfathers and grandmothers, for many generations. I said to myself then, that if I ever did become a wealthy and great man, I would not permit my children to suffer deterioration in mind and body as the result of their father's state and position. But the question kept running through my mind as to what was the real difference between the men who stood on the sidewalk and those who walked on the velvet carpets in the mansion? I concluded that the whole difference was not at all heredity, but environment and position.

I formulated in my own mind a theory that, to become a master of men, one should eschew all employment by other men, no matter how remunerating it might be. One must first be his own master and work for himself, and, as soon as possible, become the master and employer of other workmen.

That night I also threw to the winds all of my former theory about real equality between men. That theory was based upon the idea of democracy in my own country. Regretfully, I abandoned this theory. Sadly I acknowledged to myself that the world was composed of a very small class of slave drivers and a very, very large class of slaves.

If one man meets another under such conditions that he must either kill the other man or be killed, no matter what may be the natural instincts of the first man, how gentle a soul he has, how full his heart may be of love and kindness for all living things, he will, when the meeting comes, kill the other man if he can.

I was in this frame of mind on Brook Street. I had to be either one of the oppressed or one of the oppressors. I had to be either the master or the servant. I had to either take wages or give them. There came to my mind that night the saying of Jesus Christ, It is more blessed to give than to receive. I translated this saying into another one, It is more profitable to give wages, than to receive them.

I slept most of that day, going to bed after dawn. In the evening after our supper I informed George that I was going to Paris as quickly as I could, to locate our lodgings and wait for him until he came.

During the three or four weeks I was in London with George, I traveled on foot and on the rooftops of the London busses, and occasionally in a hansom, over nearly all the city, at least over scores and scores of miles of the city's streets. I traversed the Thames by boat. Being a very young tourist, I made a point of seeing most of the principal objects of interest that were mentioned in the guidebook. The things that interested me most, however, were the living things—men, women and children.

The guidebooks were mostly about antiquities. I was searching for the modern. I risked many adventures in Whitechapel and other slums, for the purpose of seeing night life as well as day life in those quarters. Always I was searching faces. Always I was making mental comparisons of these faces, not only one with the other, but those of one section of the city with those of another, and those of one social class with those of another. And the great masses of the composite physiognomy of the city with the great masses of the composite physiognomy of my own country, especially my then home city, Detroit.

Galton did not, until thirty years later, invent the word "eugenics." I knew the word "heredity." I do not believe I had ever heard the word "environment" used with a scientific significance. But, if I was in no way equipped with scientific terminology, I was thoroughly organized as an observer, an investigator, an analyst. The lesson that kept repeating itself to me was: Men and women, their physical form, their mentality, their spirituality, were none of them matters of inheritance, but all of them developments, the consequence of formative forces that began to bear on them after birth. It was decades later that I formulated, or had formulated for me, the phrase that it is "the job that makes the man."

Everywhere in London I was looking for that face or that form, male or female, that would prove an exception to the rule. Nowhere among these millions of men and women did I find such.

One evening between the hours of six and seven I was crossing London Bridge. It was at the time when the greatest tide of humanity set away from the City. There were comparatively few other walkers going my way, while thousands and thousands of men and women were trudging forward, facing me. At times, the crowd was so dense that I could hardly elbow my way through it. I stopped at the bridge side occasionally, and hung onto a parapet in order to keep my position more securely. I asked a policeman if there was anything unusual going on to cause such a crowd. He replied that it was the same every working day. The same crowd. Except that in the morning they would be going one way, and in the evening the other.

I pressed on and on until I arrived at some point near the middle of the bridge. I began to feel sick and weak and nauseated. The sight of so much humanity, the close contact with so much ugliness, misery, hopelessness, and dull blankness of vision, had oppressed me. I began to feel something like hysteria. I stopped at the bridge parapet. Clinging to it, I looked away from the crowd, and down at the river, eagerly sensing the breeze blowing up the river. I wanted to see no more of my fellow men, and said to myself:

"I am just one of these. I am one of these millions. All through England there are millions more. All the world is full of millions and millions of men and women. All but a very, very few belong to the crowd, the rabble, that suffer poverty. Their minds are blank or almost blank. The little circles of the activities of each are infinitesimally small.

"When there are so many millions of us, what matters one of us, or a thousand of us, or a million of us, even? So many as a million could suddenly and instantly disappear in death, and not for an instant would their disappearance be noted. The crowds would be just as large, the press of humanity on humanity, if lightened at all, would be lightened only to an infinitesimal extent. What difference is there between me and any other man in this crowd? Under similar conditions, they would, each of them, have been my equal; under similar conditions of birth and rearing, I would have only been an equal of these. I had no part in causing even that small distinction between myself and any one of those who were pressing on me. It was not by my will that I was born where there were open fields. It was the result of no intention of mine that my birthplace was in a new country and a freer country than England. I can hardly credit myself for any of the movements, physical or mental, that I have made. Chance has given me some items of luck that it has denied these others."

I had either not yet heard or not had reason to remember what was said by John Bradford when he saw a criminal being led to the gallows from the jail. "There, but for the grace of God, go I, John Bradford." But I clearly did appreciate the fact that, but for a lucky chance, I might have been one of those who were crowding past me.

Often enough at night I had stood under the stars, gazing upward, humbled and awed, and overcome by the greatness, the awfulness, and the beauty of that little part I could see of the universe. Wandering in the wooded place near my boyhood home, I had been impressed by the solitude and quiet, and felt myself small. On the river's brink, on the lake shore, facing the falls of Niagara, standing in the bow of a mighty ship plowing the Atlantic, listening to the trickle, the roar, the swish and lapping of the water, I had humbly meditated.

But here I was, a mere drop in the great river of seething humanity. I was myself an intricate part of the waves and eddies of the stream itself. I felt a loathing for the whole species, including myself.

I looked down at the water of the Thames. It was evening, and in the comparative dusk, the filthiness of the water was not apparent. But even if it had been, the filth of the water would have been cleanliness itself compared with the filth of this other stream in which I was involved. I yearned to throw myself over the parapet and in quick unconsciousness escape the realization of what I was and what all humanity was.

I pressed on to the end of the bridge, entered a hansom, and ordered the driver to my apartment. I refused to look forward and outward. I closed my ears with the tips of my fingers, so that I could no longer hear or see any more people. On this homeward drive I resolved more than ever before to disassociate myself from the crowd, to climb up and out and over it, no matter by what means, even though crime itself and the worst of crime should form the rungs of the ladder which I felt I must climb. If not, I would commit suicide.

I arrived in Paris sometime early in May, during the Paris Exposition of 1878.

Before leaving America I had arranged with the editor of the Detroit *News* to write letters from Europe at the rate of fifteen dollars per letter. The exposition was a perfect mine for copy. Before my quarrel with my brother I had written very little. Now I determined to earn all the money I could on my trip so that it would be easy for me to repay the money borrowed from my brother. (All my letters proved acceptable, and on my return after a six months' trip I found due me eight hundred dollars, which turned out to be my share of the six months' trip.)

I did another thing in Paris. I determined to cease to work for a salary or to depend upon little makeshifts for making money. I determined to be my own boss and run a newspaper of my own, subject to orders from no one. I had never been in the city of Cleveland, but that city was only a short distance from Detroit, where I first entered the news business. I knew the size of it and some of its character. I determined I would make my first newspaper venture there. When my brother joined me a few days later, I told him of my object, and offered to take him into partnership on certain terms. The terms were that he was to furnish the money and leave me alone, and I was to furnish the brains and make us both rich. I started the paper in Cleveland two months later, but not as its controlling owner.

On June 18, 1878, on my twenty-fourth birthday, I found myself in Rome. Naturally enough, considering my own peculiarities, I had not thought of the day as being my birthday.

In the afternoon I left my brother at our hotel and started out for a stroll. I knew little of Rome as I had not been there more than a day or two. I knew there was a street called the Corso. It was brightly lighted. There were many cafés and swarms of well-dressed ladies and gentlemen on the pavement. I walked along the Corso and perhaps strayed off the street. In the moonlight, I discovered the pillars of the ruins of the Old Forum, and beyond, the dusky outlines of a mammoth building. Dusky because the street lights were sufficiently bright to make even the pillars of the Forum appear in the shade. But I walked on down past the Forum, where there were no bright lights. Then I discovered what the large building that I had seen was. It was the Colosseum, and it was lit up by a moon. A pretty nearly full moon, I believe.

Back in my father's home on the farm I had read Byron, and there came to my mind clearly some such words as "Did you ever see the Colosseum in Rome by moonlight?" There was the Colosseum bathed in the moonlight. Yes, the eighteenth of June, and my birthday. I continued my course and entered the arena. In the middle of the floor of the great structure—then entirely unexcavated—there was a capital of one of the great pillars. It was upturned so that the top was the base. I scrambled up to the top of this old capital.

I was seeing the Colosseum by moonlight alone and it was my twenty-fourth birthday, and I had in my mind a resolution to alter the whole course of my life. I was going to become a wealthy man. I spent hours and hours reclining on this old capital, and, before I realized what had occurred, the moon had gone so low that I was in the shadow of the walls of the Colosseum.

I had read Gibbon's *Decline and Fall of the Roman Empire.* I was in Rome and had Gibbon's book in memory; every page of it seemed to be open to me. I fell to thinking of the characters that had been depicted by Gibbon. There was Julius Caesar and Octavius and Pompey, and oh! great men after great men!

I was going to embark on a great adventure. Which one of all the great men of Rome would I choose as my model? My choice was an odd one. It fell on Fabius Maximus. Fabius who was patient and who knew how to wait, clinging to the hills while the Carthaginian adventurer Hannibal was wasting the valleys. Fabius was always threatening, always menacing, but seldom if ever attacking. Hannibal conquered himself and Fabius went back to Rome to enjoy his triumph. The world belongs to him who waits if he doesn't wait too long; if he only waits long enough for his opportunity and then is quick to seize it.

How curious for a boy of twenty-four, hot-blooded, irascible in temper as I was, to start out on a career of mutiny by a process of waiting! From that day I have been ruled very largely by the resolution I made that night in the Colosseum at Rome. Let the other fellow have all the glory. Let him occupy the place in the limelight. For me I only care to have the power.

I was to wait and wait patiently for the opportune moment and then act promptly—that was to be my policy.

III

The Laziest Boy in the County

TWENTY-FOUR years to a day before that night in the Colosseum I was born on the farm of my father, James M. Scripps, a mile from Rushville, Cuyahoga County, Illinois.

I had a reputation in the family, in the neighborhood, and among the town people who knew me, as a very lazy boy. On occasion I heard myself spoken of as the laziest boy in Cuyahoga County. Instinctively, I hated and despised manual labor. I was sharp and shrewd and wise and I almost always got others to do the work that most boys did for themselves.

I was a bad boy, not only according to the views of other people, but according to my own views. I was never fully aware how bad a boy I was until I had sons of my own. I was bad about every way a boy could be bad. My sons had their faults, but they were never as bad as I was. I was sent to public school and Sunday school. I never believed anything that was told me in Sunday school or that I heard in church. I had no religious principles to guide me. I don't believe that I ever had any principles of any kind that would usually be reckoned as good. I was a poor pupil at school. I was a nuisance to all my Sunday-school teachers. I was taught to say certain prayers before I went to bed, but unless I was under observation by my mother or one of my sisters, I never repeated any of them at night before going to sleep.

I took pride in my reputation as a lazy boy. I would chuckle to myself, and would be filled with vanity because I knew that, instead of being the laziest boy in the county, I was the most industrious individual of all the boys, men, girls and women in the neighborhood. I can recall no days or hours of idleness. I was seldom seen on the school playgrounds. This was due to my physical condition. I was expert at no sport. Most boys' sports are games in which one set of boys contest with another set. In choosing sides in such games, I was always the last called, if called at all. I was humiliated on this account at times. Vain as I was of my own capacities in some respects, I was no philosopher. I vainly coveted superiority in every field. I have no doubt that my inclination to be bookish was sharpened by a desire to offset my lack of prowess on the playgrounds.

My father and mother had very strict ideas about children getting the habit of work. My earliest task was bringing in wood for the fires. Later I had to cut and split the wood. I never sufficiently mastered the ax to be able to chop a four-inch stick clear through. The most I could do was to hack around it. My ax blade never hit the same place on the second stroke. It missed by two or three inches. Where another boy would divide a stick of wood into two pieces with six strokes, I would have to strike a hundred or two hundred times. I never could cut down anything larger than a sapling. My stumps were an object of scorn and ridicule to all who saw them.

I had to drive in the cows from pasture, and to milk some of them. I could milk. That is to say, if I pulled the cows' teats long enough, I would get enough milk to satisfy myself. I could never master the art of "stripping," cleaning out the last drop of milk from the udder. The cows that I milked soon dried up. I milked in the same way I went to church: I refused to consider the important part of the transaction. While milking, I made up rhymes, and tried to scale my verses to the swish of the milk in the pail. I would do about as much milking in an hour as an ordinary milker would do in ten or fifteen minutes.

As a field hand, I was as good as or better than any other boy. I could rake hay with a hand rake or horse rake, and I could cap the hay. I could use the scythe and cradle. I could shock my wheat and oats. I could plow and hoe corn, sugar cane and potatoes.

I always liked to work in the dirt.

I felt a sense of pleasure in tackling a field of corn with my plow or my hoe. I liked to see the distance grow from the starting side of the field toward the other, as I plowed my way through. I liked especially well to do the work thoroughly. Some of the proudest hours of my boyhood life were those when on a long summer's day I covered more ground in plowing or hoeing than the hired men did. I divided up the field in as many spaces as there were men working, so that I could compare my own work with that of the others.

It was quite by accident that I learned that with two, three or four men or boys at work, the spirit of emulation among them would cause the total performance of the day to be far greater than when each had a separate piece of work. The work was best if the whole group moved together row by row, talking together, arguing about something, and generally forgetting their task.

When I was fourteen, my father began his last illness. This endured for several years. He could do little work. There was no one at home to attend to the farm but myself. I was very proud of the important position that I had obtained on this account. I had learned that, boy as I was, I could outwork a man. I obtained my father's consent to employ town boys to work with me, instead of doing the usual thing of hiring men when seasonal work was heavy.

The farm laborer's wage was usually one dollar per day. I got a number of ambitious boys from the town to come to work on the farm at twenty-five cents a day for spending money. For all of that season, however, work on my father's farm was just as much a contest as any boy's ballgame, or tug-of-war.

I spaced off in the field an equal number of rows, a space for each boy. Then we all began to race. The town boys were rather soft for hard work. As I was comparatively tough, I easily enough beat the crowd. At the end of our first effort I was so much in the lead that I was able to sit down in the dirt and laugh and jeer at my companions.

Boys' tempers are short and soon arguments among us ran high. I was accused of sharp practice, of having trained for my work when the others had not. A situation presented itself. I saw an opportunity. I diverted the argument from myself to a cousin of mine, who was the smallest and youngest of all the boys. He was also the pluckiest and most conceited, and, in a way, the most ambitious of all. Next to myself, he was best at the work. I pointed this out and taunted the others for letting the little fellow win above them. Then began the usual boyish wrangle: "I bet you this," "I bet you that," "I bet his work is not as well done as mine," and much more to the same effect.

They voted, at my suggestion, that I should stay out of the contest. Another set of spaces was marked off for each boy, excepting myself, and a new contest was tried. It was a question as to whether or not each boy did his work fairly. As I was paying the money for the work in this hoeing contest, I would act as referee and follow up all the other boys to see that they did equally fair work. I doubt if it has ever occurred to any of these boys to this day that, while they were sweating and aching, I was enjoying myself looking on.

It was rather tedious following the boys up over the ground and doing nothing. Soon enough I had my book out, which I always carried with me, and was in a fence corner reading. I told the boys to call me when they got on their last rows so that I could overlook their work.

From that time, there was no lack of boy workers on the Scripps ranch. The town boys wanted to get into the game they heard so much about. I arranged contests between individuals or groups of boys in cultivating the corn by plowing, or hoeing a potato field, a cane field or a kitchen garden or doing any other activity of the farm life, while I sat under a tree, or in the shade of some bush, or haycock, or corn shock, and read, while the contest was waged.

My mother used to say after I had grown to manhood, that a not infrequent post of mine was on a fence rail. She said that Eddie always seemed to be sitting on the fence watching the other fellows work. She added that it looked to her as though I was running my business in the same way I had run the farm.

It was on the farm that I first learned how to make money—my very own, which my father recognized that I had a perfect right to spend as I saw fit.

My father's farm was marked with the old-fashioned rail fence. These fences are very expensive in land since they occupy a very large space. It occurred to me that I could make use of the fence corners, without any loss to my father. I spaded up enough of these corners one year to make the equivalent of an acre of land. I planted this with sweet potatoes, and grew a fair crop. Another season I extended my enterprise over other waste pieces of land—odd corners, small pieces not large enough for a field—and on these I raised sweet potatoes, Irish potatoes and sweet corn. I recall that, during the year that I raised Irish potatoes, I got them into the market as new potatoes earlier than anyone else. I reaped a rich harvest.

On the farm a large part of our fuel was coal. Along the creek bottom that ran through the farm, there was a few inches below the surface a vein of very fine coal, from eighteen inches to three feet in thickness. The coal was so brittle it could not be shipped, but if handled carefully it could be brought to the open gate or stove in very good shape. It was entirely free from sulphur and such other things as ordinarily cause coal to clinker, and made a beautiful fire and burned to a clean ash.

In the fall of my eighteenth year, I got out enough coal for house use. The way we obtained the coal was to plow and scrape the earth off the underlying vein, choosing the places where the earth was thin and the valley deep. In laying out the excavation work I stripped the soil in such a large piece that when I and the men began taking out the coal, we found, unexpectedly, that not half the coal uncovered was needed. (Now, if this coal was left exposed to the weather, it would flake and become almost worthless coal dust within a year.) I obtained my father's consent to take out the coal at my own expense and sell it. While no one in the town had ever used coal like this, many of the people knew of our coal and what fine grate fires it made. It was easy enough for me to sell all the coal at a price that netted me a good profit.

Needless to say, while the coal was being extracted, both for my father and myself, I sat on the bank for the most part and bossed the job. It is possible that I might have driven the wagon in delivering the coal to my neighbors. I forget.

Another of my father's sources of revenue had been cordwood in stove lengths. We had one of those horsepower treadmills, with a small circular saw. It was the only machine of its kind in the town. I can remember my father working with this machine, together with the other men. Usually, he did the hardest part of the work himself—lifting a stick of cordwood from the pile, carrying it to the machine, and pushing it through the saw, while the other men held the loose end and threw the stick away. For a few years now the sawmill had not been used, except for house purposes. That winter I contracted to rent the outfit from my father, and from one of my brothers

I rented two very old and almost useless horses he had won in some trade. Their value to me was their heavy weight, as it was weight that made the treadmill horsepower effective.

I started out working with the outfit—at first doing the hardest part of the work, feeding the saw. Soon enough it occurred to me that my hired man ought to do the heavy work and I ought to do the light. After I had completed my first job and collected the money, I went out looking for another job. Two or three days were consumed in finding a job and moving my machine to do it. As the saw was netting me two or three dollars a day, I felt that this was waste. When I got my next job, I hired a boy at twenty-five cents a day to throw the sticks away, while my dollar-a-day man fed the saw, and I went out looking for orders. After booking enough orders to keep me going for some time, I might have returned, discharged my boy, and done my own work; but I revolted at the idea of working for twenty-five cents a day, which I would practically be doing if I discharged the boy and took his place.

I might have discharged the man and made a dollar a day, but some of the cordwood was heavy, and really that was not one of the jobs that I enjoyed, like plowing the corn, or cane cutting, or feeding the sugar mill. So I sat around and bossed the job some, stayed at home and read my books some. Since my father and mother had a right to think that I was industriously employed, they set me no other task.

I can set down almost the correct figures of this first business enterprise of E. W. Scripps. I paid $1.00 a day for the use of the machinery, $1.00 a day for the horses, maybe 25 cents for their feed, $1.00 a day for the man who fed the saw, and 25 cents a day for the boy who threw the wood away, or a total of $3.50 a day. I forget just how many cords per day I sawed, and how much I got per cord, but I well enough remember that I was making a daily profit, above the wages of two or three men. I remember standing around the stores and other places in the town, sometimes being complimented, sometimes being joshed, and sometimes being reminded of my being the laziest boy in the county, on account of the way I was making big money off of other people's work. On the whole I was far more displeased than pleased by the comments I heard. I avoided, as much as possible, public places, and frequently hid myself between two stacks of cordwood, or in some other out-of-the-way place, where I could read and not attract attention or comment.

The one person who had more to do with the shaping and development of my character than all other influences that have borne upon me, is my sister Ellen Browning Scripps. She was really my half sister and seventeen and one-half years older than I was. She was a full-grown woman before I reached the age to which my memory can carry me.

My father was the youngest son of the family, and was supposed to be the least gifted intellectually. He was an apprentice to a bookbinder in his youth, and made one or more business failures. My grandfather came to America, bought a tract of land near Rushville, Illinois, and later brought my father and his family of young children to this country. (Perhaps he had the thrifty idea they would be less costly to him here than in England.) My father married my mother, Julia Osborn of Williamstown, Massachusetts, in this country, and from her had five children. He had been twice married before, and became a widower for the second time at about the age of forty. He had two children by his first wife, and six by his second; hence, I was his thirteenth child.

Ellen was the only one of our whole family who ever had a college education. She was graduated about the time I was four years old.

I was a sickly, whining and unhappy child. About all the attention my mother could give me was a spanking or a switching when I was unusually bad. It was my sister who taught me my letters. It was she who would sit by my bedside at night before I would go asleep, or when I was ill. It was she who remembered to give me the ginger cooky and the doughnut between meals.

But having started with teaching me my letters, it was only going a step farther to read aloud to me the books she was reading as she sat minding me. I can recall some of the earlier readings. She was reading books for grownups and I couldn't understand much but I liked to hear her voice. In time I was curious to know what some of the words meant and from this my education began. She would tell me the meaning of a word whether I asked her or not.

How far I progressed in any given time I cannot tell, only I do recall that when I was nearly eight years of age, she was reading Shakespeare to me. She read Scott. She read Tennyson and Longfellow. She read many books to me which, after I had grown a little older, I read again to myself. It was an interesting experience to read these books after my understanding had fully or largely developed, and to recall the ideas I had had in my more youthful years when the same books were being read to me by my sister. The personages were not the same personages. The events were not the same events. The meaning of the words that my sister had given me had not penetrated my understanding, but had only been pegs on which my imagination hung decorations.

My sister taught me nothing of religion. Later I learned that except for one brief interval when she had been carried away at some revival meeting, she had never been in the matter of faith a Christian. Somewhat owing to the fact that I so loved and admired my sister who was not the same kind of thing the Sunday school taught us was a Christian, it was hard for me to believe anything that was said by a Sunday-school teacher or a preacher. The idea of my sister going to Hell because she did not believe a lot of fool stories made the whole Christian teaching seem to me not only absurd, but wicked. I know that later my mother complained that my sister was to blame for my being such a wicked boy.

But it was books, and books, and always books that I remember. It seems to me that others than Ellen read books to me for several years in my very earliest childhood, but my memory is mainly for her sitting reading to me. I remember her reading poetry, for example, Jean Ingelow's "The Tide of Enderoy." "Fairer woman ne'er drew breath than my son's wife, Elizabeth," or lines similar to these are running through my head, and I can remember saying them over and over again to myself. Perhaps the poem was often read to me. I was sixteen or seventeen when I first read the poem for myself, and although I could not repeat the lines word for word, line for line, and verse for verse, it was all familiar to me. In the same way much other matter that I read earlier, I found was familiar. At the family hearth, Ellen often read out loud to the family. Just when I emerged into self-reading I do not recall.

I went to school as the other boys did, but did not make much of an attempt to learn my lessons. Besides my schoolbooks, I always had some other books in my desks. It was these and not my schoolbooks with which I spent my time in school. With the exception of my sister Ellen, I knew of no schoolteacher, in my younger days, male or female, for whom I did not have contempt.

Books and more books were always sought for by me, because in them was concentrated the fruits of ages of observation and thinking. Perhaps it was my sister Ellen's reading to me from books for which she had, at that earlier period of her life, a taste, that I acquired a particular appetite for poetry. I could draw from some poems whole songs not sung. It happened that in my father's house there were very many books of verse. Parts of the Old and New Testaments were poetry to me, despite the imbecility of the Sunday school and the so-called Sunday-school teachers.

(As to that stupid automaton the preacher, I would refuse to hear, and did succeed invariably in not hearing, his sermons. As a child, I either slept or sent my mind far afield in dreams or cogitations, while the preacher hollered, pounded on the pulpit, wept out his sermon, or mumbled in prayer.)

I suppose that half, or nearly half, of all my waking hours have been spent with my eyes on a printed page. As I have a very retentive memory, I have kept nearly all that I have gathered from my reading. Still I am aware that I am a sort of jack-of-all-trades-and-master-of-none in the great field of learning.

After many years devoted mainly to poetry and all that class of literature which might be called belles-lettres, I gradually worked my way into history and philosophy. The greater part of my serious reading, for twelve or fifteen years, was history. Really, reading pure philosophy has always been, for me, a laborious task—a sacrifice of comfort for the satisfaction of knowing, and perhaps having other people know, that I was more or less familiar with certain schools of philosophy. From my fortieth year or thereabouts, I began to be interested in various scientific subjects. I included theology as a science.

There was one bit of childhood reading, however, that had a very great effect on my later life.

One day when I was about thirteen my brother James and I had a conversation in what was called "the boys' bedroom"—an attic chamber in the Rushville farmhouse where all the boys of the family slept. In the bedroom there was a little homemade bookcase, where I had gathered books I was reading and intended to read. There was a set of volumes called *Peter Parley's Tales*. The tales were all stories of crimes and romances that had often been published before. As I remember, they dealt mainly with facts of court record. The author of Peter Parley had rewritten, in very simple form, these old tales for the readers of modern times. The Peter Parley tales were written by Samuel Griswold Goodrich, 1793-1860, and first appeared in a magazine the author founded in Boston in 1826 called *The Token*. Goodrich was strongly influenced by the writings and personal friendship of the English bluestocking, Hannah More. Many of Hawthorne's *Twice-Told Tales* also first appeared in *The Token*.

I was seated on the floor in front of this little bookcase, trying to select a book to read. I had a volume or two of Peter Parley's in my hand. I was so preoccupied I did not hear the steps of someone on the stairway, and crossing the short landing to the door of the bedroom. My brother James and his wife were then visiting the old homestead. I heard the jangling of a key ring just above my head, and looked up. I saw my brother James looking down, but not at me. His eyes were fixed upon the book in my lap. From the expression on his face, he was musing; but the keys on his key ring kept on jingling as he nervously twitched his fingers. Then a strange thing happened.

(I might say here that between the boy and man there had never been any sympathy or mutual interest, and later there was always antagonism between the two. James seldom noticed me or saw me, and on not more than two or three occasions during a visit to the home did he ever directly address me.)

There was no chair in the room, so my big brother squatted down beside me and took one of the Parley volumes from me and began to turn over the pages. They were, I am sure, familiar to him. I could hardly say that he was talking to me, though it was not his habit to talk to himself. He had something on his mind, and he had the impulse to express it in words. He probably thought very little of his listener.

He began by saying he knew the old books well and that he had often been thinking of them, in later days, with a view to putting into journalism the idea that Peter Parley had in bookmaking. He pointed out that these old stories in the Peter Parley volumes had previously been written and published in book form. In the other books, however, the narrative had been told in such a verbose way that each of the stories required more pages than was required for all of the tales in the books before us. It was in order to save the time of the reader, and at the same time permit him to have a firsthand knowledge of these old stories, that Peter Parley had so greatly condensed each of them.

Now the great idea that my brother submitted to me was the publication of a daily newspaper, very small in size, with large type, and which, by reason of having condensed writing, would contain all of the news, and all of the miscellaneous matter, and even the love stories that could be found in any of the large "blanket sheets" that were being issued as newspapers in this country. For the first time, I then heard the name of Samuel Bowles, and the Springfield *Republican.* From what James said, it appeared that Bowles had already begun the work of condensing journalism.

Finally, wearying of his uncomfortable attitude, he sat squarely down on the floor, stretched out his legs, and leaned against the bookcase. He kept on talking. For an hour or more, he certainly did talk. Perhaps it was longer than two hours. I remember that I was hungry. I remember also that my awe of my big brother forbade my interrupting his stream of talk.

It was in "the boys' bedroom" that he narrated to me the whole plan of that little newspaper which he was later to found in Detroit, and which was the kernel of the Scripps newspaper concern.

IV

The Value of Being a Nuisance

WHY DID I become a journalist?

My Grandfather William A. Scripps was a journalist and part owner of the London *Literary Gazette*. He began his activities in this field a century and a quarter ago.

My great-uncle ran a little country newspaper. A cousin of mine was editor of the same paper when I was a boy. Another cousin of mine, John Locke Scripps, was one of the founders of the Chicago *Tribune* in association with Joseph Medill, and was for a number of years its editor. My brother, nearly twenty years older than myself, was the editor of the Detroit *Tribune,* a daily newspaper. Together with the other members of my family, he owned the controlling stock interest in that paper.

As a boy, as I have said, I devoted my spare time to reading. Before my nineteenth year, I never had any desire to become a journalist. I had great ambitions to become a writer of books, even a poet.

Actually, what led me into journalism was a very natural boyish restlessness to be out in the world and doing things. My home life, or farm life, rather, was anything but monotonous or disagreeable to me. Yet on one occasion, in my eighteenth year, I deliberately prepared to leave home and make my own fortune. I was not exactly going to run away from home. I knew there was no occasion for my running, as no one was going to stop me.

Some neighborhood boys and I went to the state fair together. I was carrying a carpetbag containing my few clothes and all my money savings. I did not intend to return. I wanted to try myself out and find out how well I could support myself. We boys spent two days and one night at the town where the fair was being held. On the second day I must have drunk too much pop, and eaten too much stale cake, and run about in the sun too much. Before the train had started back for home, I was sick and miserable. Then and there I abandoned my great adventure.

Some months later, a young Englishman, a cousin of my half brothers and sisters, who had been graduated as a chemist and passed through an apprenticeship as a pharmacist, arrived in America. He intended to set up as a druggist in Detroit. He had small funds. My father loaned him several hundred dollars with the understanding and agreement that I should be employed in the drugstore for the purpose of learning the business.

I was struck with the absurdity of the plan—the idea of my being a druggist, and worse, a drug clerk. Still, Detroit was a great way from our home. It was a city, and it was a field for adventure, and my brother was the editor of a newspaper there. Why, then, should I offer any objection to the plan?

One thing was fixed in my mind when I left home on November 2, 1872, to go to Detroit. That was that I would never be a drug clerk, or employer or even owner of any trade establishment. I was born with something like contempt for all storekeepers. No young English gentleman possessed a greater repugnance for "trade" than did I.

When I arrived in Detroit, the druggist had not yet opened up his shop. The carpenters and painters were still at work. I had several weeks in which to get acquainted with town life.

I carried from home a new suit of store clothes that I had bought and paid for. I wore a new overcoat which my father had bought for himself. He had no use for it, being a bedroom invalid. I had some loose change in my pocket, and sewed up in the lining of my vest, eighty dollars of my own money. This I had earned digging coal, sawing wood, and in other similar enterprises. It was my firm resolution that I was never going to part with this eighty dollars except in the last extremity of hunger and sickness. I also resolved that I would always have in hiding a sum of money that would be sufficient to guarantee my perfect freedom from the control of anyone.

(Although I have gradually amassed a fortune of fair size, I have never failed to keep a special fund that would be safe against theft or creditor, ready for immediate use. I have been unwilling to consider even large bank allowances as a substitute for my little secret hoard. There has never been a time in my whole life when conditions have been such that I have had to turn to anybody—a friend, a business agent or an employer—to get the few dollars of cash that I might need to cover any possible emergency of my own.)

James, whom I never got along with, had consented to my coming to Detroit only because of our father's request, and because of the knowledge that our father was dying. I could see plain enough that the editor of the Detroit *Tribune* thought I was a nuisance and a bother. I was well enough aware that he had no intention of making himself responsible for me. He had two young children of his own, and did not intend to stand *in loco parentis* to a redheaded, freckled-faced, country lout of a brother.

Although I had not planned to be a newspaperman, I had read a great deal, especially English books, about literary men who had started their careers as humble attachés to newspapers. I knew that I was far from fitted to enter journalism or any other literary field. I could not write a legible hand. I could not write a straight line across a sheet of paper. Spelling I was no good at. I had not acquired the habit of either speaking or writing correctly. I knew I needed apprenticeship for my literary calling; and I assumed—rightly enough, I know now—that a newspaper office was the proper place for such an apprenticeship. I intended to worm my way into employment on the *Tribune.*

James would not have me on the paper, but my brother, W. A. Scripps, was foreman of the job-printing room. I knew I could easily enough work my brother Will to get what I wanted. James, as president of the company, was of course Will's superior officer; but these two brothers seldom agreed. In little things, Will often had his own way, much to the discomfort of James.

Finally the carpenters, painters and cleaners got the interior of the drugstore ready for occupancy. My druggist employer and I took possession of the premises. I was set to work washing windows and bottles. I helped fill some of the bottles. We installed a soda-water fountain, and I was told how to manipulate it. In a few days, the drugstore opened for business.

We opened our drugstore on a Monday morning. On Saturday the druggist told me what my wages were to be. I think he said a beginner ought to get fifty cents a week. On the first Saturday night, the druggist left before the closing hour, and instructed me to turn out the lights and lock up. I did so. I had not been paid my wages. I walked out of that store determined never to come back again as an employee, and that is just what I did. I said nothing about my leaving to anyone. I just did not turn up Monday.

I forget how I spent my time for the next few days. I was pretty well disgusted with life. I wrote my father that I had quit the drug business. I spent some time on the docks along the river; not exactly looking for a job, but sizing up the situation. I thought it might be a nice idea for me to try a few weeks or months of sailing.

It is truly wonderful how little money it takes to feed and clothe and house a youngster who knows nothing about money spending, and who has not yet learned to do anything for appearance's sake. I know that I could well have afforded to go on several months without earning anything. But I was hunted up by one of my brothers. I went to my brother Will's house to live, and went to work as an office boy in the accounting room of the Detroit *Tribune.*

I spent a few weeks in the counting rooms. It was evident that I was not learning any literature by sweeping out the office, making fires, selling papers over the counter to newsboys, occasionally taking an advertisement, and generally running errands. I struck. Then I got my first job in a printing shop. As office boy, I got three dollars a week. I helped myself very little here. I was set to work holding copy for a proofreader, or trundling a cartload of printed matter down to some outsider. I had to sweep out the job room as I had the front office. Again I struck. I recognized that I had made some headway in getting experience, but I wanted to learn something about books.

I felt that sticking type out of the case, or running presses might lead to better things. In those days, most reporters and editors graduated from the case. Nearly all the newspaper reporters and other writers in Detroit were ex-printers. I got rid of the cart-trundling business, and was allowed to set up some very cheap, plain dodgers. I was even allowed to learn how to kick a Gordon press. (This was a little press run by a foot treadle, and was used to print such small things as business cards, etc.)

My brother Will about this time began to make use of me as a bill collector. So long as this work did not consume any more than my idle time, I did not mind it. In fact, I liked to get out into the air and on the streets. It was soon enough discovered that, generally, when I went after money, no matter how hard the customer was, I brought back the amount of the bill. Then it occurred to the powers-that-be that I might come in handy to collect a lot of their old hard bills from bad customers. Instead of having to collect a few fresh accounts, I was given whole sheafs of old bills that nobody else had been able to collect. I was a glorious success at this. I began to recognize that I was not only valuable, but valued.

But bill collecting and literature are two entirely different callings.

I became dissatisfied. I did not kick. I did not say I was going to strike. I just quit the office one Saturday night and went off by my lonesome to think things over.

A few weeks later James found me and promised me eight dollars a week if I would come back to the office. He said he would hurry me along as rapidly as he could into some reporter's job, where I could learn the rudiments of journalism. It was with a feeling of no great content that I went back to learn to be a printer.

I did work with the printers' stock a great deal. I worked with all the presses. By actual work, and close observation, I learned something of all the processes of the press room and the composing room, and how to use the different machines. I never became an expert as a type sticker. Even in those days, when printers were paid by piece, and comparatively large wages, I doubt if I could have earned fifty cents a day as a printer. I also recall that I was constantly doing greater or less damage to the presses. Had the foreman of either the press or composing room been dealing with me as an ordinary apprentice, I would not have been able to hold onto my job for the day.

Then, on Easter morning, in 1873, a fire started in the *Tribune* office, and the whole building burned down. From this fire started not only my career as a journalist; but from the ashes of the old *Tribune* building sprang up perhaps the greatest and most effective journalistic institution in this or any other country.

Soon after the fire, the insurance was adjusted. The *Tribune* had recently put in an expensive printing press. Before this, the paper had been printed on a job press. In the job-printing office there were many presses, large quantities of type, and a great quantity of all sorts of material. Insurance had been taken out about a year before the segregation of the two properties. It was not blanket insurance, but itemized. When it came time to adjust the insurance, it was found that all of the job-office property had been fully, if not over-insured. Type that had been insured as new type was now old. Presses insured on the basis of their new value had become obsolete and partially worn. The result of the insurance adjustment left my brothers, James E. and W. A., with more cash than they ever had before.

The fire was a blessing to them. James and W. A., who were sole owners of the job-printing plant, decided to part company after receiving their insurance. After the separation James had, I believe, about twenty thousand dollars.

The *News* was started on August 23, 1873. Only a few weeks later, the great panic of 1873 broke. Instead of proving a disaster to the new paper, it was one of the causes of its early success. The *News* sold on the streets at two cents a copy at a time when all the other papers' street sales were for five cents. The average wage of an ordinary laboring man at that time was about a dollar a day. To people who only earned a dollar a day, the cost of a daily paper of the old type was altogether too great. With the hard times of the panic came the necessity for general economies in the *News*. Being a new paper, it had of necessity adopted a low advertising rate. For the sake of economy alone, many merchants transferred some or all of their advertising to the *News*.

The *News* was a success from the start. In less than three years its income exceeded outgo. From a date not many weeks after the *News* started, it had a circulation of about five thousand daily. This, I believe, was larger than was the circulation then of the Detroit *Free Press*, the Detroit *Morning Tribune*, the Detroit *Morning Post* or the

Detroit *Evening Tribune.* All these newspapers had been established institutions for many years. From that date circulation steadily increased, showing that the public favored this kind of journalism.

At first, the *News* was published in the form of a four-page paper, with six columns to the page, each column eighteen inches long. The actual size of the *News* was from one-quarter to one-sixth that of other Detroit papers.

I have never seen economy carried to such lengths as it was during the whole period of the existence of the Detroit *Evening News.* Why, even the paper that we reporters had to write our copy on was always used twice! After we had written our articles and sent them to the printer, on clean paper, the composing-room "devil" rushed to gather up all of the copy paper. With a pencil he drew two marks across the written pages. He returned them to the writers, so they could use the other side for fresh copy.

I never saw any copy produced by my brother that was not written on the inside of an open envelope, on the inside of wrappers in which other papers had come to the office, and on both sides (one side at a time) of such papers as wrappers of books, etc., that came into the office. He made it his business to open the mail, whether letters, papers, books or periodicals. He then carefully laid aside all of the envelopes, etc., which he had straightened out, and pressed them under some heavy book, for his own use and that of his editors.

We had another custom, the primary object of which was to save wages, but later maintained to save loss by theft. As soon as work was finished in the editorial room and the presses began to run, my brother James would go to the press room himself. There he counted out and sold the papers to the newsboys and carriers, taking the money or tickets or checks that were sometimes given in exchange. When he was unable to do this for some reason, either I or my brother George took his place. For many years some member of the family or some particularly trusted member of the editorial staff delivered papers from the press room to the carriers and newsboys.

In those days of the early seventies, a printer who would make "pie," or drop type on the floor would be sure of discharge. Proof-reading was always done by some member of the editorial staff, with the assistance of the foreman. The last ounce of printer's ink was scraped from the bottom of the barrels. There was no contract for outside parties to make our gum rollers for the press. The foreman of the press room and his helpers had to do the work in addition to their other duties.

There was one other source of saving, in which my brother George took the greatest delight. His bent for economy was so extreme that it could not be distinguished from niggardliness. In those old days, there were no typesetting machines. Printing in newspaper offices was paid for by the pica—so many cents for each thousand ems. Each printer had his "slug number," as it was called. When he had set up a piece of copy and put it into type, he placed under or above it what was called a "slug." It was a strip of metal on which was cast a number, and it was this slug that he put atop that part of the column of printing matter he set up. Generally from four to twelve slugs would divide the matter into a "galley," which would hold one column of type. The office "devil" took two proofs of this galley of matter, put one proof on the foreman's hook, and the other he brought to the proofreader.

At the end of the day, the foreman took his proofs and cut them into pieces corresponding to the amount of matter marked by each printer's slug. Then he gave to each printer this little piece of proof paper. The printer took his pieces and pasted them together in a strip called his "string."

The printers of those days, in most cases, were dissipated men. There were many tramp printers who would work a day or two and then tramp on. Even the regular printers were given to spending their money daily as fast as they earned it.

The office rule was only to cash "strings"—that is, pay the printer for his work—once a week. As the printers often wanted their money sooner, it was their habit to sell their "strings" to some fellow printer or some speculator in the office. They were sold at a ten per cent discount. My brother James ruled there should be no speculators in the office, but that the cashier in the counting room would buy all "strings" at the usual discount. My brother George acted as cashier. In his shirt sleeves, he used to measure these strings of improvident printers with a long brass measuring stick. He would haggle with them often over a few lines of difference that might have been caused by the printer leaving too large a space between one "take" and another. (A "take" was the amount of type set up for one particular piece of copy, and hence marked with a "slug.") There was no use for any smart printer to try to get a few extra cents out of George by leaving wide spaces in his pasting operations.

The discount on a Monday's "string" was ten per cent, and it was also the same for any other day in the week. Any printer who wanted to cash his "string" and get full value would have to wait until the closing hour of Saturday afternoon for his money. It used to cost a great deal of money to set type by hand. There were a great many improvident printers. The composing room expense of the Detroit *Evening News* was, for many years, cut down from three to five percent by this system of cashing "strings" at a discount.

Were the big newspaper institution that has grown out of this paper, to become the Scripps newspaper concern, as economically managed as the Detroit *News* in its earlier days, and the *Cleveland Press* in its earlier days, it would yield a net profit today fully three times as great as it now yields.

My own job on the *News* had very little to do with news writing or any other kind of writing at first. In Rushville I had sold ice, coal, potatoes, and had taken orders for sawing wood. When it came to canvassing for subscriptions for a newspaper that no one had ever heard of, my genius as a salesman immediately became strongly apparent. I and other young men on the paper blocked out our respective districts, agreeing not to compete with each other in these districts. From the first we began to meet daily and compare notes. Then it was discovered I was getting more subscribers every day than any other four or five canvassers.

I found, after a little practice, that I could get almost anybody to set down his name to an agreement to pay ten cents a week for a newspaper. I learned later, to my cost, that it was far easier to get a man to agree to pay ten cents, than it was to get him to pay up. I was very much interested in the work of getting up my routes. After I got my first two hundred subscribers (all that I could possibly carry) I found there were still a good many days before the paper would start.

It occurred to me there really ought to be no occasion for my doing the hard work of racing through the streets with a bundle of papers under my arms. I could hire someone else to do this work for me. I made an experiment to see how long it would take me to run over my route, mimicking the actual delivery of a paper. Later I got a bundle of old copies from the *Tribune* office and ran over the route delivering these. Then, I began to experiment with other boys. I found that I could do about double what the average boy was willing to do. I began bargaining with the boys. I found that I could employ, for a dollar a week, a good strong boy, who could and would deliver for me a hundred papers each night.

As a hundred papers cost me six dollars a week, and my collection was ten dollars, I figured that I would net three dollars for every boy I employed. I proposed to do the collecting myself, in a leisurely, gentlemanly way. By the time the *Evening News* started, I had more than a thousand subscribers, and a staff of ten boys, each of whom had been taught their routes.

I was so busy with all these things that I could not think of being a reporter at the start. I told my brother so. But, in the first issue of the *Evening News* appeared one article that I wrote myself. It made me very proud to read it. I suppose I read that item fifty times. I forget what it contained. It really did not matter to me. The words in it were my words, and the words were in print.

Soon enough I got my circulation system organized, and paid up to the *News* my little back bills for the papers, and began to make a fair profit. Of course my real profits were nothing like what they showed on paper. But soon enough I was making ten dollars a week, then twenty, then forty and finally fifty dollars a week. I think it was only a few months after the Detroit *News* started that my income, or my profits, was greater than that of the highest paid employee, the advertising manager. My income was higher even than that of the owner.

I became a successful businessman. I put on a silk hat. I went to a hotel to live. My brother James showed, in every way, his very high regard for his kid brother. He began counseling with me and taking my advice in all sorts of editorial and business matters. It was he who first revealed to me the importance in the editor of a newspaper keeping in close touch with the retail and wholesale vendors of the paper itself. It was I who could tell him, within twenty-four hours, whether or not a certain article had struck a popular chord, and when a certain line of editorial policy was met with disapproval. I enjoyed a fairly long period of swelled head. I knew that I was the most influential man in the office of the Detroit *Evening News.* (Never, as long as I remained in Detroit, did I fall from this high estate.)

Yet I was ashamed of my success, because it was purely on the business side of the newspaper. In those days I did not recognize what a tremendously valuable education I was getting—such an education as few, if any, great or small editors have had in preparation for their journalistic work. I determined, nonetheless, to get into journalism. And that soon. I would be a real journalist. A writer.

I had my business going nicely, and time was hanging heavily on my hands. I hung around the city editor's room, meeting reporters and studying the peculiarities of their personalities. I chummed around with the printers. I talked with my sister Ellen, who handled the exchanges and got "filler" material for the paper. I bought drinks for those editors who would drink, and furnished them with cigars, and even eats. I was beginning to formulate a plan. I no longer needed a salary as a reporter. I made two, or three, or four times as much money as any of them did.

I began organizing my business, and put a superintendent in charge of it. I told my brother, who had been reproaching me for my idleness, of my action and my plan to enlist as a cub reporter, working gratis. He pooh-poohed my idea. He said I was cut out to be a businessman, and not a writer. He threw before me some of my own pencil notes that I had sent to him. They were hardly legible, the grammar was execrable, and the spelling was in the highest degree phonetic.

He broached another subject. He had tried several times to get the *News* circulated in the country districts around Detroit, but had failed. He said that, as I had been so successful in Detroit, I had better take that up. I thought the matter over a great deal. In those days, especially in the West, there was no systematic method of obtaining country circulation for newspapers. In every town there was a drugstore, which kept a sort of newsstand. Papers were sent there. Such as were sold were paid for. The unsold copies were returned to the office. A few people subscribed for their papers by the year by sending the money directly to the office, and getting their papers by mail.

I thought out the scheme of having single routes in all the little towns, and several routes in the larger towns, and delivering newspapers in these places as they were delivered in the city. My brother made the proposal that for the first 1,000 circulation I got in the rural areas, I would get $250. I was to pay all expenses. If I got 2,000 circulation, I was to get $500; if I got it up to 3,000, I was to get $750, and thereafter I would get $750 for each additional thousand subscribers.

I went at the scheme with a rush. I had my plans all made before the deal was agreed to. The towns that were first taken were along certain railroad and boat lines, and each transportation route was to be taken as a whole. I had my canvassers employed. But before setting any of the other men to work, I went out myself.

My experience in the city was good training. But, oh! what a difference there was in those days between the city man and the country "jay." In the city I was lucky if I nailed one customer out of every four persons I attacked. In the country towns, I got nearly three people out of every five, and I recall instances where I went into a town and got every man and woman I talked with to subscribe.

I had to become an expert in the physiognomies and other peculiarities of my prospects. I knew at a glance the man who would subscribe and pay for his paper and who would probably continue to take the paper. I knew at a glance the man who would subscribe and would not pay. I knew at a glance who would take the paper for a week or two, out of curiosity, and then drop it. I knew those who were a total waste of time.

I set myself a task of getting fifty names a day, or three hundred a week. I would sometimes do two or three small towns a day. I would sometimes spend several days in one of the larger towns. Now, my compensation did not depend on the number of subscribers I got to sign certain little documents. It depended on the number of people who would take the paper regularly and pay for it. If I got a thousand subscribers in a month, and they paid for the paper, I would get $250; but, if during the next month half of these people should stop taking the paper or stop paying for it, I would have to make up for these and get a lot more, in order to get my second thousand. As the number of subscribers constantly increased, the greater would be the volume of the number of quitters. So it behooved me, above everything else, to get a carrier I could rely on to do his work continuously after I had started him. Next I would want as a carrier a boy who would be keen to keep his old subscribers and get new ones. Beyond this, I wanted a boy who—either on account of his popularity or the popularity of his parents or parent, or on account of public sympathy for such parent—would be supported and encouraged by the community. The best type of boy I found to be a ten- or twelve-year-old son of a widow who had other children, and who was known to be worthy and a hard worker. Who, in fact, had the sympathy of the community. My experience taught me that more than half of my success depended upon the right kind of boy to carry the papers.

I started in with a rush, as I have said, and inside of three months I had gotten up to the $750 per thousand subscriber payment. The whole thing was too easy, after the method had been discovered. Had I been shrewder I would not have boasted so much. Especially, I would not have told my brother all of the secrets of my success. I think James made a mistake, however, in greatly underestimating personalities, and overestimating methods. He did it in this case. (As long as he lived, it always seemed to me that he was trying to make silk purses out of sows' ears, always trying to build up success with a method, instead of with a man.)

By this time, I was not only deriving a fair income from my city routes, but had become possessed of about $3,000, a considerable part of which came from my rural circulation work. In fact, I was rich. When James, with an eye to his own interests, advised me that he was going to lay me off the country work so that I could give more attention to building up my city routes, I was quite satisfied.

When I quit the country work, James offered it to another reporter on the paper. He told him how well I had done. James offered him a sliding-scale compensation—but at about one-third of the amount he had been paying me. Not merely this reporter, but other people were put at this work. The method I had discovered and invented was a good enough one, and the country circulation of the *News* continued to grow for years, although more slowly after my quitting.

James E. Scripps was in no sense a natural-born editor; he was not a literary man naturally. He told me once that he was entitled to great credit for having learned what he had learned of books and literature and for becoming an editor, because of all things in the world which were most distasteful to him, he said literary pursuit was the worst. He said it required great force of will on his part always if he had to read any book for more than an hour. Reading always put him to sleep.

I am the half brother of James E. Scripps. I like books. I like literature. I never wanted to be an editor. I never wanted to be rich. I just wanted to write things for other people to read. I had an ambition to be a poet! Think of that!

Was it my blood and breeding that made me an editor, or was it the family tradition, my grandfather, my cousin and my brother? I think it was family tradition. I think, too, that some of the talks that J. L. Scripps gave me when I was a freckle-faced, redheaded, barefooted boy on the farm at Rushville kindled some of my ambition.

I once personally knew quite well a man named John Young, who lived near Lexington, Kentucky. He was a great horse breeder. He told me that at the time of his speaking he owned one quarter of all the thoroughbred mares in the world. I remember what John Young told me:

"I don't care who the sire of this or that colt is or who the dam is. I want to know what kind of cousins the colt has. If nearly every one of the colt's cousins have been purse winners, that's the colt I want to buy, and having bought, I won't sell except for a high price. The dam and the sire may both be slow as the seven-year itch, but if the colt's cousins are all right then I have got a good chance of getting a purse winner."

There are all sorts and conditions of men and women who are closely related to me by blood. By John Young's rule, I should be classed among the country storekeepers, bankers, preachers, at the best. The man who is always looking for evidences of trustworthiness of the law of inheritance is always able to find a great ancestor of a great man, and a great scoundrel as the ancestor of a scoundrel.

A great deal may be learned by finding out how many great men have great scoundrels or poor, mean scoundrels as ancestors, and how many poor, miserable scoundrels have had great and good men for their grandfathers and great-grandfathers. I have in my veins exactly one-fourth the blood of my grandfather, and I believe one-eighth of the blood of John Locke Scripps. I have an idea that if my horse-breeder friend had depended entirely upon his knowledge of the traits of his colts' cousins, and not at all upon his own eye, to size up a colt, he would have gone broke long before he owned anything like one-quarter of the thoroughbred mares in the world.

V

I Buck My Big Brother

I CANNOT NOW fix the exact date when I became a practicing newspaperman. I can only guess backward from the winter of 1876 and 1877. I know that at that time I was legislative correspondent for the *Evening News* at Lansing, Michigan. Before going to Lansing, I had been city editor of the *News* for a little time, and before that I had served more than a year as a reporter on the paper.

This session of the legislature opened just three years and four months after the first issue of the *Evening News*. If I had been city editor for four months, that would leave three years between the time the paper started and my editorship.

After I was laid off my country work, I went to my brother and told him that at last I had determined to become a reporter. Again he pooh-poohed me, and stated that I would only succeed in making a very poor reporter out of a first-class businessman. I told him that was my affair. I gave him an ultimatum: I would go to work on the *News* or go on one of the other papers in the city. And I left him. I went to the city editor, Mr. Michael Dee, and told him I was going to be a reporter. He had been coached by my brother, and laughed at me, and sneered at me, and damned me for a fool. He said he only wished he had my chance and my capacity; that he would not be burning up his good gray matter as a hired man.

Dee had a weakness for free drinks, free lunches and free cigars from an all-around easy mark, such as I was. When he refused to employ me, I imagined he was only carrying out orders. I went out and bought a cheap pine table and a chair. I set them in the local room, and I sat down by it with a pad of paper and began practicing rewriting articles from other papers. I told Dee I was ready to do anything he wanted done in the way of getting news. I would be copy boy for him. I would run errands between the office and the reporters who were out on assignments. I would go to fires. I would, in fact, go and do anything he did not have anyone else to do for him.

To have a free messenger boy in the office in the days when there was no telephone—a messenger more than six feet long, more than half legs, easily able to walk four miles an hour and to run twice as far and never tire—was something of an acquisition. For free smokes, and free drinks, and all sorts of flattery (and this Irishman did love flattery!) I got lots of errands to do. I met people, and made every acquaintance I could. Because I was a Scripps I got consideration that would never have been given to an ordinary messenger boy. I had a big nose and a pushing habit. I was always asking questions of everybody. It was not possible, under the circumstances, for me to fail to get many tips and pointers. Sometimes I would be able to write out what I had learned with sufficient definiteness to enable the city editor or some other reporter to make up from my contribution an item, and even occasionally an article.

I went to night school to learn to write better and to learn to spell. I doubt if I gained anything by this at all, and abandoned it after a few months. But always I was working with my pencil and a pad of paper; writing imaginary items, or rewriting and condensing articles and items from any paper that came handy.

Damned Old Crank

On most evening newspapers some member of the staff had to arrive early in the morning and cut up the morning papers, select items of local interest and put them on the editor's desk. Then he was supposed to rewrite, in the briefest possible form, the items that appeared in the morning paper. It was my brother's theory that his little evening paper should have in it everything that all the other papers, morning or evening, had, over and above the news of the day that came by wire or was gathered by the reporters.

This rewriting was always a tedious job. There was always grumbling from the reporter who was assigned this task for a week. There was one man on the staff who was particularly vicious on the subject. He was the best writer we had, a big Scotsman named Ross. He kept very irregular hours, was a regular nighthawk in fact, and could not endure early rising. I made it a point to get down to the *News* office every morning before even this man came, and, with an extra set of morning papers, I would begin the rewriting. I would then compare my stuff with the other fellow's as he did his rewriting.

One day on Ross's turn for the morning work, what I had always expected happened: he was nearly half an hour late. I had done nearly all the rewriting myself, and suggested to him that he might find it easier to fix up my copy than to do all the rewriting himself. He grabbed my sheaf of copy to look at it, and went to work dressing it up. After two or three pages, he began to grunt with satisfaction. Then he compared my clippings (they were "follow-up" stories) with the original papers, and found our work was done before anyone else had come in. He turned to me with a string of curse words, damning James E. Scripps for being a pigheaded old fool, and the city editor, Dee, for being some sort of a damned Irishman, and said that I could do that work as well as anyone else in the office, and that it was a damned shame for a man like himself, Ross, to be required to turn out such chicken feed.

When Dee came in, Ross convinced him that my work was nearly good enough. After that the other reporters, in succession, took to staying away in the mornings, and I became the actual rewrite editor of the *News*. It was not many weeks before I had gotten the knack of doing the routine courthouse and city hall work. I was then a full-fledged cub reporter.

But it was in the office that I was strongest. I began getting to the office even earlier than had been usual with me. I not only did the rewrites, but laid out the follow-up clippings and suggested the name of the reporter for the assignment. In a short time I was really the assistant city editor, with Mr. Dee only supervising and inspecting my work. The city editor began coming to the office later and later. Relieved of a great deal of the routine work of a city editor, he was able to let himself out, as he particularly liked to do, and write brilliant articles himself. It was not many months before he was only titular city editor and I was actual city editor.

My brother James, acting as editor of the paper, made it a point never to allow a word to be printed in the *Evening News* until it had passed under his eyes. He soon enough discovered both the amount and the quality of my work. He also had a trick of taking stock of his writers. Every day after the paper was off, he sat down and marked the paper, putting on every article and every small item the initial of the man who wrote it.

One day he called me in and told me that it was hard work for him to keep track of the local room, and asked me to do this part of his paper marking. I remember how astonished I was after marking up my first paper. More than half of the local matter, which included the rewrite, was actually my work.

In the meantime I had taken to rewriting telegraph and general news, thus relieving the managing editor of a large part of his work.

The end of my first year was approaching. During this whole year

I had received no salary and no recognition of any kind. With the aid of the plant foreman, a fellow named Matthews who was a great admirer of mine, I undertook to mark up the whole paper. James E. Scripps was very fond of clippings. He held that a great variety, not only of subjects, but of authors, in any one newspaper was good for the paper. I often scolded him and quarreled with him for leaving out perfectly good local matter in order to put in some article he had clipped or condensed from a New York, Boston or Chicago newspaper. Against these clipped items was the mark "clip." In time, I gathered a number of papers of consecutive issue wherein items credited to E. W. Scripps amounted to from one-fourth to nearly one-half of the whole paper.

At the end of the year, I took these papers to my brother James, and told him I had finished my apprenticeship, and that I was now ready for business. He chuckled and grinned and said he thought that was about right. He immediately wrote out a check for $520, at the rate of $10 a week salary for the whole year I had served. Fifteen dollars a week was about the average salary of Detroit reporters.

I also had a serious talk with my brother on another matter. I informed him that his so-called managing editor was an old stick, that his work on the editorial column was so stupid that it made all of us of the city staff ashamed of it. I pointed out some brilliant examples of Mr. Dee's writing, and suggested the appointment of Dee as editor and editorial writer. Dee was getting $30 weekly as city editor, and would gladly take the editorship at the same price. We had a perfectly good city editor on hand to take Dee's place for $15 a week.

Dee got his promotion, and I got mine.

The staff of the *News* in those days was about as wild and reckless a bunch of newspapermen as I have ever known gathered in one room. The staff was the reason the paper thrived so lustily. My brother, by purest chance, gathered on his staff a group of men who surprised my brother, surprised the community, and even surprised themselves, by their brilliance of mind and force. Named in the order, not of their merit, but of their emergence into conspicuousness, these men were:

R. B. Ross, an ex-printer, ex-hobo, ex-Confederate captain, ex-blockade runner, ex-country editor who had failed. He was a great big six-foot-two Scotsman who looked tough, as he had lived for many years before what could be called a very rough life.

Michael Dee, an Irishman, ex-printer, ex-reporter of a Chicago newspaper, and an ex-editor of a daily paper founded by labor unionists in Detroit. He had a brilliant mind. He was a poor city editor, but a magnificent writer of local copy and of editorials.

Thompson J. Hudson, a man of mature years even when the *News* started, a lawyer who had failed at being a lawyer, a politician who had failed to get a remunerative office, a humorist and a droll, a philosopher, and a writer of books who had become wise by his reading and his observation.

E.W. Scripps, who, even before he became a writing journalist, had established himself as a member of the local-room gang, and who acted as a sort of go-between and intriguer between the local staff of the *News* and its editor and owner, and who, later as *de facto* editor, and then city editor, tried to exercise no control or government over his staff at all, but incited every man on it to raise as much hell as possible.

Henry Little, who could imagine more things than ever could possibly happen, and whose fiction was better than most reported facts.

With a staff like this, it is not surprising that our paper was, for those times, flagrantly sensational, the *News* had a number of libel suits. It frequently got mulcted for heavy damages. Yet a funny thing happened. So great was the popular interest in the subjects we wrote about and were sued for, and so great was the public's sympathy with the *News* in these fights, that each of the suits was accompanied by large increases in circulation and prestige, and hence, advertising returns. Instead of a sag in the profit line, there was an upward trend.

The Detroit *Evening News* was practically the founder of what is known as "personal journalism." Rich rascals found that, as far as the reporters of the *News* were concerned, they were living in glass houses, and that they had no means of protecting themselves from public exposure. This applied to rich men who were affected with petty meannesses, so-called respectable men in political offices who were doing wrong things, clergymen who had faults that unfitted them for church service or even decent society, professional men—doctors, lawyers, and even judges on the bench—who had depended upon the cloak of their respectability, or position, to cover a misdeed.

The Detroit *News* gained a reputation almost nationwide for its attitude. About this time the Scripps family was described by someone as "a tribe of Ishmaelites, whose hands were against everybody, and against whom everybody's hands were raised." My brother was a timid man. How keenly he felt this reputation nobody outside his family knew. He felt and said he was a victim of circumstances over which he had no control, that he was being damned for deeds that he had never done and had never wanted done.

One time the scallawag staff of the *News* elected a mayor of Detroit, practically over the dead body of its owner.

The central figure in this election was a young man then coming into prominence in Detroit, William G. Thompson. Thompson had come from somewhere in the East, was a member of an aristocratic family. He had married, in Detroit, the daughter and heir of one of Detroit's wealthiest citizens.

Thompson was naturally a sport. He was bright and intelligent in a way. He got into the game of politics for fun. He was a crony of Ross's, and a companion of that roistering Scotsman in many of his orgies with both men and women of the sporting life. Thompson was genial and amiable, and liberal in furnishing entertainment to our crowd on the *News*.

At the time of this mayoralty election, the town was surprised at the gall and impudence of young Thompson in presenting himself as a candidate for mayor. He ran against one of the oldest, most respectable and well-to-do of the city's residents, a man whose patronage and condescending friendship had won my brother to him completely.

The first gun of the campaign was fired by the *News* in the form of an editorial, written by my brother himself, favoring his friend.

The next thing was a war council in the local room of the *Evening News*. We decided that we wanted Thompson for mayor. The question was to elect him. Even Thompson's own party papers were giving him lame support. With the influential *News* against him it would be reckoned that his chances were hopeless.

I brought the local crowd the orders directly issued to me, that the local staff must heartily support my brother's candidate. How to obey this order, from the editor and owner, and at the same time support our man—that was the question.

It did not prove such a difficult problem when it was submitted to such a coterie. We were well acquainted with my brother's disposition to be obtuse on some subjects. We still better knew that the editor lived such a secluded life that he had in no way been touched by politics or even by the people of the city themselves. We knew that he was so hard at work—sixteen hours a day—in his office and at home, with the details of the business, that he could never give a second thought to any subject after he had decided and given his orders. We proposed to elect Thompson for mayor by abusing him roundly when he proposed something the public would highly approve of, and by praising his antagonist for doing those things and being those things that we knew the public would detest.

After our first conference, we retired to Ross's living rooms and sent for Thompson to join us. He entered into the plans with enthusiasm, and told us he would see to it, not only in his public speeches, but in all his perambulations about the city, and in his activities and associations, that we would be furnished with mines of copy suited to our purpose. He agreed that he would invent things himself, and allow us to draw on our own imaginations for other things to say about him, so that we would have plenty of material for denouncing him for doing and being what would please the voters—"the great rough masses of the horny hand," as he called them.

His opponent, on the other hand, was to be trailed. His meetings with bank directors, his attendance on social functions, the splendor of his home, the number of his servants, etc., were all to be dwelt on in such a commendatory way as not only to tickle the candidate's vanity, but to gain as well the complete approval of his social set.

This was the background of the constant pre-election duel between the editor of the paper and his assistant editor, the editorial writer, and the local room gang. My brother was wonderfully pleased with what he considered the hearty and cordial co-operation of the local room with his editorial policy.

Election day came, and Thompson won out by a magnificent majority. It is possible that no one but Thompson and the local staff of the *Evening News*, prior to the election, even dreamed of the result.

I suspect that James later waked up to the trick that had been played on him. For, from a certain date later, he was always suspicious, not only of the local room as a whole, but of me in particular. He selected one editor-in-chief after another, in order to find some man who could control the local staff. Yet he did not dare to fire one of his local men, all of whom were proving their tremendous value by causing the *News's* circulation and influence to grow so rapidly.

I imagine that one cause of my brother's long and bitter antagonism to me was the memory of the suffering he had once gone through because of my activities as city editor.

The only result of these activities, as I have said, was to advertise the *News* more extensively as being enterprising, and gain for it a larger and larger circulation. Finally, it dawned on the respectable citizens of Detroit—the victims of our "personal journalism"—that the only way to squelch the Scrippses was to put some of them in jail. They began to talk about criminal libel suits.

James told me that he proposed to turn the *Evening News* into a corporation, in order to avoid personal liability or criminal libel. Those were the days when a speaker had characterized corporations as things that "had no souls to be damned, nor noses to be punched." James said he did not mind civil suits, even when damages had to be paid, but that he could not endure the idea of being convicted as a criminal.

For James to think was for him to act, unless there was someone at hand to restrain him. Almost immediately he set about to incorporate the *News*. Despite his long experience as a newspaperman, James knew little about the law. He soon learned that under Michigan law a corporation would have to have five stockholders and five directors. James was averse to stock companies. What he really wanted was a closed corporation, a corporation with all the advantages of a partnership.

He said the *News* must be in large blocks, with no share worth less than $1,000. He did this to reduce to a minimum the danger of stockholders parting easily with small shares. He proposed to incorporate the *News* for $50,000. When it came to selecting the stockholders, his desire for a closed corporation led him to confine the stockholding to the family. It was necessary, of course, to reduce the holdings of his two partners, my brother George and sister Ellen. George insisted on keeping his full one-third of the whole concern. To do so, he would have to have sixteen and two-thirds of the total shares. We finally induced him to take sixteen shares. James took thirty shares. Two shares were allotted to Ellen, one share to me, and one to John Scripps

Sweeney, a cousin, and a most valued member of the business staff.

Although the *Evening News* was incorporated for $50,000, it had actually cost—as the books showed at the time of incorporation—$30,000. The new stockholders were assessed $600 for our $1,000 shares. This incorporation took place some forty years ago. I have held my one share of stock ever since. It represents two per cent of the value of the whole property. I think there have been very few cases where any investment paid the investor so well as this $600 paid me. My first year's dividend was not less than ten per cent of the amount of the investment. Each succeeding year, from that time, my dividends have grown larger, until the year 1914, when they amounted to $6,000 or more.

My brother James and I have had many bitter quarrels since that time. More than once in the early days he suggested that I sell my share of stock to him, and that Ellen should sell hers to him also. But for the last thirty years of his life, I must say he has never intimated any desire to get hold of my stock. I think that both sentimentality and a certain kind of superstition prompted him in his desire that I should keep this stock. This year (1915) it is earning six per cent on $120,000. I doubt not that I could sell this stock for $120,000. I am reasonably certain in my own mind that this stock will go on increasing in value, for another generation, at the rate of six to ten per cent in value, besides paying big dividends.

This little $600 nest egg of mine has proved to have had other great values. Had I not possessed it, I would not have had the collateral that was absolutely necessary for me to put up in order to borrow the money for my share of the Cleveland *Press* on its foundation, in the fall of 1878.

In fact, if my memory serves me right, this $600 is the seed from which has grown the whole of my present estate. I cannot recall any other capital that has come into my possession (excepting one block), that did not come directly and lineally from this one share of *Evening News* stock. Other money I had made prior to this time seems to have slipped away from me, lost or spent, and not carried over into any future business enterprise. I suppose it all went into my social education, which was largely composed of love affairs.

(That block of my fortune which I speak of as deriving from other sources than my first investment in the *Evening News* was an inheritance from my brother George, who died in April, 1900. This inheritance amounted to about $750,000.)

I believe that during the first twenty-five years of the existence of the *News*, James E. Scripps never even got near the position of being able to control his own newspaper's policy. He fretted and complained often on the subject; and, many times, reproached me for having been the instigator of a perpetual and irrepressible rebellion. I used to maintain to him that it was only because he had been unable to control his staff that his paper had succeeded. He said, in contradiction, that his staff could have done just as brilliant work and made just as popular a paper had we proceeded along the lines that he wanted.

About thirty-five years after the founding of the *News*, James E., through one of his sons-in-law, became owner and controller of the Chicago *Journal*. This property proved a mighty loser. My brother tried to do in Chicago what he had always maintained that, but for my treachery, he could have done in Detroit. He was trying to make a great and powerful paper by making it extremely respectable—that is to say, respectable to capitalists and corporate interests.

The paper got into very bad shape. I had met my brother in Chicago, in the early days of this century, to discuss several business matters among them, the subject of the Chicago *Journal*. We were talking about whether it would be wise for the *Journal* to be turned over to me, to be managed and controlled in conjunction with my other papers. My brother James preferred to keep the controlling share of stock, but was willing to bear even a greater proportion of the costs than his stockholdings required.

We were both stopping at the Great Northern Hotel in Chicago. I had a suite of rooms in a corner in a way that projected out to look down on the main thoroughfare. My parlor had a large circular window looking down on this street. Just at that time, there was prevailing one of those mighty labor union strikes that so often afflicted Chicago. It was a teamsters' strike.

A riot broke out in the street below while James and I were standing at the open window. The noise was terrific. While James looked down on the mob, his face was working with disgust and anger. He kept jingling his keys in his hand.

"Oh, Ed," he said, "I only wish I was mayor of this city, or some other city, when some such thing as this was going on. I would sure enough teach these fellows a lesson that they would remember, as would every other workingman in the city."

To shut out the noise, I closed the window, and we went back and settled down on the sofa to continue our talk.

"I know that you meant what you said just now," I told James. "It is because you are running a paper here in Chicago from the standpoint of a man who thinks as you do that you are losing $200,000 yearly. We might as well drop the discussion of the *Journal.* I will never waste any of my time trying to run a paper which you control. It was hard enough in the old days to run the *News,* when you were too poor to risk your chance for success by discharging men who understood and sympathized with just such poor devils as those rioters in the streets below."

VI

Bad Habits, I: Wicked Women, etc.

A MAN'S LIFE story that does not include a fairly accurate synopsis of his sex experience is, to be trite, like the play of *Hamlet* with Hamlet left out. When you consider that man's chief role in this earth stage is the continuance of the existence of the race, it is easy to see the absurdity of leaving out of a life story that which is, biologically speaking, the sole object of that life's existence.

On my sixteenth birthday I measured myself and found I was a full six feet tall though I weighed scarcely one hundred twenty pounds. I was long, thin and gawky. The beard on my face began to grow before I was fourteen. I sometimes shaved but I was clumsy about it and always cut my face so I preferred to resort to the barber. But what was the good of shaving? I wore rough clothes. I never went to parties. What was the good of wasting my time and my money in barbershops? I rarely shaved.

I was redheaded, and I had a great mop of hair. It caused me to spend twenty-five cents every time the barber cut it, so I let it grow. To say I wasn't vain because I didn't dress well or shave and keep my hair trimmed, would be to say something false. I became quite proud of my great mane of auburn hair and even the silky, thin beard which grew on my face. Yes, I was proud of my personal appearance.

There was an old, a very old woman living in a cottage near the building where I used to go to school. The old woman had a niece or a grandaughter. She was a homely little creature. When I happened to be in the post office with a lot of the village youth, girls and boys (the boys dressed in store clothes and even wearing white collars), one of the girls told the party, to plague me, that a few days before she had been talking to this drab. She reported that the girl had said, "I don't care if he is redheaded. Ed Scripps is the prettiest boy in town." Now this must be as nearly as possible a true story. I wasn't flattered by what she had said about me. In fact I was mortified. She was a poor, and poorly dressed kind of a girl. If one of these village aristocrats had said the same thing of me I would have swelled with pride. So it appears that I was not only proud but decidedly vain.

So far back as I can remember, I was sex-conscious. I suppose most men had the same experiences, although I judge from what many have told me that each one has considered his own case unique, or nearly so.

I doubt if the exposure to temptation for boys in the country is less than it is in the city. I sometimes think it must be greater. Girls or young women are to be found everywhere who are only too willing to give instructions to young boys.

My youthful experiences, and the conditions around me, were such as to cause me considerable anxiety. Injunctions to secrecy and instinctive modesty constantly impressed me with the idea of my wickedness. My first idea of the meaning of the word hypocrisy was coupled with these first experiences of mine. It seemed to me that I was a hypocrite, and that a great many other young fellows around me were also hypocrites. We pretended to be what we were not.

Whether or not continency in young boys and young men is possible, I have no personal means of knowing. It certainly did seem to me that it was impossible, and that I really had no right to blame the temptresses, although they certainly seemed to take the leading part in our mutual transgressions.

There were girls, and girls! I thought.

As a young man I was exceedingly diffident in my relations with those whom I considered nice girls of my years. The consciousness of my own transgressions was always accusing me. I always felt not only embarrassed, but guilty of wronging these nice girls and young women by associating with them. Shortly after reaching adolescence I sought to escape this embarrassment for a time by avoiding the companionship of young women whom I thought above my own moral class.

(From time to time I had expressed to women of mature age my conviction that the woman and not the man was the real pursuer. Great subtlety on the part of the woman in this pursuit may be the chief cause for the commonly expressed—though perhaps not commonly believed—idea that the man is always the brute and the woman the victim.)

I determined when quite young to escape from this continual self-condemnation and temptation by marrying early. Romance, of the ordinary Anglo-Saxon storybook variety, had played but a small part in my life. My mind was so set on this utilitarian view of marriage that there was little room for play and the development of what is alleged to be romance. I sought a mate. I sought diligently. I had my youthful ambitions and no doubt that the future held for me a worldly position that would require my wife to be above reproach and beyond the suspicion of having had anything like a loose past. I fully expected to hold such a prominent position that inevitably the past life of myself and my wife would become known. But for this, I would have cut the Gordian knot of all my difficulties by marrying some young woman with whom I had been intimate.

As time went on, and the history of my amours extended, I came to feel that it would be hopeless for me to try to conceal my past, and that I would do a great injustice to any pure woman who should marry me without complete knowledge of my past. Over a period of several years at least I discussed this subject with myself. I finally concluded that all the nice girls in the world would have to go unmarried if they did not marry men of my own character. I determined, when the time came, to assert my right and marry the nice girl.

At least I have been enough of a gentleman never to commit adultery. Nor have I ever been the party to blame for the first step in an immoral dirction by any girl or young woman. I had been very early in my life instructed on the subject of venereal diseases, and the lasting effect on any victim of such a disease. In one respect at least I was physically pure. I was not the carrier of any poisonous germs.

When I finally determined on my right to marry any girl of my choice, if I could win her consent, I chose a somewhat different course from that which I had pursued for a few years. I had had a number of experiences with young women who "knew how to take care of themselves." As I had considerable to do around the theaters as a newspaperman, I had a rather wide acquaintance among actresses. I had not been very careful in the matter of showing myself publicly with young women who, though not of the demimonde, were still not above suspicion. I adopted a course that might be called temporary monogamy. I chose a mistress who was as little inclined to public reproach as I was myself. One result of this was that I had far more time and freedom to devote to the society of nice people. It was now certain that I would not be in danger of having my propensity for bad company exposed by casual encounters, or by the general talk of men of all classes and women of some classes.

I made a number of efforts as one might say to reform myself and be entirely continent. They proved entirely vain. Conditions being as they were, it was physically impossible for me to practice celibacy for more than a very brief period of days, or, at the most, weeks. During these periods of torture—for they were nothing less—I felt more debased than at any other time, because my mind was so preoccupied with the subject as to make me feel all the time that I was unclean clear through to the core. Intelligent and perfective work in my profession was impossible. Walking and running, rowing and swimming, the most violent kind of exercises, had to be kept up by me all of the time to make existence endurable.

Prior to this reforming of my customs, I had never given thought to dress or any of the accomplishments supposed to be the possessions of young men who are attractive to young ladies. I now began to pay much attention to my dress. Clumsy, awkward and loutish as I was, I undertook to learn dancing. I studied the carriage and expression of the young beaux. I practiced, before the mirror, various poses, and gestures, and facial expressions. I made a business of trying to make myself into a dandy.

I always had, because of my position, some sort of acquaintanceship and companionship among nice young ladies. I set out deliberately to widen as far as possible this circle of acquaintanceship. But all the time I was looking for a wife.

It must not be supposed I grew to young manhood without the usual number of heart affairs. I had known several young women who were nice, and with whom, for a greater or shorter period of time, I thought I was in love. Even with the other sort of girls, there had been several who had attracted me immensely. In fact, I had been at times violently in love with them, notwithstanding my relations with them and my knowledge that they must have had similar relations with other men.

After I had already taken the necessary first steps toward the accomplishment of place and position, I felt my advances to various nice young ladies were acceptable, were surprisingly acceptable. I recognized soon enough that my eligibility, or supposed eligibility as a husband was valued more highly than my natural or assumed graces. This realization, so far from humiliating me, rather gratified me. I preferred to have my position recognized as being desirable, rather than my person. I thought none the less of a girl when I believed that she had sense enough to appreciate my position, and my ability greatly to improve that position. I felt extremely vain on more than one occasion when a "managing mamma" took an interest in my attentions to her daughter.

The first of my successes at about this period involved a certain very well-to-do Israelite whose home I frequently passed. This man had two pretty daughters. One of them I thought was really extraordinarily beautiful. In those days, I was very much attracted by a beautiful face. It was easy enough to get an introduction, and I was warmly welcomed by both daughters and mamma. I soon enough was paying constant attention to the beauty. The father found out about me, and undertook to find out more about me. It was a serious matter for him, an orthodox Jew, to think of the possibility of a gentile son-in-law. He was a large stockholder in the Michigan Central Railroad. James F. Joy was then president of the railroad, and H.B. Ledger was treasurer. As a newspaperman, I knew both these men. Mr. Joy had been, for a number of years, an intimate of my brother's; it was easy enough for the father of my sweetheart to discover who I was, and the kind of family I belonged to. Mr. Ledger was a rather grave and serious sort of young man (then in his early thirties) and, on my coming into his office one day, he spoke to me on the subject, much to his embarrassment. I was in the office of President Joy a few minutes later, and he, rather jokingly, complimented me on my thrift and told me he was not throwing any obstacles in my way. He intimated that he had told one of his friends if I should follow in the footsteps of my elder brother, I might be considered a desirable party.

I was by no means sure of the girl herself. It seemed to me that she was very fond of being seen in public in my company. She liked especially for me to take her to the theater. As in those days I had entrance to the theaters without charge, I was able to gratify her love for the stage without seriously depleting my narrow finances. I had my doubts as to whether she was attracted by my position, by the fact that I was a gentile, or by my personality. I had become conspicuous, both on account of the beauty of my companion, and because she was a Jewess. My friends and acquaintances began to joke me too much for my comfort by calling me "Abraham." They warned me of the great physical pain that I would have to endure in order to become acceptable to a Jewish family.

There were few Jews in Detroit in those days, and I think there had been no intermarriages between Jews and gentiles. All this set me to thinking pretty hard. I thought I was very much in love with the girl, but I was embarrassed by two conditions: I hated to make myself a marked man by marrying a Jewess; and, from the standpoint of my poverty, her father could be reckoned a very wealthy man. I had a tremendous aversion to the idea of ever being, in any way, inferior to my wife. It was simply intolerable for me to think of that old man exercising influence over me, directly or indirectly through his daughter. But I think the main thing that scared me off was the taunts and jests of my friends and associates who called me "Abraham."

I have always been ashamed of this incident in my life. The girl was so exceedingly pretty, and she was so very nice and kind to me.

About this time, something occurred to take me out of the city, and keep me away for several weeks. When I returned, I did not again return to see the girl.

Some years later, when I was sitting in my editor's room in the office of the Cleveland *Press,* two cards were brought to me. I recognized the man's name and remembered him very well. He was a Detroit citizen, wealthy and prominent. I did not know his wife. It seemed to me his wife had died; but the other card was evidently that of his wife. I sent for them. They came into my room. I knew that there was no particular occasion for this man's calling on me, but when he came in with his wife, I immediately recognized the reason. She was my old friend, the Jewess. She was six or seven years older than when I knew her, but she did not look it. She was still beautiful, very beautiful. The gentleman told me that his wife had been the occasion of their visit to my office, that she was an old friend of mine, that she was determined not to leave Cleveland until she saw me, that she wanted to see me in my office and nowhere else.

She had waited a long time to marry, and then had married an old widower with two or three children. She came and took a seat beside me at the desk. On two or three occasions, when her husband was looking away from us, she gave me a very hard, and, I thought, reproachful look. As I sat there with her, I felt my face fairly flaming red and hot with shame. That woman knew I had deserted her because she was a Jewess. I believe that she came and dragged in her old husband with her for no other purpose than to give me a bad quarter of an hour. She succeeded in not only giving me a bad quarter of an hour, but many and many a one since.

I know I was not desperately in love with her. If I had been, I would not have treated her as I did. What I was ashamed of was that I had been afraid of the jeers of a lot of very useless young men, and because I had been so careless in trying to attract her regard without giving any thought to the result.

My general reputation, however, caused me a lot of trouble. Once, when I was editor of the Cincinnati *Post*, I was called on in my office by a young woman in whom I had once been very greatly interested. She told me that she had come to Cincinnati to resume our old relations.

"It's impossible," I told her.

She insisted.

I told her that she must leave me immediately.

She was a beautiful divorcee, and had been, I believe, very much attached to me, notwithstanding the irregularity of our alliance.

She informed me in a very decided way that she would not permit me to cast her off.

Since I had been in Europe and had not seen her for more than two years, and since our parting had not been caused by desertion on my part, I did not consider the matter one of "casting off." I was struggling mentally against my propensities, and against nature that was crying out within me. The temptation to give way was tremendous. I felt that I could not trust myself to too long a siege, so I determined to close the incident in the only way that I felt it could be permanently closed.

I knew that I could not be considered an object of blackmail. I did not believe the woman wanted to blackmail me, in the sense that she wanted money. I had known of her life from the time I had last seen her to when she visited me in Cincinnati. She was well-provided for by a lover who possessed considerable means and wanted to make her his wife. He finally did.

I directed that an official from the police department be called for. At the same time I directed that the reporters of the three other papers in the city be called in. I then told the woman that I proposed to make a holy show of myself and secure it complete publicity.

She did not believe me.

The police officer, the reporters, and my business associate, Mr. Milton McRae, all appeared on the scene to join us, within a short time.

McRae was frightened at what I was about to do. He protested that it would be a great injury to the paper. I told him that, injury or no injury, this matter had to be settled then and there and forever.

I told the plain-clothes detective and the three reporters that for some time, up to a period of two or three years before, the woman who was present and I had been intimate. I said that the period of intimacy had closed by mutual consent, and that she now had returned determined to take up the old relations and had made a disagreeable scene.

The story was a short enough one. It was sufficiently sordid and vulgar to cause me considerable pain in relating it.

I then told the woman there was nothing more she could do, and that she had better leave. The officer informed her that she must leave or submit to arrest. He pointed out that her action was clearly illegal, and that, according to her statement, her purpose in Cincinnati was to disturb the peace.

There was no scene, no tears and protests. The woman had been surprised by my actions, which was natural. On the other hand, I think she was gratified at the prospect of the publicity she was to get and at the prospect of her name being coupled with mine. Furthermore, I think I lost nothing of her respect—a certain sort of devotion that such women have for their lovers—by the course I had taken.

With a smile on her face, a friendly smile rather than otherwise, she parted with me, and announced to the officer that she would go with him to the station.

McRae's first business was to accompany the officer and the woman. He said the officer soon convinced the woman that her remaining in Cincinnati would only be disagreeable to her. Then McRae furnished her with sufficient money, bought her a ticket and put her on the train.

McRae's next business was to attempt to suppress the account that I had given to the reporters so that it would not be published. He appealed directly to the publishers of the other Cincinnati papers for their consent not to publish it.

One of them said he would not publish it if I personally requested him not to. Another said he would not publish it if none of the other papers would.

Mr. Murat Halstead's reporter came back to me to see if I had made the request. I told him it was legitimate news, but that I did not intend to publish it in my own paper. I told him that Mr. Halstead, as editor of the *Commercial Gazette,* was the only person to decide whether or not an item of news should be published in his paper. I sent word to Mr. Halstead that, in a similar case where he and his family might be involved, I would not suppress such an item of legitimate news, at his or anyone else's request.

The article was published in both the *Enquirer* and the *Commercial Gazette.* It was given sensational headlines. Both of the papers, as I remember, did me the justice of giving my statement as to why I caused the arrest—that is, my resolve to live, thereafter, a clean life.

The incident attracted considerable attention throughout the country, and a number of papers published the story in one form or another. One of the nation's leading papers devoted to it a column on its editorial page, headed "Divorce without Marriage."

McRae, when he failed in having the article suppressed, was completely discouraged. He sought me out in my Cincinnati hotel and told me I had ruined the *Post* beyond redemption.

I told him that I had caused myself considerable trouble, and made public an incident that would probably return to plague me as long as I lived. But I added the belief that I had still done a far better thing for myself than I would have done had I either submitted to the temptation of resuming intimacy with the woman, or attempted some shameful and cowardly course to eliminate her from my life. I also told McRae that he need have no fear of the *Post* suffering. I said I believed that among the class of men that he had to deal with—the businessmen of the community—there was perhaps not a single individual who had not, at one time in his life, been embarrassed with a mistress. I told him that most of these men had made large sacrifices, either of money or principles, to hide their shame, and all of these men and the general public of men would rather admire me and envy me for doing something that each of them lacked the courage to do.

McRae afterward told me that when he started out the day after the incident, after the morning papers had published the news of it, he dreaded meeting his customers. However, he admitted that as he went down the line he found things much as I had said they would be. Some of his customers joked with him about the incident and laughed. Others spoke with some admiration. Even those very really or affectedly pious men expressed their satisfaction with the man whose deeds coincided with the principles enunciated by his papers.

The incident was not a nine-day wonder. It was hardly a twenty-four-hour wonder. It does not occur to me that I have ever heard of anyone speaking of it. When, some two years later, one of the papers took up the old story and published it the paper was universally condemned.

There were other cases where events did not proceed so far as in the cases I have mentioned. My career was not that of a universal conqueror. On two occasions, proposals of marriage by me were turned down cold, as the boys would say.

I can recall four actual engagements of marriage. In each case I had proposed marriage in good faith, and believe that I was accepted in good faith. I think there were no less than three of these cases wherein the young lady changed her mind. And, in the one in which I changed my mind, I was reduced to a pitiable state of embarrassment and shame in breaking off the match. This time it was not only that I had lost all feeling of affection that had temporarily affected me, but I had found out that there had been several cases of insanity in the family. This young lady later went on the stage, against her parents' will, and developed a reputation for being very eccentric. This, I thought to myself when I heard about it, was only a form of the family mental trait.

I have told enough of my experiences to indicate how natural has been my development. For many years I have sought to avoid as much trouble as possible, by avoiding whenever possible, all association, either business or social, with women. I learned that whatever may be the capacities of other men, my capacities as a ladies' man are so small that they are not more than enough to do justice to the one woman who has a right to all that I can give.

I met my wife in a little village in South Ohio. She was the only child of a Presbyterian minister of that section. My wife's father was, I think, one of the most simple-minded, unworldly-wise men I ever knew. I thought that, inasmuch as I could not speak of such things to the girl, I ought at least to let her parents know what sort of man the suitor for their daughter's hand was. I felt called upon to do the un-American thing, namely, to ask the girl's father before asking the girl herself. I undertook to do so one evening, when the old gentleman and I were alone together. I intended to make a rather long speech of it, and explain a good many things. I wanted to say to him, myself, all of the things that he or anyone else might possibly hear of later.

As my courting had been carried on entirely in the girl's home and in the immediate neighborhood of the village, my father-in-law was not at all surprised when I came to speak of the subject. Of the several sentences that I had spoken, all that he seemed to have heard was that I wanted to marry his daughter. From there on he took the words out of my mouth, and stated that he only had one question to ask me, and that was, whether I had ever been divorced. As I was twelve years older than his daughter—I was thirty-one, and she nineteen—it was evident to him that there had been plenty of time for me to have had previous marital experiences.

It seems that, just at that time, there was considerable attention being paid, by the ministers, to the question of the propriety of divorced people marrying, or of ministers marrying one or the other of the parties who had been divorced. I was rather stumped for a reply to this question. I had wanted to tell him how many, many separations I had had; but I could not honestly tell him that I had been divorced.

I made two or three more futile efforts to make a clean breast of the situation. It was all in vain. So I let him go happy and contented with the thought that his girl was going to marry a man who had never committed the sin of being divorced from his wife.

VII

Bad Habits, II: Alcohol, Nicotine, etc.

FROM THE time I took my first drink of alcohol on my twenty-first birthday, until I was well along in my forty-sixth year, I drank so much whiskey, not on what are called "sprees" but in steady tippling, as to cause every doctor I had spoken to about the case to believe I was a liar when I told about it. They declared no man could drink so much as I said I drank and live for more than a year. I think that during this twenty-five years rarely did a day pass that I did not drink alcohol to the equivalent of more than four quarts of whiskey. I was a forty-drink-a-day man.

Traveling on the railroad cars, I always had a large flask of mixed water and whiskey under my pillow, so that during the night I would drink at least a pint of whiskey. At home I always had a decanter on the table at my bedside with a siphon or a bottle of plain water. For nearly twenty-five years, I believe that day and night I was never entirely out from under the influence of alcohol.

When I was fourteen a very good old cousin of the family, the Sunday-school superintendent in Rushville, a very pious and very zealous man in all things moral, founded a Good Templar Lodge in our community. Its aim was to redeem drunkards, to keep boys and young men from acquiring the habits of drinking and smoking. Somehow I was induced to join the lodge. A part of the initiation ceremony was a solemn oath taken by the candidate: "Never so long as life lasts will I use alcohol or tobacco in any form."

I had often sipped my father's wine, many bottles of which were kept in our cellar. I was quite familiar with the taste of Scotch ale. I rather liked both of these beverages.

A few days after joining the Good Templar's lodge I had a slight cold. My father's favorite remedy for colds was a glass of hot wine, well-seasoned with spices and sweetened. I detested the stuff, and when on this occasion I was ordered to drink it, I pleaded my temperance vows. This made the old man very angry. He was not only angry with me for having taken the step without consulting him, but he was angry with our old Sunday-school superintendent cousin for having inveigled me into the lodge. My father contended that no minor child should be required or even allowed to bind himself by oath. Someway the matter was settled and I ceased to be a lodge member. But while I was in the lodge I heard a great deal about what was said on the bad effects of alcohol and tobacco on growing boys.

In severing my relations with the Good Templars I made a resolution that I would not indulge in tobacco or alcohol until I was twenty-one. On the evening of my twenty-first birthday I walked into the bar of the hotel in Detroit, and took a small wine glass of the mildest possible claret. I also bought a very small and mild cigar.

When I was a young boy I had tried to smoke a cigar once, and took violently sick. I had no intention of running the least risk of suffering from tobacco sickness and so on my twenty-first birthday I smoked not more than one-half inch of my cigar. Next day I took another cigar and no wine, and of my second cigar I smoked about an inch. It was a week or more before I consumed the whole of a small cigar by continuous smoking. Later I experimented in wines, stronger and stronger, and found I got no effect with a single glass. Finally I took in one draught a glass of lager beer. I didn't like the bitter, harsh taste of the stuff. I then tried a small glass of whiskey. I was advised by a senior of many years that if I diluted it well with water I would feel no bad effects. My first glass of whiskey might have been pure water for all the effect it had on me. Among the set of young men who were my associates, no one was really a man until after he could get drunk and until after he had other experiences.

I never really acquired the habit of getting drunk, but before a year was over I could drink many times more glasses of whiskey than any of my associates without any feeling of inebriation, and without much feeling of stimulation. I learned to keep away from champagne and never to take another drop of liquor after I felt the premonitory symptoms of inebriation. Accidents have happened when I have taken too much, but in all my more than seventy years, not more than a dozen times have I ever become even unpleasantly stimulated. On each of these occasions I was made terribly sick in the stomach and suffered from terrible headaches.

During the twenty-five years I was continuously under the influence of alcohol, I attended to my business affairs I presume successfully. Some of my immediate associates knew that I was a very heavy drinker; but in attending to my business and coming into contact with very many other people, men and women, it appears to me now that none of these even suspected that I was drinking anything.

Just as I was growing to be such an outrageous toper, I was growing in my use of tobacco. My usual consumption of tobacco was some forty large but mild Havana cigars a day.

It was in my forty-sixth year that I realized that whiskey had finally gotten the advantage over me. By the time I was forty-six I was almost blind. My body had become weak and flabby. The flesh on my legs and arms had shrunk so that when I was stripped or wearing a gymnasium or bathing suit I resembled one of those ridiculous little figures that the artists paint and draw as brownies. My skin, from my feet up to my waist, and on my arms and hands, had lost nearly all sensitiveness. When I touched the bare skin of my leg with my finger or with a pencil I received only the impression that a man in ordinary condition would feel were he to touch his foot with his shoes on. There was a perceptible tremble in my hands.

I waked up to the fact that I must quit drinking or die soon. I engaged a physician to travel with me and to be with me continually. With him, and with other physicians, I tried to overcome my alcoholic habit by the use of other drugs. However, I made no progress in the way of recovering my health, although I did reduce my tippling to two quarts a day.

As I have said, my eyesight was almost gone. I had to depend on others to read to me even the most important documents that required my signature. I was able to write some sort of a signature, although I could not see it. My secretary would place my hand at the point where I was to begin writing; and then, blind as I was, I could, by force of long habit, make a complete and fairly good signature.

I really felt the need of my eyesight more than anything else. My oldest son was then in his fifteenth year. I determined to make a last herculean effort to hang onto life until this son should reach his majority. An oculist and another doctor, together with my personal physician, made a thorough examination of me, paying particular attention to my eyes. They reported that, with great care on my part, I might prolong my life for the six years I desired. The question was whether or not I could stand the shock of entirely giving up stimulants. Of course, the question in the minds of both the doctors was whether or not I had sufficient force of character and resolution to quit drinking. A number of other physicians had given up my case entirely, and had told my personal attendant that there was nothing to be gained by my torturing myself by abandoning the use of alcohol. These doctors from Cincinnati told me that I could continue drinking with moderation, and, with great care, could reasonably hope to live for the few years I desired.

"But about my eyesight?" I asked. The oculist said there was only one possible hope of my escaping complete and permanent blindness, and that hope rested on my entire abandonment of the use of alcohol and tobacco. He frankly told me, however, that my case had proceeded so far that he would make no promises. He stated further that there was not more than one chance out of three or four that I would ever gain sufficient eyesight to read even large type with powerful lenses.

When I suggested that the shock of complete abstinence might kill me, they did not give me too much assurance. They both did say they had great hopes for my constitution being strong enough to stand the shock, and that their faith in my constitution was based on the fact that I had, for so long, drunk such enormous quantities of whiskey and still lived. One of them said that any man who could live for a year under the conditions that I had been living under for many years would have to have a most remarkable constitution and natural vitality far in excess of the average.

I could then continue to drink and live, but be blind. I could abandon whiskey and tobacco and have one chance out of three or four of being able to see a little.

I emptied my pockets of cigars. I removed the box of cigars from the room I was in. I called for a drink of ginger ale. From that time, for a period of three years, I drank no beer, wine or whiskey. For eighteen months I did not touch tobacco.

There was no shock at all as the result of my breaking off my drinking. Of course, I had the craving. On only one occasion did this craving become so strong as to cause me almost to break my resolution. I think this was the third day after I had taken my last drink. I begged my personal physician to let me have just one drink. Perhaps for a half hour or so we strove together on this matter. In the meantime, he had induced me to take a dose of morphine in some form. I think it was a big dose, as it put me to sleep. But from that time, I felt nothing like the compelling craving.

At Asheville, North Carolina, I rapidly recuperated in general health. I rode much in the open air, and walked a good deal. I made many acquaintances, and often enough I would go to the bar in the hotel with them, and while they drank whiskey and beer and wine, I would take my tipple in the form of ginger ale or Vichy water. I was much encouraged by my rapid recovery of health. The numbness I had felt in my hands and feet disappeared, my hands ceased to tremble and my eyesight very rapidly improved. I could see to walk alone. I could find my way about the hotel alone, climb the stairs and even begin to recognize faces.

One day a bellboy brought me a telegram. There was no one in the room to read it to me, so I opened it and took out the message. When I held it up I was surprised to find that I was able, with some difficulty, of course, to read the entire message myself. I think that for a number of months before this I had never even attempted to read anything printed or written.

Besides my secretary, who was with me at Asheville, I had employed an old gentleman to come in and read to me in the afternoons and evenings when I had leisure. It was probably a full year before I completely recovered my eyesight—that is to say, so that I could read with spectacles. Prior to my blindness I had never used spectacles.

The night of my discovery of the recovery of my eyesight, I determined to celebrate by a little game of poker. The same two doctors that went with me to the barroom sat in the game and there were several others. All my guests smoked. The smell of the smoke had its effect. The craving for a cigar was almost more than I could bear, and after a half hour the game broke up and I went for a walk.

It was about fifteen years before this whiskey and tobacco episode that I contracted ophthalmia in one of my eyes while traveling through Mexico. This presumably was the result of using a towel that had not been thoroughly cleansed and disinfected. On account of the extreme pain I suffered with the eye, the doctors found it necessary to use morphine by injection. There was hardly a square inch on the surface of my body that was not swollen as the result of needle pricks. The disease was cured, but I had contracted the morphine habit. Unless I had a dose injected into me two or three times an hour, I suffered as much pain in my eye as I ever suffered when it was diseased. At that time I had not been married a full year. My wife was traveling in Mexico with me, and there was already evidence that in a few months I would become a father. It would not do for me to permit myself to be a morphine addict. I can truthfully say that it was fully one hundred times harder for me to get over this morphine drug habit than it was for me to lay aside both whiskey and tobacco.

I have on a number of occasions had friends and even medical men praise me for my strength of character and will, and yet I never felt myself entitled to any of the praise which was given me. In both the morphine and the whiskey episodes, the alternative in each was so extremely horrible that it seems to me a man of even the weakest will and smallest amount of self-respect would be compelled to do as I did. Of course, it hurt in both cases. The ordeal was great, but for me to presume to claim any credit would be ridiculous.

After all, I did only what I had long before determined to do, conduct myself as a gentleman, and I think no one who even pretended to be a gentleman could, under circumstances such as mine were, fail to do what I did. Both of these experiences were of great value in the development of my personality. I learned how easy it was for any man to do what he wanted to do, provided he really wanted to do it badly enough. It is a common saying that no man knows what he can do until he has to do it. I know that I have been very largely a creature of luck. What is luck, good or bad? Who knows. I don't know. Is it not a fact that I was fortunate in my young manhood in acquiring the liquor-drinking habit? If I hadn't acquired it, I couldn't have exercised my will power in breaking it. Perhaps that which another would call my misfortune of having my eyes affected in Mexico was after all a very fortunate thing for me. Had I not become a morphine addict, I would never have discovered the potential strength and the usefulness of exercising my will power.

It is said that necessity knows no law. I have had so many necessities that if I have not become lawless I have learned that in the great multitudes of laws, conventions and social codes, there is always to be found, by the earnest seeker, some law that is an antidote to some other law. There are several ways of killing a dog besides choking him on butter. There are so many ways of doing everything that it is not at all difficult for the determined man to find some way that does not contravene any statute law or even any common law or custom.

This matter of drinking reminds me of a talk I had with my mother when I was in my fortieth year. She said that her father, who was a terrible toper, waked up to the fact one day that he was setting a bad example for his sons, and that on that occasion he resolved never again to touch alcoholic liquor or tobacco.

"Eddie," she said, "from that day on he never smoked and never drank. Why can't you be like your grandfather in that respect, like you are in so many other respects?"

In reply I asked my mother what my grandfather's age was at the time of his reform. She sat for a moment, evidently trying to recall instances that would fix the date. For example, she said, "Your Uncle George was then such and such an age and George was so many years younger than, and my father so many years older than me, etc."

Then turning to me she said: "Why, Eddie, he was just sixty-three years old."

"Very well," I said, "Ma, I promise to do just as good as my grandfather did. When I am sixty-three years old I am going to quit drinking and smoking."

She both sighed and laughed.

VIII

Some Outlandish Rules for Making Money

AFTER OUR European trip, George and I arrived in Detroit late in September, 1878. I wanted to begin my life's achievements. I had been an apprentice too long. It was time for me to begin the real work of life.

A few days later found us in Cleveland. We went there to take stock of the town, with the view to starting a newspaper. A few days was long enough to satisfy me that it was a good town for what I wanted to do.

In Detroit we began negotiations for the founding of a new paper in Cleveland. James was flatly opposed to my assuming the responsibility of editorship of the new venture. To this I replied that I knew well enough my capacities, and that he knew them too. I told him that if the Scripps brothers did not finance me, I would find someone else who would. (Might I add that after our European experiences, I felt that George would follow wherever I led.) I told James that I was no longer going to work for wages, nor was I longer going to depend largely for my subsistence on the fifty or sixty dollars per month that I was still getting from my old route-carrying business of the *News*. James, of course, would not consent to my leaving. I knew well enough in what high esteem he held my ability.

We agreed to start the Cleveland *Penny Press* with myself as editor, and my cousin, John Scripps Sweeney, as business manager. George preferred to remain in Detroit. We decided that the capitalization of the paper should be limited to ten thousand dollars and that the name of the firm should be Scripps and Sweeney. George A. Scripps and James E. Scripps were each to have a thirty per cent share of the business, and Sweeney and I were each to have twenty per cent.

By nature, I am always on the rush to get things going and get them done. Sweeney was a good second for me. The result was that we had rented an office, bought and set up a press, and outfitted the printing office in such time that the first issue of the *Press* hit the streets on November 2, within sixty days from the date of my landing in New York after the European trip.

The *Press* was distinguished from its contemporaries in those days in that it suppressed nothing and published nothing to gain the favor and approval of those people in the community who flattered themselves that they were the better classes. It owed its early success, too, to its two young managers, men of remarkable vitality and vigor. These men had been trained and disciplined in the office of the *Evening News* in Detroit, as few other young publishers ever have been trained and disciplined. The *Press* had the advantage of adopting, by necessity, the James E. Scripps methods, such as the most extreme economies, cash payments and cash collections; a system whereby statements were made at the close of each day's business, showing the exact receipts and disbursements, advertising earnings, actual paid-for circulation, etc.

Almost by accident, the *Press* got for its first editor a man who had a genius for the calling, hardly suspected by himself, and not at all recognized by others. (Difficult as it may be for me to tell the truth, the whole truth and nothing but the truth in my autobiography, as a rule—it is none the less easy to be frank sometimes.)

What's a good editor? I don't know. There is only one way of determining a man's ability to make a newspaper, and that is by giving the man a chance to fail or make good as an editor. What particular quality should a successful editor have? There is nothing in the looks of a man, there is nothing to be learned from conversation with him, there is no peculiar set of habits that indicate the capacity of a candidate for editorial honors and responsibilities. A successful editor is simply a man who knows by instinct how to cater to the public and give to it the kind of reading matter it wants, and, at the same time, set up in the public mind a movement or thought which will tend to cause a large proportion of the public to think as the editor thinks on public questions.

Almost from the first issue of the Cleveland *Press,* its editor succeeded in catching the public's attention and the approval of a large part of the community. The *Press* was a little five-column sheet selling for a penny. This was counted by the public sufficient reason for its popularity. This miniature sheet contained the substance of every important or noteworthy happening in the city of Cleveland, state of Ohio, the nation and the world at large, for the twenty-four hours previous to the hour of publication. Little, if any, more space was given to an item of the day of publication than to an item of news that had been printed in the morning papers. It was the idea of the Peter Parley tales. A reader of the little *Press* could be sure that he had missed nothing in the news way that he could have found in one of the larger morning or evening papers of the city. Three-fourths of the contents of the *Press* was little more than a series of brief articles. But every day, or almost every day, there appeared in the *Press* short articles, never exceeding a column in length, dealing with subjects and news events such as none of the other papers published. Or an article dealing with subjects and news items in a way different from that used by other papers. Some examples:

When a very wealthy man named Leonard Case, a citizen of Cleveland, died by committing suicide—chloroforming himself in his bed—the other papers recorded his sudden death due to heart disease. He had left his estate to be devoted to the founding of the Case School of Applied Sciences, and the papers devoted columns to the laudation of the deceased, and especially to the munificence of his gift. The *Press* simply recorded his death, the manner of his death, and the cause leading up to his suicidal act.

A young son of a very wealthy iron manufacturer was arrested by an ignorant policeman because the youngster was drunk on the street and had had a fight with a prostitute in public. The clerk of the police station recognized the prisoner, and entered an alias on his blotter. Although all the reporters knew of the incident, the *Press* alone published the item, giving the young man's real name. He got no more space than if he had been a dock roustabout, and no less.

A wealthy merchant, who was the largest advertising customer in all the Cleveland papers, had the bad luck to get involved in a divorce suit. He asked all the local papers to make no announcements in their news columns of the court proceedings. The *Press* published the news concerning this divorce suit, treating it exactly the same way as it would handle all other items of court news.

I was myself arrested by the agents of the Society for the Prevention of Cruelty to Animals, because I had ridden a horse after it had cast one of its shoes, and that, too, on hard pavements. The *Press* published a news item concerning the arrest, giving the editor's name. The story neglected even to plead as an excuse that I was myself unaware the shoe was cast or that injury was being done. In police court, I pleaded guilty and paid the fine.

It was because the *Press* published such items as these and many more, treating rich and poor, prominent and obscure, alike, that the *Press,* almost from the start, was charged with being sensational. The *Press* did not publish scandalous gossip. I do not recall that anything salacious was ever printed, except in cases of court procedure where an accurate report required such.

It had been customary for Dee and Ross and some of the other reporters on the Detroit *News* to give undue prominence to the conduct and misconduct of well-known people. I had recognized that as a fault. I knew that there was a great desire for notoriety and publicity among members of the smart set at that time, and that, however much members of that group might protest, they were invariably more pleased than angry with the publicity given them by the *News.* I made up my mind that the *Press* would not pander to snobbery by either unduly lauding or unduly condemning any of the smart set.

In Detroit I had some experiences as a reporter that made a deep impression on my mind. I often observed there the great suffering caused the mothers, wives, sisters and daughters of the city by publication of the misdeeds of their menfolk. When I took over the Cleveland *Press,* it was with the resolve that I would always keep in view the womenfolks, and that, so far as possible in carrying out my thoroughgoing system of journalism, I would avoid making any woman cry. Everything else being equal as between any two items, or any two ways of writing an item, I would prefer the item that would not hurt women, or the way of preparing it that would hurt them least.

I recall a trying experience of this sort. A woman came to me for the suppression of a perfectly legitimate piece of news, and one that I could not consistently leave out of the paper. Her husband had been guilty of some offense, and had been arrested. She told me the other papers were going to suppress the item. She said her attorney had told her that if publicity could be prevented, the judge who was trying the case had promised great leniency. He had even held out hopes that there might be no prosecution at all. The man was very well-known, and mouth-to-mouth gossip had made the event notorious or was sure to make it so.

I told the woman that the notoriety would be increased rather than diminished by the suppression of the story by the newspapers. I added I felt I had no right to conspire with a corrupt judge and prosecuting attorney to prevent the punishment of a man who had committed a crime. I was aware that my publication of the item was going to cause a great many women to weep, and was going to make certain the conviction and punishment of the criminal. Later the lawyer came to see me. Another person brought a verbal message from the judge. Other women appeared, and there was a great flow of tears. But the item was printed. No sooner did I see it in the forms than I took my hat and left the office and went off for a long walk into the country, pondering deeply. That evening I almost resolved to abandon journalism.

But I was a willful, headstrong, and determined young man. It was not in me to conceive failure. I would have what I wanted, and would get what I wanted in the way that I wanted it. I was engaged in founding a newspaper. My whole mind and will were concentrated on this one thing. There was only one thing worth while avoiding, and that was failure. Had there been 999 chances out of 1,000 of losing my life by proceeding along the course that I had determined on, and only one chance for living and hence succeeding, I think I would not have hesitated.

I must confess something more. I believe if it had been necessary for me to break every statute of the state of Ohio in order to accomplish the end I had in view, those laws would have been in great danger of being broken. When a man is fully prepared to take any risk or pay any penalty in order to accomplish some one thing, it rarely occurs to him that a man has to take any risk or pay any penalty. In those days I was never conscious of an effort to push my paper by choosing one side or another in any political issue or any other matter of public contention. I am sure that I did not make my great effort of propaganda for the full development of labor unionism in Cleveland for the purpose of winning the good will and patronage of workingmen. I was only chuck-full of opinions and ideas that were more the result of emotional activities than of reasoning. I had a newspaper under my own control, and I just turned myself loose on the public.

The Cleveland *Press* taught me the truth of some paradoxes. As editor I was always on the side of the workingman and the poor man, right or wrong. I was always against the rich man, whether I was right or wrong. I had an almost instinctive hatred for all men in power, whether the power was derived from political sources or based on economic successes. Although my father was a tradesman I had acquired, perhaps through my extensive reading of poetry, an extreme aversion to trade and tradesmen. If I hated the millionaire, I despised the shopkeeper. The only kind of poor man I could never sympathize with was the poor man engaged in trade. My antipathy for, my contempt of trade were such that my mind was always biased against that very class of the community on whose patronage nearly all the newspapers of this day depend for a living. I mean advertisers.

One reason I have always hankered to keep my papers small in size was that by doing so it was possible to make so large a profit from the sale of the paper that only small additions from the advertising department were needed for its support.

To the merchants of Cleveland, my attitude was always that of contemptuous disregard. Between two articles or two items, everything else being equal, I preferred to publish the one that would directly or indirectly offend or work injury to the business of some merchant or merchants. Very likely I never referred to them in those days as merchants, but only as storekeepers. This attitude of the *Press* was a startling innovation in Cleveland, and oddly enough, this very attitude of the *Press* toward that part of the public who pays the advertising bills had the effect of bringing speedily comparatively large returns from the advertising department. I said "oddly enough" but should have said "naturally enough."

At first much effort was made to bring pressure on us by the advertising public. In 1878 it was the custom of Cleveland daily papers to give to every moderately large advertiser a tremendous amount of "puffs." They would not only puff the merchant's business itself, but they would puff the merchant and the merchant's wife and daughters. Every advertiser on the ordinary Cleveland newspaper could depend upon a good-sized notice in the reading columns for the birth of a baby in his family, or a death, or a marriage, or a social gathering at his house. The *Press* always refused to publish such items, or, if it noted such events, it was generally with the object of ridicule, or at least of making the public laugh.

For decades, this line of conduct of the *Press* made it impossible for the businessmen of Cleveland to think of exercising any influence whatever in the editorial or news columns of the paper.

Newcomers to the business world of Cleveland had many shocks. Accustomed in other cities to another style of journalism, they took it for granted that their patronage of the *Press* would gain for them certain favors and privileges. There were two instances I recall especially. Both occurred several years after I had left Cleveland and had ceased to have anything much to do directly with the local management of the paper.

After I had come to live in California I received a letter from a merchant who had recently entered the Cleveland field, and who was a very large advertiser in the *Press*. He complained of the treatment he had received at the hands of the editor of the *Press* when he had made a request. He told me he wanted to see me about it when I was next in Cleveland. When I did go to Cleveland I had forgotten all about my correspondent, but the *Press's* customer had not forgotten. He came to my hotel and told me his story. I asked him how much he was paying the *Press*. I expressed doubts on the subject, and told him to go and get his contract. He did so. In the meantime I obtained a duplicate copy from the office of the *Press*. Then I led him on to talk and to bluff as I knew the salesman in him would certainly dictate. He said he would never renew his contract until he had been apologized to.

"I suppose you are sorry now that you are under contract," I said. He said he certainly was. I asked him why he did not ask for cancellation of the contract. He said he had, but that he was bound, and the *Press* would not cancel it. At the right moment I got him to offer, or rather to insist on the cancellation of the contract. With his consent, I tore the two contracts up, and then ordered him out of the room. I told him I would discharge any man from the office of the *Press* who ever took any more of his business.

I forget how the incident was finally concluded. I suppose that in this case, as in others, I consented to take his business again at a higher rate.

Another time a large firm was involved, one that has many stores in a number of cities. I had newspapers in several of the cities where these people had their stores, and they patronized these papers. When they finally opened up in Cleveland, they immediately became the largest advertisers in the city. At that time, the *Press* was not only the principal advertising medium in that city, but had a circulation larger than all of the other papers combined. It was just the one paper in which these people had to advertise if they were going to do any business at all. Their concern was entirely new in Cleveland, and had established no good will patronage, and their whole campaign depended upon skillful and very costly advertising. Their local manager was a fresh, pushing, energetic young fellow. At the time, I think they were paying the *Press* several thousand dollars a month, and were the largest advertising customer the paper had.

The young manager began very quickly, to demand not only privileges, but rebates on his bills on account of typographical errors, or for other reasons. He was a tricky sort of fellow, and somewhere in his past fields of operation had learned how to manipulate copy and proofs so that it was impossible to prevent typographical errors.

At that time Milton McRae was acting as general manager of the *Press,* and Willis Thornton was manager of the advertising department. Mr. Thornton told me of his troubles. It appeared that the written contract between the *Press* and the store had not yet been signed, because of some defect in it.

I sent word for the manager of the store to come to see me. He failed to appear. I ordered his advertisements out of the paper. Then he came to see me. I told him that he had come just too late. I said I had learned that he was a damned scoundrel and a trickster as well as a fool bully, and that I had sent for him to read him a lecture; but that, as he had not come when I called him, I had nothing more to tell him. He started some impudent talk and I ordered him out of the office. He sassed back. As I got up, he saw something that caused him to grab his hat and disappear.

I then notified Mr. McRae and Mr. Thornton that I would discharge either of them or any man connected with the *Press* who would either solicit an ad from that firm again or permit one of its advertisements to appear in the *Press.*

Some time later I saw a copy of the Cleveland *Press* in which this firm's advertisement appeared. I wrote to Thornton. He replied, as I remember, that Mr. McRae had gone over his head, and had, through one of his employees, taken the advertisement. Thornton added, however, that the store had made the first move and that, furthermore, it was paying extreme rates, rates considerably above the contract rates. As president, I immediately removed Mr. McRae from the general management and disciplined Thornton for not reporting it. I directed that no more contracts should be made with the firm until it changed its manager. The store's management was changed; and for a number of years, and probably now, the store's advertising appeared in the *Press*. I do not think that any further attempts were ever made by this firm to defraud or influence the *Press*.

"It was easy enough," one might say, "to deal with a big customer in the highhanded way that I speak of, after the *Press* had become so strongly established." But it was in the very youth of the *Press* that its editor and business manager practiced the identical course in dealing with the paper's advertising customers. John Sweeney was literally a terror in the eyes of Cleveland advertisers. His exactions went so far that at times even I interfered with him. Instead of John Sweeney being bulldozed, he was bulldozing everybody else. His attitude was, That's my price, those are my conditions, take it or leave it!

But, as I said, I was unconscious of any plans or rules in the early days of the *Press*.

So far from trying to impress my own personality on the newspapers, my endeavor was always to incite every man to impress his personality on the paper. Instead of showing myself much in public, I invariably chose that my paper should be represented by someone other than myself. I kept my name out of the paper always. Even the staff of the Cleveland *Press* never regarded me as their employer, their chief, the man who was directing the paper itself. Each staff member was allowed to produce about whatever copy he wanted to. My business, in the early days of the *Press*, was to select what I wanted to print. My editing of copy consisted simply in cutting it down so that I could get an article that would occupy the least space. Soon enough I even left this work for someone else to do.

In those days, as in later years, I chose to think much and do little. It was in moments of emergency or days of trial that I came forward, unfatigued, to encounter some difficulty, the possibility of which I had long contemplated, and hence was prepared to meet.

I used to complain to my brother James, when I saw him in the Detroit *News* office, grinding out copy that I considered inferior to what could be produced by a three-dollar-a-day man. I would find him going over exchanges, classing items, and reducing the number of his words with a pencil and pasting them onto copy paper to be used by the printers. I used to tell him that with a thousand-dollar daily capacity, he spent more than three-fourths of his time doing a three-dollar-a-day man's work.

My brother James, needless to say, had his views about me. Knowing my own habits, especially my workless habit, he for years held the conviction that all of my journalistic successes were pure accidents, and that the papers I was nominally running would be the gainers if they were not burdened with the salary I received. In fact, so thoroughly was he convinced of this idea that on two or three occasions he acted accordingly, and removed me from positions of control.

I was always ready then, and always have been ready since, to do four men's work or a dozen men's work in a day when there was any occasion for it; but I was always seeing to it that such occasions for great efforts on my part were very, very rare. I was always careful to sleep as many hours as I could. Rarely have I gotten out of bed in the morning because I thought it was time to get up and go to work. I always felt it was more essential that I should be fit for work when I got up than that I should get up at any time.

Any ordinary person would have been justified in believing that, whoever was making the *Press* go, certainly I was not that person.

Why, even when I have been observing myself and analyzing my own actions during the past thirty or more years, I have often questioned my own ability. It would seem to me that I did so little myself that my various successes must have been accidental. However, as time has passed, and as on occasions I have abandoned the superintendence of my newspapers for years together, I have come to realize just how effective I have been and how absolutely necessary my work was, for years together.

I have said elsewhere that I have spent pretty nearly half of all my waking hours with my eyes on some printed page; I am sure that from the time I was twenty-four more than half my days have been spent with no conscious thoughts or attention to business of any sort. Judging by the number of days and number of years and the actual things I have done in journalism, it almost seems to me that the whole of my business career has only absorbed a small fraction of either my time or my thought. The practice of journalism seems to me, even now, to have been an unimportant incident in my life.

The first issue of the *Press* came out on November 2, 1878, exactly six years from the day I left the farm at Rushville. Some time in March, 1880, I went to St. Louis to start the St. Louis *Evening Chronicle*. Thus, I devoted only sixteen months to the founding of the Cleveland *Press*. I remained in St. Louis for about a year. Early in the spring of 1881, I was removed from the management of the St. Louis paper, and returned to Cleveland. There, in a desultory way, I acted as editor-in-chief of the *Press*.

On November 2, 1881, with my sister Ellen, I started for a trip abroad. I was thus in Cleveland for six months. Add to this six months the total of sixteen months and it appears that, all told, I spent twenty-two months either as actual editor or nominal editor of the Cleveland *Press*. From the day I started to Europe until today (1925) I have been, with the exception of one brief period, in actual control of the

Press. During these years I have not spent as much as thirty days in Cleveland. Therefore, the *Press* has cost me twenty-three months of actual residence in Cleveland and firsthand direction of that property.

It is my conviction now that the Cleveland *Press* is a far greater property and a far more influential organ of public opinion than it would have been if I, from November 2, 1878, up to this time, had directly managed its affairs.

In my actual running of the *Press*, I reverted to my boyhood scheme; I either sat on the fence and watched the other fellows work, or else I took my book and went off by myself to read and dream and plan or otherwise amuse myself.

It is true that I had a determination to make the *Press* a success. Aside from that I had no particular plan. I simply lived from day to day. Sometimes I worked hard. Always I was a hard thinker. Often I did not work hard at all, or was not conscious of working hard. I quickly fell into the habit of coming to the office late and leaving early. I forever sought and found excuses for leaving the office and leaving my work for others to do. I always took along books to read, went into the country, and stopped at some rural hotel. I spent a good deal of time rowing and sailing on Lake Erie. Sometimes I would leave the office for weeks together. I doubt if, after the first few months, I averaged more than two or three hours a day in my editorial room. Sometimes I wrote in my hotel room. I wrote articles in a row-boat, drifting. But even the time given to this work was infinitesimally small. I used to say I carried my business under my hat and that it was when my hat was on, whether I was riding, driving, rowing or sailing, that I could do far more effective thinking than when sitting at a table, either in my office or at a hotel.

I knew my *Poor Richard* but I didn't agree with him. This resulted in my leaving many things undone—many things that I believe were better left undone. I have found by my life's experience that the big things accomplished in life, or the really important ones, are very few indeed. Doing a few important things that are right, and are right at the right time, and doing them thoroughly, is the important thing.

I know I very seldom gave any orders to my staff on the *Press*. More often I offered advice or suggestions. Recently I saw a copy of a letter written by R. F. Paine to some young man employed in our concern in which he said that, during the more than thirty years he had been in my service, he had not received more than six orders from me.

Although I have been personally responsible for the founding or purchase of not less than forty newspapers, I doubt if I have directly given a total of five hundred orders to all the men employed on these papers. My life's work has mainly consisted in selecting a few score of men, studying each, and then offering them opportunities and inspiring them, by my talks and letters, each to develop what was best in him to the highest extent.

I hold very strongly that the world owes no human being a living, that society owes nothing to any individual member of itself. Only that human being who can support himself or herself, beginning at the age of adolescence, is entitled to a place in the world at all.

This is nature's law. This is the law that governs all other living beings except humanity, and in the end it inevitably must govern humanity too. The individual man who lives contrary to nature perishes. Any society of men, whether it be a community of small numbers or of national proportions, must suffer the penalty of any and every infraction of natural law.

The individual and the social body may—each and both of them, the one for a longer time than the other—violate nature's law for some time without suffering the death penalty, but the delay, the postponement, of the penalty is only that, only a delay or postponement.

Some other maxims that I have employed in my business, and which I commend to others interested in money-making, are:

Some Outlandish Rules for Making Money

1. Never spend as much money as you earn. The smaller your expenditures are in proportion to your earnings the sooner you will become rich.

2. It is more blessed to pay wages than to accept them. At least, it is more profitable.

3. Never do anything yourself that you can get someone else to do for you. The more things that someone else does for you the more time and energy you have to do those things which no one else can do for you.

4. Never do anything today that you can put off till tomorrow. There is always so much to do today that you should not waste your time and energy in doing anything today that can be put off till tomorrow. Most things that you do not have to do today are not worth doing at all.

5. Always buy, never sell. If you've got enough horse sense to become rich you know that it is better to run only one risk than two risks. You also know that just as likely as not the other fellow is smarter than you are and that whether you buy or sell, in each case you run the risk of getting the worst of the bargain. By adopting my rule you will diminish by one-half your chances of loss.

6. Never do anything, if you can help it, that someone else is doing. Why compete with one person or many other persons in any occupation or line of business so long as it is possible for you to have a monopoly in some other field?

7. If circumstances compel you to pursue some occupation or to follow some line of business which is being pursued by some other person, then you do your work in some other way than that in which it is done by the other. There is always a good, better and best way. If you take the best way then the other fellow has no chance of competing with you.

8. Whatever you do once, whatever way you undertake to do a thing, don't do the same thing again or don't do the thing in the same

way. If you know one way to do a thing you must know there is a better way to do the same thing.

9. If you're succeeding in anything you are doing, don't let anyone else know of your success, because if you do some other person will try to do the same thing and be your competitor.

10. When you become rich, as you will become rich if you follow my advice, don't let anyone know it. General knowledge of your wealth will only attract the taxgatherer, and other hungry people will try to get away from you something they want and something you want to keep.

11. One of the greatest assets any man can secure is a reputation for eccentricity. If you have a reputation of this kind you can do a lot of things. You can even do the things you want to do without attaching to yourself the enmity of others. Many an act which, if performed by an ordinary person, would arouse indignation, animosity and antagonism, can be performed by a man with a reputation for eccentricity with no other result than that of exciting mirth and perhaps pity. It is better to have the good will than the bad will, even of a dog.

12. Never hate anybody. Hatred is a useless expenditure of mental and nervous energy. Revenge costs much of energy and gains nothing.

13. When you find many people applauding you for what you do, and a few condemning, you can be certain that you are on the wrong course because you're doing the things that fools approve of. When the crowd ridicules and scorns you, you can at least know one thing, that it is at least possible that you are acting wisely. It is one of the instincts of men to covet applause. The wise man regulates his conduct rather by reason than by instinct.

14. It is far more important to learn what not to do than what to do. You can learn this invaluable lesson in two ways, the first of which and most inspired is by your own mistakes. The second is by ob-

serving the mistakes of others. Any man that learns all the things that he ought not to do cannot help doing the things he ought to do.

15. Posterity can never do anything for you. Therefore, you should invest nothing in posterity. Of course your heirs will quarrel over your estate, but that will be after you're dead and why should you trouble your mind over things which you will never know anything about?

16. A man can do anything he wants to do in this world, at least if he wants to do it badly enough. Therefore, I say that any of you who want to become rich can become rich if you live long enough.

17. After what I have said it goes without further saying that you should save money. But no man can save himself rich. He can only make himself rich. Savings are capital. It is only by doing things that one learns how to do things. It is only the capitalist who handles capital that learns how to handle capital profitably. The more capital you have the more skillful you become as a capitalist.

18. Fools say that money makes money. I say that money does not make money. It is only men who make money.

19. There are two cardinal sins in the economic world: one is giving something for nothing, and the other is getting something for nothing. And the greater sin of these is getting something for nothing, or trying to do so. I really doubt if anyone ever does get something for nothing.

(Don't marry a rich wife. Women are what they are. At best they are hard enough to get along with. They are always trying to make a man do something that he doesn't want to do, and generally succeeding. When a woman is conscious of the fact that she has furnished all or any part of your capital, her influence over you will be so great as to be the worst handicap you can carry.)

20. If you're a prospective heir of your father or some other relative, you should also consider that a handicap. I would advise you to refuse to be an heir.

21. Despise not the day of small things, but rather respect the small

things. It is far easier to make a profit on a very small capital invested in any business than it is to make the same proportion of profit off of a large capital. It is true that after you have learned how to make a profit on a business that shows small capital, successively, as your capital grows, you learn how to handle it profitably. Then the time will come when the greater your capital becomes in this way the greater your proportion of profits on it should be. And, for an added reason, as your wealth and skill grow rapidly, your so-called necessary expenses grow much more slowly and in time cease to grow at all, so that beyond a certain limit all your income and added income becomes a surplus, constantly to be added to your capital.

22. It is far easier to make money than to spend it. As it becomes more and more difficult to spend money, you will spend less and less of it, and hence there will be more money to accumulate.

23. The hardest labor of all labor performed by man is that of thinking. If you have become rich, train your mind to hard thinking and hold it well in leash so that your thinking will all be with but one object in view, that of accumulating more wealth.

It is true that a man cannot serve both God and Mammon. If your only sin is to obtain wealth then you should devote all of your service to Mammon.

IX

I Kill Henry Chisholm

ONE MORNING in the late seventies I arrived by boat in Cleveland after a visit of several days in Detroit. On my arrival at the hotel I learned of a momentous event in my young life.

During my absence in Detroit, a young man had been arrested for his part in a brawl with some woman on the street. At the police station he was recognized as Stuart Chisholm. There were then in Cleveland two brothers—Henry and Stuart Chisholm—who were the principal owners of the Cleveland Rolling Mills. Both of these brothers had sons. The son of Henry, the elder brother and principal owner of the company, bore the name of Stuart H. Chisholm. The son of Stuart Chisholm was named simply Stuart Chisholm.

My star reporter on the *Press* was a brilliant writer named Maurice Perkins. One of his reporting rounds brought him to the police station and he was told the young man who had been arrested bore the name of Stuart H. Chisholm. Perkins, it turned out, was wrong. The item we published constituted a technical libel on the Stuart Chisholm with the H. in his name. This one had been affected injuriously by our report of the misconduct of his cousin.

I had by then become used to libel suits. While I was annoyed by the misadventure, I was not greatly alarmed. When I arrived at the office, after breakfasting at my hotel, I was greeted by a scene of turmoil and excitement. Henry Chisholm, the richest man in Cleveland and father of the innocent Stuart H. Chisholm, had sent for Perkins. The messenger who called assured Perkins that Mr. Chisholm recognized that only a slight error had occurred. When Perkins got to Chisholm's office, however, he was set upon by a crowd of Chisholm's employees. These dragged him to a back room, took all his clothes off, and painted him with black paint from the top of his head to the soles of his feet. The paint was the kind used in painting iron. To complete the job, the paint had been poured on his head. Then Perkins had been thrown out of the office, picked up by someone and taken to his home.

I knew enough about such matters to know that unless Perkins was immediately cleansed, death would almost certainly result quickly. I hurried to Perkins' house to find that he had been scraped pretty clean, that a doctor had superintended the operation and that Perkins had been put to bed.

Perkins was a tall, lean, cadaverous young man with a very weak constitution. The nervous shock of his attack brought on a violent case of hiccoughing.

Though I was terribly angry, I still had my senses about me, and recognized that this outrageous assault made by Chisholm was a thousand times worse than the innocent mistake of a reporter could possibly justify.

I found that Perkins' mind was clear. I cleaned up the room and got from him the story of the whole transaction. I told him Chisholm had made a terrible mistake. I added that Chisholm had, in his ignorance and anger, almost committed murder, and that soon enough his friends and attorneys would tell him this, and that there would thereafter be a great effort made to settle up with Perkins and hush the whole matter up.

Perkins' face lit up; he saw prospects. I knew Perkins as the kind of man who would settle for a very little money, and I knew I could not rely on either his good sense or any promises he made to me. I then told Perkins I would guarantee him a settlement of at least five thousand dollars. I told him I thought he could get much more if he would let me send him a lawyer to advise with him. I got Perkins' pledge that he would not settle at all, after I told him I stood prepared to give the five thousand dollars if no one else did. As I left him, he was still hiccoughing. I told him that after the shock wore off his hiccoughing would stop, in all probability. I advised him, however, not to try to stop it, and not permit the doctor or his wife to dope him for the purpose of stopping it. He gave me a wink that convinced me that he was "on"—as the boys would say.

Immediately I went to the lawyer that I had determined to employ, and sent him posthaste to Perkins. I then returned to the office. I had engaged an open carriage in order to save time. As I neared the office I saw the whole street in front was jammed by a mob of men, who were on the point of riot. My driver, alarmed, did not want to approach too near. He said he had heard it whispered around that the crowd was going to mob the office of the *Press* and gut it. I taunted him with cowardice. I told him to force his way through the mob with the carriage. I stood up in the seat, holding on with one hand, and holding my pistol with the other.

The crowd was neither very enthusiastic nor very angry. It consisted entirely of Chisholm's rolling-mill employees, who were simply under orders. I saw no hostile faces among them. On the contrary, I saw what I might well have expected—only friendly and encouraging glances. The *Press* had, from the first, been a very popular paper in Newburg, as that section of Cleveland was called where the rolling mill was situated. These men knew that the *Press* was the workingman's friend, and they had also heard of the assault on Perkins.

But they were under orders, and I think there was no doubt they would have obeyed them, and mobbed and gutted the office, had there been no serious obstacles to overcome.

I knew that the next step of the enemy would be to resort to more legal methods. I felt certain there would be arrests for criminal libel. Luckily there were a number of property holders among our employees, so it was easy enough to arrange with them for bail for anyone on the staff who might be arrested.

Sure enough the deputy sheriff appeared with warrants for my arrest and Sweeney's arrest, on the charge of criminal libel. I took my bondsman, the sheriff, and my partner in the carriage and immediately went to the courthouse to give bond. This was an hour or two before noon.

When I returned to the office, I found all work suspended. Another sheriff was on hand to serve a warrant on me by "attachment," for fifty thousand dollars damages. In bringing the civil suit, the Chisholms had sworn that I had no property within the jurisdiction of the court except the property of the Cleveland *Press*. They argued they were entitled to attach what property I had.

I urged on the sheriff that no damage would be done if the men were allowed to go on with their work. I said none of the property would be moved. But he replied that his orders were to prevent anyone touching any of the property that had been attached until all of it had been inventoried and bond given by me. Then, and only then, would the whole property be turned back to me again.

It was Saturday. It was easy to see the designs of my prosecutors. They wanted to delay the inventorying to such a late hour that no return could be made, and no bond given by me, until such a late hour that it would be impossible to publish the *Press* that day. Since we were a daily only, it was presumed we would not appear on Sunday.

I asked who the appraisers were to be, and was told by the sheriff that he did not know. By this time I had engaged as my attorney

Judge R. F. Paine, father of a boy on our staff who later succeeded me as the editor of the *Press*. Judge Paine knew my rights, and demanded and got immediate action.

Then appeared on the scene a pair of appraisers who could be depended upon by the Chisholms to embarrass me to the fullest extent possible. One of these was the famous Edwin Cowles, owner and editor of the Cleveland *Leader* and the Cleveland *Evening News*. Mr. Cowles was a former editor of the Cincinnati *Commercial*, and was the most influential newspaperman in the state. Cleveland and Ohio were great Republican strongholds, and every politician in the city of Cleveland and the county of Cuyahoga, was thoroughly subservient to Cowles. The other appraiser was William Gleason, formerly of the press room of the Cleveland *Plain Dealer*.

I met these two men and told them I was sued for fifty thousand dollars. I presented them with documents showing the price of every article in the office—in fact, I showed them recent bills for same. Since the whole stock was nearly new, I told them they could appraise the whole property in five minutes. However, they stood on their rights to inspect every article from the roof to the cellar and place a value on it.

As no headway could be made in the office, I started in at the task of finding bondsmen. Although the suit was for fifty thousand dollars, it was required to furnish bonds for double that amount. In those days there were no bonding companies. Although I had only been in the city a short time, I had made a number of acquaintances, some of them prominent in a way, and wealthy. These men liked my paper and frequently came to me to praise me for my honesty and fearlessness. Naturally I turned to them for help. Naturally enough, they deserted me in my hour of need. All of them, every last one of them.

I wasted several hours in this vain effort to get bondsmen. Suddenly I had an inspiration. If my friends had deserted me, who were the next people to turn to? Why, I said to myself, the enemies of the Chisholms. It was plain to me that the Chisholms must have enemies. Such a violent-tempered man as Henry Chisholm, I knew, must have flocks of them. Just as he had been driven to an act of possible murder, and just as he was attempting to bully me, he certainly must have been guilty of many another such act.

Judge Paine had departed, giving his kindly advice to be patient and let the law take its course. He had returned to his office some six blocks away from mine. No sooner did the idea come to me of appealing to Chisholm's enemies than I ran for my carriage and ordered the cabman to take me at full tilt to Paine's offices.

I found the old man sitting out on the pavement in front of his office. I jumped out of the carriage, ran up to him, and asked: "Judge, what rich man or men do you know in this town who hate Chisholm as bad as Chisholm hates me?"

The old man looked up at me curiously, and then settled down to think. In less than a minute he slapped his knee, chuckled, and threw back his head in a loud guffaw.

"Come on," he said, "I will go with you and get him."

There was an old fellow named Samuel G. Baldwin. He was a professional bondsman for prostitutes and thieves. He owned a large amount of property in what would now be called the red-light district. Paine told me he had at least five hundred thousand dollars of just that kind of property. He lived only a few blocks from Paine's office, in a shabby little cottage, with an old wife. Baldwin and his wife were dressed and were apparently living in a style that could be well afforded by a day laborer.

Now Judge Paine had remembered that many years before, Henry Chisholm and Sam Baldwin had a lawsuit in a justice court. This was long before Chisholm's wealth had grown into such large proportions. Chisholm's anger was aroused by something Baldwin said on the witness stand. Chisholm, whose temper was even hotter then than it was in my day, slapped Baldwin on the face as he left the witness stand. Chisholm was a big man; Baldwin slight and comparatively weak.

In less than five minutes we had Baldwin in the carriage and all three of us drove to the courthouse where Baldwin signed my bond for a full hundred thousand dollars. This made it unnecessary for the appraisers to finish their work in my office. We took one of the deputy sheriffs with us, carrying an order to the appraisers to cease their work, and an additional order turning over to me the property.

By about midafternoon I was out of the clutches of the sheriff. We were in fairly good shape, since from the beginning of the trouble I had set Henry Little, Bob Paine and other members of the staff to writing up a full account of the whole proceedings. Particular stress was laid on the treatment of the reporter Perkins. Between jumps, I had written much myself.

By the time I got my own office released, most of the story was set up in type. Since my printers could not work with my type, I had taken them to a neighboring job office. By paying liberally, I had gotten use of the job office's type. After it was set up, it was sent over to the *Press* in galleys. The printers there went on with the story furnished by me of my efforts and final success in the way of getting my office back.

Not one other paper in the city, morning or evening, contained one word about all that had been going on about the *Press*. The nonappearance of the *Press* on the streets at its usual early hour occasioned much comment. By degrees, and in more or less exaggerated form, the story had been passed from mouth to mouth so that the whole public was curious.

It was nearly 6:00 P.M. when the first copies of the *Press* got on the street. Meantime, John Sweeney had been making all due preparation for getting a big circulation. He gathered together hundreds of newsboys, and had carts and carriages ready to carry the newsboys to the outlying districts of the city.

From the time I got my press going until perhaps midnight we kept on printing papers, with the result that that day the circulation of the *Press* was many times larger than the average daily circulation. Large numbers of additional copies were struck off to be sold Sunday. Before Sunday night came the story of "The Shame of Chisholm" was known by every resident.

Henry Chisholm was a great man in his community. He was deemed a very respectable man. He was a deacon in the principal Baptist church. I was told at this time that Chisholm's fellow members of the church refused to take communion with him because of the incident.

Perkins kept on hiccoughing. He was examined by doctors. Efforts were made to get him to settle. Various sums were offered. He was sorely tempted. To a man getting fifteen dollars a week, a roll of bills of about five hundred dollars looked like a fortune. I had great trouble to keep him down.

When the criminal libel suit was tried, I was acquitted.

A short time later the Chisholm suit against the *Press* was discontinued, and Chisholm paid Perkins five thousand dollars through my attorney. The incident was closed. The *Press* had acquired tremendous prestige. The little paper had beaten the richest man in Cleveland in a fair stand-up fight, and this had a lasting effect.

On the Monday following the fight, I prepared a condensed statement headed "The Crime of Chisholm," or something like that. The length of this article was about one-third of a column. It was set up in italics, and, I think, placed at the head of the so-called editorial column. It was published one day, and the next, and the next, and continuously until the final settlement had been made with Perkins by Chisholm. Every day the *Press* appeared with this short article printed in italics. I proposed to keep the story alive, to remind the people of Cleveland every day what Chisholm had done.

At first, I had no idea of punishing Chisholm himself, directly, by the publication of this article. My idea was to hammer the story into the public mind to such an extent that anyone who got into the jury box, in the trial of the criminal libel case, or the civil libel case, would know all about the beginning of the row, and would have his mind refreshed on the subject up to the time he entered the jury box.

I have no means of knowing the effect of this peculiar course of mine on the jury or the court.

Mr. Chisholm was a Scotsman, a man of great force of character, a remarkably obstinate man. He was not the kind to surrender under fire. I heard that his friends and members of his family were begging him to acknowledge his defeat, pay Perkins' damages, and make peace with me. I also heard of his stern refusal to show any signs of weakness.

After the criminal case had been tried and I had been acquitted, I heard that Chisholm's health had been so affected by this incident that he had gone to bed a sick man with a doctor in constant attendance. One day there came to my office Mr. Chisholm's doctor and the president of his bank. They told me the incident was costing Chisholm his health and probably his life. I replied bitterly that Chisholm had shown no mercy to the poor weakling Perkins and was entitled to no mercy from Perkins' employer and friend.

The doctor, who was also a pious man, reminded me that I could show my greatness in giving evidence of mercy. I told him that wisdom was just as much a characteristic of greatness as was mercy, and added that justice was even a greater virtue than mercy. I said Chisholm had proved, by many of his acts that I knew of, that he was not only a man of violent temper, but of a low standard of integrity, and that his word was not to be relied on. I told them that if they could find a single man of good standing in Cleveland or Detroit, where I had come from, who would declare that Ed Scripps had ever broken his word, I would not only do as they wished, but would pay Perkins' indemnity myself.

"Now, gentlemen," I said in conclusion, "you go out and make yourselves busy hunting up my record, and when you have found a man who has any reputation at all who is willing to make an open declaration that I have ever lied, come to me with him and I will drop the case."

We then sent for Chisholm's chief attorney. I told the two men that if this attorney went to Chisholm's bedside and brought from him a message that was satisfactory to me, I would take up the case with them. I trusted the attorney, since very early in the case he had called on me trying to settle the whole matter, and had frankly and candidly declared his client's actions had been utterly inexcusable.

I honestly believe the attorney visited Mr. Chisholm. He returned with the message that Mr. Chisholm was a dying man, that Chisholm was really a Christian, and that he wished to right the wrong he had done and prepare himself for death. I had my doubts about what was reported to me about Chisholm's physical condition. I had met him only a few days after the assault on Perkins. He was a large, robust man of approximately sixty. It seemed to me impossible that his health could so suddenly have failed. His doctor told me he had no organic trouble, that the sole difficulty with him was his mental suffering on account of public humiliation.

I sent for my attorney. The proper documents were signed withdrawing the suit for civil damages against the *Press*. The banker and lawyer went to the bank with me and I received from them five thousand dollars in currency. They took my receipt for the sum and a statement of what the money was paid for.

I then went to Perkins' house, accompanied by the banker and lawyer. We found him in bed. He was still hiccoughing. I handed him the money in the presence of the banker and lawyer, and took the precaution to get Perkins' receipt, which I also had the banker and lawyer witness.

I dismissed the two other men, and, after they had left the room, I told Perkins to quit hiccoughing and get up and dress and go back to work or go off on a frolic. He quit hiccoughing, and chose to go off on a frolic. I saw no more of him for several weeks, and until after he had spent more than half the money he had received.

A few weeks later, Chisholm died.

I was shocked by the event. I believed then, and believe now, that had Chisholm's attack on Perkins killed Perkins, and had Chisholm been successful in suppressing my publicity and hence avoided public contumely, he would have lived many years longer, a leading and respected citizen of the city of Cleveland.

I may be mistaken, but I never believed that simple remorse killed Mr. Chisholm. But neither have I ever had any doubt that Chisholm's death was caused by me. Had I taken a pistol and shot him to death, I would have felt no more and no less responsibility for that death than I have ever since felt. It is true that I did not know I was killing Chisholm when I was killing him. Nonetheless I believe that had I known that I was killing him at the time, I would have pursued the same course. I believe I would have felt no more remorse, no more guilt, under those circumstances than I have since felt, and I have felt none.

I believed then that I was not only doing what was right, but that I was actually performing a public duty.

X

Shooting Irons and the Blair Eye

DURING MY first ten years as a journalist, it was a not uncommon thing for editors to be shot, and for editors to shoot other people. Horsewhipping of editors was sometimes indulged in, and more often threatened. Only once was a message brought to me that I was to be shot at sight. Whether that man ever saw me after that or not, I do not know. I know I never saw him.

Even in these later years there have been physical encounters between roughs and some of the Scripps editors and reporters. In the early days of the *Press* in Cleveland, I had several almost physical encounters. I did not seek them, nor did I try too hard to avoid them. I had sense enough to know the danger of my situation. I was not so much afraid, I think, of other people as I was of myself. I knew that I would kill any man who ever struck me a blow or offered me an extreme insult, and that it would be hard for me, under some circumstances, to justify my act. I never shot anyone, though.

I have often wondered if I am a physical coward. As a small boy, redheaded and freckle-faced, I was the kind of boy you might expect. I dearly loved a fight. But along about my fourteenth year I was attacked by a mild form of rheumatism. My knees swelled so that at times I had to use crutches. My ankles were weak and painful at times. I had a bad right shoulder, the shoulder to which a boy's fighting arm is usually attached. I had fought with perhaps every boy that would fight at all in my school, and with most of the boys in the neighborhood.

One evening I met in the road a boy who enjoyed as well as I did a good fist fight. Of course, the fight followed the meeting. My knees gave way and I had only one arm to strike with and that was my left. That boy gave me a good beating before I was able to convince him by drawing up my trousers and showing my knees that I was a cripple. However, the word went 'round that I could no longer fight. The number of lickings I then took would be enough to discourage any fighter.

I had long recovered from this defect before I began my career in Detroit. Here was a water-front section, and my business carried me there frequently. I saw many a bloody fight, and I hated to contemplate what would occur to me if I had to become involved. Soon enough this happened. I had grown tall and stout, and had a particularly long reach, but I had lost the art of boxing if I ever had it. But I knew that in that section of the city the man who didn't want to fight was sure to have to fight. The man that was licked by one man would be licked by another and another and many others. My antagonist was no more skillful than I was, but he was a tough, and he had no sense in his bullet head. I came out of the encounter if not the victor, at least with a very few bruises, having given a good account of myself.

Several years later I had to encounter both knives and guns with my own gun in my hand. After this experience I began practicing with my pistol at a quick draw and learned to shoot from the hip. I had no desire to be a crack marksman. My favorite target was a gatepost. I felt pretty sure that if I could hit a gatepost three times out of six, I could feel equally certain that I could hit a man as many times.

I made no secret of my gun practice. I once knew an attorney who gained a national reputation as a fearless man and a good gun fighter. He had killed one man. For a time this man frequently visited me, and whenever we would go out together he was always practicing with his pistol. He told me the occasion of his pistol practice: that he was engaged in a trial where he had every reason to believe someone would try to kill him. My friend was very careful to take aim and always held his pistol at arm's length. I told him I thought he ought to have read enough dime novels and seen enough of real life in the Far West to know that his greatest safety would depend on shooting first. A week or two after his last visit with me, this attorney was shot. That he was not killed was due to his good fortune and not his good sense. For twenty years, up to a few years ago, I ceased using my pistol and practicing, though I always had with me or near me a weapon for emergencies.

One day sometime later one of my sons came to me and told me he had heard that an attack was to be made on me at the first convenient opportunity. At first I felt scared. Then I took my pistol and went off to a quiet spot where there was a telephone pole. I stepped off a distance of thirty paces and drew my gun. I attempted to hit the target. I knew the persons whom I might expect to attack me and the conditions under which I would probably be attacked. I knew also that I would have time. I shot five cartridges that were in the cylinder and hit the telephone post three times. I reloaded and practiced time and again, sometimes only registering two shots out of three and sometimes four out of six. But with the gun in action I shot quickly. There was no longer any tremble in my hand. I went back to my regular affairs and learned a few days later that the fight had been called off by intervention of the chief of police. I was an old man by that time, but during the whole of my life I have never killed a man, and never to a certainty can I say that I even wounded one. I really wanted to kill a man who deserved to be killed.

I have been engaged in such employments and I have traveled so far away and in so many distant parts that I have had to encounter dangers on several occasions. The only thing I have feared for a long time is that in some emergency I might get scared—and badly scared. I am old enough not to desire a longer life. When a few years ago, after a thorough overhauling by a group of doctors that I had called to pass on my physical condition, I was told I might live ten or twenty years more, I was discouraged rather than encouraged by the verdict. I do not want to live any such long time. Yet when my time comes, unless it comes in some fortunate way, I am afraid that the nearness of death will scare me and cause me more mental suffering than any physical pain that I can bear.

My life has been threatened on more than one occasion. I have preserved it only by alertness, preparedness and bluffing. My most useful weapon in frightening some would-be assailant has been—I know not how to describe it!—a facial expression that always appeared when I was very angry or when I found myself in a desperate situation. This peculiar look of mine had something to do with a cast in my eye. This is a very common peculiarity of the Blair family, to which my mother belonged. It is even called "the Blair eye." My mother had this cast in her eye; I have it; and my oldest son, youngest daughter and one of my grandchildren have it.

The first occasion when this peculiar facial expression was brought to my attention was in my rooms in the Wendell Hotel in Cleveland. In my sitting room there was a large mirror. I had slept late. A note had been sent me from the office telling me to "look out!" as a certain person had made a serious threat against me. I called for my breakfast. While the waiter was bringing it, I dressed and started walking up and down my sitting room thinking of the case and how I would handle the emergency.

By chance, as I was facing the mirror, I looked up and saw my own face. I will not say it was distorted with anger and excitement; but, pale as it was, there was such an expression on it, and especially such a look about the eyes, as to startle me. It seemed to me that my face was the face of a stranger and a very dangerous man. I strove to retain the expression on my face and study it for a while. Then, by an act of will, I smoothed out my features and saw myself normal. Time and again I practiced this change of expression. For the first time, then, it occurred to me why big strong fellows had backed away from me.

I forget the outcome of this experience, but I have never forgotten what I saw in the glass that day. Nor did I ever forget how, even without the artificial aid of the glass, to resume the expression. Several years after this discovery I was in a riot in which a number of people were fighting. A dozen or so men turned toward me and started to attack me. They came in a sort of half circle. I always carried a pistol. I knew I would kill somebody if I was touched. I think that every man who saw me at that moment was convinced of the same thing. We were in the anteroom of a courtroom, a comparatively small space. The crowd came up to perhaps a couple of yards of me. My hand was was moving toward my hip pocket. In an instant the circle stopped. There seemed to be a blanching of faces. "He's going to shoot," someone screamed. The crowd fell back, turned and ran, and in an instant I was alone in the room.

I have had a number of such experiences with individuals and groups. I have seen fists clenched and ugly looks on other men's faces. Yet no man has ever struck me or applied a foul epithet when face to face with me.

XI

My Toughest Customer: Myself

IN 1881, in the middle of my twenty-seventh year, the doctors condemned me to die from consumption. In those days it was believed that consumption was incurable.

By that time I was fairly well off. I had, from my holdings in the Detroit *News* and the Cleveland *Press*, an income of about ten thousand dollars a year.

The climate of Cleveland was considered very bad for all pulmonary troubles. I had read of the Sahara Desert having the most satisfactory climate for this sort of trouble.

I asked my doctors if it would be all right for me to start immediately for Africa. One of them asked me about my family affairs. I told him they had nothing to do with my going anywhere or doing whatever I wanted to. He replied that he thought Africa would be as good a place to die in as any other. I had been having serious hemorrhages.

I didn't expect to die. I immediately informed my sister Ellen what my intentions were, and she as promptly volunteered to go with me, and in a few weeks we were on our way to Algiers. When I left America that fall, it was with the firm resolve that I would never again return to my native land. I had learned enough about Europe, on my earlier trip with my brother George, to think that it was a much more desirable place to live in than America.

Notwithstanding my wide experiences for a young man of twenty-seven, I was in many respects only a great boy. I thought that I was old, and wise, and disillusioned, and perhaps near the end of my life, if what the doctors said was true. This possibility, as I said, didn't impress me much, however.

It will be remembered that my boyish dreams were of a literary career. Circumstances had forced me into a business career. I was determined to return to my boyish dream of pure literature. Ellen and I first went to England and remained there for two or three weeks. Ellen was visiting some of her relatives, on her mother's side. We also had a number of relatives in common on my father's side, and we visited some of them.

My slight knowledge of England prompted me to believe that English governmental institutions, both national and municipal, were far superior to American institutions. I was determined, when I got well, to establish myself permanently in England, or perhaps France or Northern Italy. The little I had seen of the two latter places before had charmed me greatly.

From London we went to Paris, and thence to Marseilles. We continued by steamer from Marseilles to Algiers.

Either I did not have tuberculosis to start with, or else my constitution was such as to enable me to recover from it quickly. Within three months after landing at the port of Algiers, I had ceased not only to have hemorrhages, but even to cough much. I weighed 120 pounds when I left New York, and within four months was up to 180 pounds.

After about six months I left Africa and returned with my sister, traveling through Italy, Switzerland, France, Belgium, Holland, Germany and Austria, through the whole of one summer.

We went to the Mediterranean, through Spain, and on to Tunis.

We went to Cairo and traveled through the Holy Land on horseback to Beirut. We went clear around the Mediterranean, visiting Ephesus, Smyrna, Constantinople, Athens and Corfu. Sometimes we stopped at Lake Como, and other times went up to spend a few days at Lake Garda. All the time I was constantly on the lookout for some place to make my permanent home.

I was nearly two years altogether on this trip. I paid particular attention to national governmental affairs, and city government. I was interested in army and police methods. I was twice in England, and made a number of friends there.

I finally concluded that, while still convinced of the evils that existed in the United States, as a democrat I could find no more satisfactory homeland.

During the last few weeks of my stay in Europe I decided a number of other things. Whatever might have happened had I begun sooner, I decided, I was no longer fit for a literary career. I was nearing the end of my twenty-ninth year. I had for many years indulged excessively in drink, and was always involved in one or more affairs with women. I had arrived at the conclusion that a real, lasting love affair was impossible. I had also arrived at a condition of absolute disgust for all women with light morals.

I dedicated myself to the determination that, when I put foot on American soil again, I would abandon drink and companionship with loose women. I would go to work for the sake of work, for the sake of having something to do to escape boredom. I determined also to seek out some nice woman near my own age, to whom I could candidly acknowledge my own past, marry her, and rear a family of children.

I had no particular plans in a business way. I was not even sure I would take up newspaper work again. I was only determined to do something and do it hard, and live a decent, clean, temperate life, and join the common herd of American businessmen. I wanted to burrow down, as it were, into the middle of the mass of common people, and be one of them and do all that the best kind of people were doing—working hard, living soberly, and bearing responsibilities as a husband and father. I had come to the conclusion that no man could be a complete man who didn't live a man's life completely.

For two years I had been traveling. I hadn't been actually loafing, because I had been reading much, and I had seen so many sights that I had actually become sick of them. But still such work as I was doing was not satisfying to me. I felt the need of expending a greater amount of energy.

I had also become satiated and disgusted by my own habits. To a large extent, I kept all my resolutions for several years. I never entirely gave up drinking, but I did drink only temperately. I was extremely chaste. There is nothing like hard work, mental or physical, to overcome bad habits and appetites.

I think that the second part of my business career, which began with my return from Europe in 1883, was successful mainly because I was not working for success in business so much as I was working to overcome my natural and acquired dispositions.

I have passed rather lightly over the period of my second tour abroad. This is not because it was unimportant in my life, but because the really important things that happened to me were internal developments rather than external happenings. So much have I always valued the educational effect of my various trips abroad that I have urged (so far vainly) my sons to travel extensively outside their own country.

On this trip I read much, mostly history and daily newspapers and other current publications. My sister and I were simply tourists. We carried no letters of introduction with us. It was only occasionally and by chance that we met people of distinction. I may admit here that I experienced often a feeling of mortification because, while my sister found it easy to meet with and easily become acquainted with men and women of some distinction, I found myself generally regarded as a sort of wild, rather impossible kind of American youth. It is true that I was assertive enough to secure attention from people I found myself with, but such attention as I received was not, as I recall, complimentary. I quarreled with a great many people with whom it would have been better for me to have kept peace. I was harsh and exacting with servants in the hotels, on boats and on railroad trains. While I fully recognized my lack of good breeding, I had then, as I have always had, a disposition to boast and bully. This resulted from a desire to attract attention to myself. I wanted to learn things of people. I was impatient at the slower method of quietly and modestly ingratiating myself. Until I could obtain recognition, I could not obtain that attention which should make other people communicative with me.

I spent altogether about five years of my early life in foreign travel. I have no recollection of their being anything like holidays or time devoted to pleasure. Rather it seems that all my days spent in foreign travel were strenuous days. Perhaps I never worked harder in my life than I did during the eighteen or more months that I was traveling with Ellen. I read enormously. I concentrated my efforts on learning French and German. My sister took up Spanish and Italian. I became fairly proficient in French, but never got far enough along in German to make it easy for me to read the language. Most of my solid reading, while abroad, was in French. I also reread Gibbon's *Decline and Fall of the Roman Empire* in this period.

I observed critically. I compared what I had read with what I saw. I compared what I was learning during my travels with what I had learned, and seen, and thought in all of those years of my life that had gone before. I generalized even more than I analyzed. I was formulating my convictions. I came to conclusions, made final decisions. I returned to America a matured man. I had served my apprenticeship, and had been through many sorts of schools of experience.

Physically, I was completely recovered. Mentally and physically, I felt myself fit and strong. I felt myself fitter and stronger and better equipped than any man whom I had known in America, and perhaps quite as well equipped as any other man whom I was to find on my return. I had lost a whole lot of my youthful vanity and conceit, too, in spite of what I have said in previous paragraphs. I was no longer ambitious. I did not want to become great or even to acquire the reputation for being great, which is a very different thing. I simply wanted to work and do things. I wanted to become more human. I wanted to cast off some of my peculiarities and eccentricities. I wanted to cease playing any sort of role. I wanted to find a wife, and become an everyday sort of a father of a family. I was weary of all my philosophy and all of my thinking. I did not care to learn any more about anything.

XII

Undialectical Materialism

As I say, I came to a number of conclusions, principally about social and economic and political matters. If I never became a socialist, it is largely because I don't know much about socialism. I have never to this day read Karl Marx, although I did read Ruskin and some of the writings of William Morris. During the past twenty or thirty years I have read much of socialism and have had quite a number of very intimate friends who were socialists. One or two of them were practically anarchists.

During those early days I was a radical, it is true, but my radicalism consisted in my disgust with and even hatred of the bungling capitalist and employing classes. I was not really deeply moved by sympathy for the poor and the unfortunate. My antagonism was directed against those people in America who have had such splendid chances and as a whole have made such a miserable failure of their opportunities.

I was nineteen when I was interested in a certain corporation that employed skilled labor. The workmen declared a strike. There were less than forty laborers, nearly all known to me personally. I had little respect for their wisdom or common sense. The strike began. It was significant of my self-conceit and my cheek that I went before the board of directors and told them that I had a way of breaking the strike if I were permitted to do certain things. I laid out before them my plan, which seemed to them good.

Inside a week I had replaced every striker with as good a man as himself. No matter how! Then the old workingmen came to me to tell what their agreements had been and what their present hardships were. As I said, I knew all of them personally. At their solicitation I visited a number of their homes. I saw things that made me feel ashamed at the part I had been playing.

Without saying anything to the old-fossil directors, I undertook to make the acquaintance and learn something about the character of the strikebreakers. All or nearly all the strikers were married men with families. Every one of the strikebreakers was unmarried and comparatively young, some of them very young. By one means and another I and the old workmen persuaded every one of these newcomers to leave. In order to save the faces of the dignified, superior men who formed the directorate of the company, the old workingmen made some concessions in their demands and were allowed to return. It was not more than two weeks later that business as usual was going on in that institution. The men whom I had been dealing with were members of the union. For the first time I learned from them what unionism meant and what its history had been. And then I had had this experience with the directors, who were really not directors at all, but merely old foo-foos, who were themselves directed by an employee manager.

From that time on in such a small way as I could, I have been leveling my guns at the employer class, whether they be capitalists or mere borrowers of capital.

My purpose in life—or at least my uppermost purpose—has been to serve the common people of my country. Consistently, in season and out of season, have I advocated the cause of the workingman—at least, the man of small income and means. It has been a great disappointment to me, and a greater discouragement, always to have had impressed upon my mind incidents that went to prove that poverty has been caused, mainly, by the ignorance and unwisdom, and the lack of force, of my clients. I have deeply and maturely considered the subject of education as a remedy of poverty, as a bulwark against oppression. Alas! I have been able to discover no remedy there. Education, or that which passes for education, appears to be absolutely ineffective.

I am not a socialist. I can see hope in socialism no more than I can see hope for socialism. To me, socialism seems to be another word for absurdity. But on the other hand, capitalism seems to me to be tragedy—a tragedy to be all the more fearful the longer its denouement is delayed.

I have faced this problem of socialism with instinctive sympathy and comprehension, and rational repugnance. There is no place on this world or the known universe for peace. There can be no progress, nor even any life, except that it be the fruit of struggle, the offspring of death. The justice that we prate about is not divine justice or natural justice, but the whispering plaint of wearied, outworn, never-resting, always-suffering humanity, whose belief in Christly and other religions is fathered by a wish to evade the inexorable, the greater justice.

Why does a man want wealth? Why political office? Why ecclesiastic dignity? Why a prominent position in society or in a community? Why many friends?

Why do men throw themselves so wholeheartedly into business? Why, after a man has obtained a complete competence, does he continue to struggle in business and continually, time after time, jeopardize all the enough that he has for the chance of gaining more than enough, which he considers possible? Why do young men run foot races, and in groups, struggle one group against another—on the diamond in a game of baseball, and on the gridiron in a game of football? Why do boys box with bare fists or with gloves, and why is it that one nation wars against another? Why do clergymen preach and professors teach?

It has been suggested to my mind that there may be one all-sufficient answer to each and every one of the above questions, and thousands more questions.

Why does the sun shine, giving light and radiating heat? Why does the apple fall to the ground? Why does the vapor arise from the lake? To these questions and many thousands more, one answer might be sufficient.

The answer? *Force.*

So far as we know, force is everywhere in existence, and is as infinite as space and time. From both the religious or supernatural, and the materialist point of view, the soul or mind of man can be defined as force (whatever other definitions may be applicable to the same thing).

The mind of man can only exist in expressing itself in force, and the body of man is either a dead body, or else is in every one of its parts expressing itself in force, and existing only and because of this expression in all its multitudinous forms of activity.

The mind of man is force, expressing itself in *direction,* and perhaps in many other ways. That part of force which is a man's mind or soul, whether it be a collection of many forces, or is one indivisible and eternal force, must continue and must have *direction.* The desires for wealth, political office, ecclesiastical preferment, or social preeminence are each of them directions of the force of the mind. Force cannot be annihilated. It can only be diverted from one path of collision with another force.

Men strive for wealth, for position. They strive on the market and on the battlefield, because men are forces. Only things that are dead and inert can be directionless and devoid of force. If force is ubiquitous and eternal, there can be nothing dead and nothing inert. A granite boulder may only differ from a human being in the direction of its force expression.

Peace. What condition does the word peace signify? Peace is a definition of something that is not existing. Peace signifies an absence of conflicting forces or directions in men's minds or souls.

But mind or soul is only force, and force must have direction. Can all force—for example, the forces that are represented by human mind and body—exist and have direction, and not be in conflict? The physicist might with reason declare that theoretically such might be the condition, but at the same time, he would have to declare that nothing discernible in the universe, material or spiritual, indicates that forces ever took parallel lines in the same direction. On the other hand, both physicists and metaphysicians might go so far as to argue that if force did not express itself by encountering other force, it would not be force at all. Such an imaginable force might be equal to that other figment of imagination, deadness or inertness.

Eternal peace indicates the absence of conflict or friction, struggle. It means that imaginary thing called death, or inertness. Even if the minds of some men yearn for death, for annihilation, for the Buddhist nirvana, their yearning is no more effective than is the child's desire to grasp the moon.

Life and peace are antitheses. Men will war against one another, many against another many, so long as men live, for exactly the same reason that the sun radiates heat and light. A dead sun will not radiate heat and light, but the sun we recognize is the antithesis of a dead sun. In fact, a dead sun is not a sun. Nor would a peace-keeping, nonstruggling entity be a man. Such an entity would be something never seen on land or sea, something that would be impossible both to imagine and logically explain.

Yet because I am human and normal, and hence weak, and because I suffer in myself and in seeing others suffer, I am driven, despite my will and my reason, to join my kind in their protest against the inevitable, and hence I fight in the ranks of the socialists: an almost hopeless unit in a hopeful army. Nothing in the world could make me happier than to lose all my convictions, even at the cost of all my possessions.

I wonder how many other men there are in the capitalistic class who are even-minded with myself in this? I have an idea that the very greatness which is required to make oneself a great capitalist requires, by implication, such a mental attitude. Perhaps only those capitalists are naturally vicious who enjoy, by inheritance or other accident, that power of capitalism which they did not originate.

From what little I have read about socialism—and nearly all that has been from the pens of its critics—I have discovered no practical plan for the elimination of the unfit and for the domination of the fit.

I am convinced of the eventual development of government along a line apparently pursued by socialists which will have for its goal something as far from the ideal of its propagandists as is the institution of the present-day Christian church different from the spirit and teaching of Christ.

The desired end of socialism seems to be to obtain at one and the same time the satisfaction of the social instinct and purely physical necessities, without having to pay the heavy price of serfdom for it. I believe that the obtaining of this end may be practicable and that socialism, as it exists, is an experimental effort in this direction which is bound to result in great progress.

Yet the whole theory of socialism, as it stands now, is based upon the assumption that the world's natural opportunities are so small that it is possible for any number of men in combination to monopolize these opportunities.

Further, socialism is based really upon a spirit of conservatism, of nonproductiveness. The effect of socialism would be that society would not only be satisfied with the knowledge it at present possesses, but that there would be no increase by discovery of new fields of human activity. The socialist would take possession of the world—material and social—as it exists today, and divide it up into shares, and thereafter have society continue to exist upon the product hitherto accumulated, taking no further step forward into the undiscovered and virgin fields of opportunity.

Poverty, real or comparative inequality in the matter of property possession, is not caused by oppressive great men, bad government and bad institutions. It is only caused by lack of knowledge, lack of intelligence and the reckless wastefulness of the individual.

If poverty is not criminal, if the ordinary poor man is not a criminal, it is only because a lack of knowledge or a lack of desire "to get on in the world" is not criminal. If the average poor man is not a criminal, I and men like me having ability to understand things and to know conditions, would be criminal if we allowed ourselves to be afflicted with poverty.

Perhaps I would be doing better if, instead of devoting my energies to denouncing wealth and inspiring the masses to jealousy and revolution, I would devote my whole efforts to an attempt to teach men that each individual is able by industry, self-instruction and economy to make himself and his family independent of and free from injurious oppression on the part of the wealthiest, most covetous and greedy of his fellows.

(Editor's Note: The material in this chapter was written in 1914.)

XIII

"Whatever Is, Is Wrong"

I CANNOT PRETEND that I went into journalism because I had a call to serve humanity. No idea came to me in my early days as a newspaperman that I owed the public a duty. I cannot even now recall the time when the idea first dawned upon me that I was working for others than myself. However, I learned, as every editor of a successful newspaper does learn very soon, that an editor has an extraordinarily great influence on the public, and that the influence may be for good or ill.

I will give myself credit for having from the very first sufficient moral bias to cause me to do good rather than evil.

It took years for me to develop to the point where I was willing to sacrifice any great immediate temporary advantage for the purpose of doing a public service.

I do not think that I ever became thoroughly intrenched in the habit of altruism until I had learned by experience that even if honesty was not the best policy, it was a policy by which at least a newspaper editor could not only enjoy business success but something still more valuable—the confidence and respect and even the affection of a large part of the public.

"Whatever Is, Is Wrong."

As time went on and the fruits of my experience accumulated, I learned that it was so easy to be successful by simply being honest and altruistic as an editor, that I could win more easily and more surely and enjoy more leisure and (I must admit it) enjoy the excitement of battle on occasion, by being so than I could by any other course.

The necessity, then, of my profession has fixed upon me a habit of being a good citizen, a habit so confirmed by long years of practice that it has acquired all the force of an original instinct.

The profession of journalism is a peculiar one. Its *raison d'être* is public service. A man who believes in what he is doing can and generally will succeed. A man who does not believe in what he is doing may be successful, but will find it very difficult. It is possible for a hypocrite, by exercising constant self-restraint, to appear to be as good as the most sincere moralist, but it is awfully hard work.

The editor who wants to serve the public finds it easy and enjoyable work, and comparatively easy to retain the public's good will. The editor who wants to serve only himself and plays a role for the purpose of fooling the public for profit, finds it extremely difficult day after day and year after year in all emergencies of temptation and personal irritation so to control his actions as not to reveal his true character.

Preachers of the gospel and editors of successful papers both must preach good moral doctrine. It is one of my guiding principles as a journalist that great wealth is not a blessing either to the nation or to an individual. Capital is a danger; large capital is never acquired by individuals as a result of perfectly fair play.

Capitalists must exist, but the danger of their existence can be minimized by constant attacks and public ill will. Keep the capitalist busy defending what he has got, and the very activity enforced upon him makes him a better citizen and more considerate neighbor and employer. Capitalists resting secure behind the fortifications of ancient and obsolete, or modern, corruptly obtained laws, become vicious, arrogant and harmful alike to themselves and the community.

New brooms sweep cleanest. No great harm to the nation, and hence the vast majority of its citizens, would be suffered by the elimination by lawful process of the wealth and privileges of the present plutocratic governing classes. France lost nothing and gained much by the elimination of the old regime, and the bloody terror of France was a health-giving surgical operation. The people of the United States should be taught that there are perfectly lawful and proper and moral ways of ridding themselves of their present masters. Old laws that protect wealth and property if improperly acquired or uselessly employed can be substituted in this democracy by laws that will work no such evil.

The people of the United States should be taught that there should be a revolution in the country, a lawful revolution, a revolution of laws, and they should be taught how best to obtain this revolution.

Organized labor is an effort in this direction. Organized labor is not socialistic, though it cunningly but unconsciously trades on socialism. There is more room for individualism in labor unionism than in any form of democracy yet invented. But the individualism of labor unionism is a different kind of individualism. Individualism is understood by the purely commercial or capitalistic class in only one form, and a low form. Its one expression is the right of every man to get richer than his neighbor. The individualism of labor unionism is the individualism of real democracy. In labor union organizations, men obtain positions of power and influence not as they do in our present commercial republic, by mere possession of wealth, but by force of character and intellect and by the greater force and the nobler one of justice and good will toward their fellows.

The possession of wealth, no matter how much, whether it be

greater than a competency or only a competency, whether it consists of land and goods, of money in the bank, or paid up or partially paid up insurance policies, weakens every man that has such possessions, makes him a more selfish man, a more timid man.

As a newspaper owner I believe that a newspaper's income should not only be great enough to pay its going expenses, including the wages and other compensations necessary to secure and retain the employment of men of considerable ability, but they should be great enough to guarantee a profit, in ordinary times, of such dimensions as will rapidly make a reserve fund.

A newspaper fairly and honestly conducted in the interests of the great masses of the public must at all times antagonize the selfish interests of that very class which furnishes the larger part of a newspaper's income. It must occasionally so antagonize this class as to cause it not only to cease patronage, to a greater or lesser extent, but to make actually offensive warfare against the newspaper.

In order to maintain a newspaper's entire independence, it is necessary that the newspaper shall be so conducted that its revenue from the advertising class will be the smallest possible that the class can afford to get on with. The advertising patronage that such a newspaper has should only be a result of the necessity of the newspaper's patrons to get publicity for personal or selfish reasons.

The man who carries a gun, and is known to carry a gun, seldom needs it. The newspaper whose reserve of capital is large, and is known to be large, is almost wholly free from the danger of boycott by advertisers who would certainly resort to pressure in order to subdue a newspaper whose treasury was small and whose existence depended from day to day upon its advertising patronage.

The first of my principles is that I have constituted myself the advocate of that large majority of people who are not so rich in worldly goods and native intelligence as to make them equal, man for man, in the struggle with individuals of the wealthier and more intellectual class.

The press of this country is now, and always has been, so thoroughly dominated by the wealthy few of the country that it cannot be depended upon to give the great mass of the people that correct information concerning political, economic and social subjects which it is necessary that they shall have in order that they shall vote and in all ways act in the best way to protect themselves from the brutal force and chicanery of the ruling and employing class. I have sought to give these people all that information which will strengthen them in their unequal contest with their masters.

In furtherance of this latter policy I have sought to teach the common people the value—even the necessity—of combination. Although I fully recognize the many evils inherent in trade unionism, I have advocated its extension, the perfecting of its discipline, and its comprehending political activity.

Whenever there is a contest between the ruling classes, including not only employers but government officials, on one side, and the wage earners, the poor men and even the moderately well-to-do men, on the other side, I have chosen to be the associate, friend and fellow striver of the second party.

I have assumed, for purposes of guiding my own conduct, that the first party is mainly wrong and the second party is of more than questionable worth and morality.

I have assumed that there are enough other newspapers and enough other forces arrayed against us to insure that no general and far-reaching injustice will result even from the temporary successes of men and measures in my party that are intrinsically bad.

I do not "stand for men"—all men—as Henry George is said to have done. I have been an uncompromising partisan of that great majority of our people who are strong only in numbers.

It is not one of my journalistic principles to reform all the political and other social movements of our people. Even when I cause to be published arguments and matters of fact, the purpose of which is to persuade the masses of men to be temperate or totally abstemious in the use of liquor, it has not been for the purpose of saving souls. It has only been for the purpose of making my partisans more efficient in their struggle with their antagonists.

In a municipal contest between the great majority of the citizens—the working class—and the capitalistic element, I would aid my partisans even did I know that their success would give the city poor government and that the success of their opponents would give the city good government.

In fact I have not a whole series of journalistic principles. I have only one principle, and that is represented by an effort to make it harder for the rich to grow richer and easier for the poor to keep from growing poorer.

It can be said, and it can even be proved to the satisfaction of most men, that there is no difference between my business principle and the business principle that governs the majority of newspaper owners; and it also can be said and proved to the satisfaction of the same people that the ethics of my journalism are no better than those of the most venal and selfish of my profession.

It can be said that the net results of making money in order to make an independent newspaper are the same as if I were to make my newspaper serve only to make me money. It can be said and be believed by very honest, serious-minded men that it is no less wicked to be radical partisans of one party than it is to be radical partisans of the other.

Lately I have talked much with my sons about the future of my concern. I have said to them:

What is the fundamental principle and spirit of one of my newspapers? It is everything that is human. It is nothing that is remarkable. This principle, this spark of vitality and vigor, is a moral principle. As a whole body, my newspaper concern is as full of corruption, of weakness and immorality, as is any human being.

But, despite the existence of all these elements, there also exists the moral principle of protest. It is and always has been in evidence by reason of iconoclastic activity. If there is anything in it that is constructive, it is hardly discernible, even to me. So much of my newspaper work has been that of protest against what is, and that of effort to destroy existing conditions, that there has been little time or energy to direct toward constructive work.

Against what has this spirit and activity of protest been directed?

It has been directed against all that is in social organization.

As against the old thesis that "Whatever is, is right," I have set up the antithesis that "Whatever is, is wrong" and must be changed.

Otherwise there can be no human progress; otherwise there can be only stagnation, inertia and perhaps retrogression.

I have protested against the governmental system that had to be wrong because it was old and had originated under conditions of society, of material development or lack of development, and of ignorance of the science of today.

I have protested against undemocratic government carried on under the false name of democracy.

I have protested against too great usurpation of power on the part of the rich and the intellectual that is used to oppress the less fortunate.

I have protested against the inequality of opportunity.

I have protested against outworn theology and superstition, against old creeds that were almost universally repeated and proclaimed hypocritically by nonbelievers.

I have protested against all sorts of authority, save that exercised by a man for the sole purpose of benefiting mankind—against all authority that was not based upon the immediate and voluntary and present desire and wish of those who submitted to the same.

I have protested against all sorts of legislatures whose members obtained position by corrupt practices, by chicanery, by false pretenses.

I have protested most especially against the rule of the lawyer and the usurpation and oppressive use of the power of the courts.

I have protested against the claims of the court to the sacredness of their office.

All of the things I have protested against socialism protests against. Perhaps because there has been no occasion for protest, I have not protested against most of the claims of socialism.

Incidentally, I will say that my belief is that there would be few left in the ranks of socialism if all of those men that are now reckoned as socialists but who only consent to be in the ranks of socialism because of their aversion to the wrongdoing of monarchy, aristocracy and plutocracy, were taken out.

Thirty-five years ago, as a journalist, I was as unformed, undeveloped and plastic as a newborn babe. The spirit that moved me as a journalist, however, was the spirit of protest. It moved and exercised itself unconsciously—that is to say, unconscious of any purpose well-defined or even possible of definition. I had no end in view. I can almost say that I was absolutely deficient of any conscious or unconscious general or particular moral principles such as I recognize myself possessed of today.

I just grew by fighting—fighting because it is in my nature to fight, and fighting that which, whatever it was, antagonized me. It was natural that I fought that which most antagonized me, although I did not for a long time stop to think what particular class of people and conditions were antagonistic to me. I resented authority, and as authority found itself in the hands of usurpers, I fought the usurpers, selfishly and egotistically, never recognizing, for a long time at least, that there was a real principle at stake, that there was anything else at stake excepting a personal victory. I hunted and fought instinctively, as the wolf and the lion and the fish in the sea hunt and fight; because it was my nature, as it is theirs, to hunt and fight and devour prey.

Therefore, in considering the moral principle upon which one of my newspapers stands, no mistake must be made based upon the supposition that any Scripps newspaper rests on the broad foundation of a large and well-ordered body of ethical principles.

Because I was a poor man and a workingman, and because I felt that in common with these other poor men and workingmen I had natural rights that were being trampled upon by richer men and more intellectual men than myself and my fellows, I fought in the blind fury of resentment. I fought so furiously that I passed out of the ranks of the poor and oppressed and advanced well into those of my opponents, still cutting and still slashing, but still holding my own, preferring rather to remain alone in my own little role than to join forces with the new men I had around me, as against my old associates, and refusing also to give up the spoils of my bow and spear to return to those I had left behind me, groveling in their slavery and in their misery, grumbling much but daring not enough.

Just as I, as a man, had found myself isolated, surrounded by a host of enemies that I chose to be enemies, courted by those whom I would not have as friends, so has my newspaper organization advanced well into the ranks of great and powerful combinations and corporations of intellectual men.

What has the future in store for me and my newspapers?

I cannot stand still, and they cannot. Standing still means stagnation, torpidity, disease and death.

We can only go back to our old friends by submitting to slavery. We can permit ourselves to be absorbed and to become a part of the militant, the fighting aristocracy, that little rank of the few and mighty who stand holding almost all the world of humanity at bay while we are enjoying wrongly acquired possessions.

Not for long will we be allowed to occupy our position of splendid isolation. Not for long can we keep our hearts in sympathy with the slaves of whom we are the champions, if we live in splendid palaces and feed around princely tables.

In what will we be different from other princes of power? Already we have grown suspect to our followers and supporters. Already have our followers and our equals grown restive of our position among them and isolated from them. It is only a question of time, perhaps, until our position will be the hardest of all. We will become the common enemies of both contending forces.

Capitalism will desire to destroy us, the disturbers of their peace. Serfdom will recognize us as not of their kind, and will join their old enemy in an effort to destroy us.

We must either fight on farther and climb to greater heights, or retreat and be destroyed as cowards—who should be destroyed.

The whole press of the United States, outside of the Scripps newspapers, with perhaps a few exceptions—journals of comparatively little influence among the governing classes—is now subject to and dominated by capitalism. This press has, for the most part, been founded by men who, temperamentally unlike myself and my associates, were fit members of the army to which they now belong. It is impossible for these men to be absorbed and assimilated without their newspapers' being destroyed as properties.

It is my conviction that it is impossible, even if we were willing, to join the army of plutocracy, since the mere fact of our attempting to join with these people would, by the destruction of our properties, eliminate us from the capitalist class.

Our position might be likened to that of Cortez in his invasion of Mexico; to that of Caesar, who, landing in the island of Britain, burned his ships behind him; to that of Napoleon, who kindled the flame of war in Europe and could only exist, being a soldier, so long as warfare continued.

We can only hold together, having supporting us the army of our followers, so long as we fight hard and fight and win battles for them: so long as we fight against privilege and successfully by degrees transfer some of the privileges of the few to the many. We must maintain our army by giving them booty gained from the common enemy.

It is the opinion of the founder of the Scripps newspapers that there is only battle ahead, and certain destruction behind.

It is my opinion that the certainty of continual victory as the result of fighting is as great as the certainty of destruction as the result of retreat.

The political world of the United States is ripe for and prepared for change, revolutionary change, and it is waiting only for leadership that can organize; the leadership of a man, of a band of men, who has or have all the weapons and all the ingenuity, the capacity for stratagem and tactics of the dominant class, as well as the sympathy and confidence of the great mass of the dispossessed.

This is a time for great men, for brave men, and for men who know how.

XIV

I Hire Some Christians

I HAVE OWNED many newspapers. I have owned papers in cities that I have never visited. I have met residents of all the cities in which my papers have existed, however, and have found that I have as many different kinds of reputation as I have newspapers. The people who know these newspapers have formed their estimates of me by what they know of the papers themselves. As no two of the papers are alike, it is not strange that I should find so many different estimates of myself.

Of all the reputations I have won, that which pleases me most is the reputation I have won on account of the Cincinnati *Post.* Friends from Detroit and Cleveland regard me as a wealthy man. Friends that I have met from Cincinnati regard me as a good man, a good citizen, and an honest and courageous man. They may or may not know of my being wealthy. It seems that my wealth, or lack of wealth, has no bearing on their estimate of me and my character. I imagine I have fewer enemies in Cincinnati than anywhere else that I have published a paper, and that such enemies as I have respect me highly.

The *Post* was not originally a Scripps paper. Late in 1880 two brothers named Walter and Albert Wellman founded in Cincinnati a journal called the *Penny Paper*. It was published from a job office. It had lasted for a few weeks when Walter Wellman came to Detroit to ask my brother James if he would be interested in backing the new enterprise. My brother was greatly attracted to Wellman, who was a very capable young journalist. He made a bargain with him whereby the Scripps interests would advance ten thousand dollars in capital and take sixty per cent of the corporation that was to be formed.

I was then editor of the St. Louis *Chronicle*. In response to a letter from James I came east to Cincinnati to superintend the formation of the new company. I was then in favor with James, and was permitted to take up some stock—ten per cent, I believe—in the new company.

After a few weeks I went back to St. Louis. Shortly after this I was removed from my St. Louis job by James and sent back to Cleveland. While in Cleveland it was understood, however, that I was to look after the new paper, called the Cincinnati *Post*.

Sometime early in the summer of 1881, a wire from Wellman informed me that he had been arrested for blackmail, and asked me to come immediately to his assistance. I went to Cincinnati, and found Wellman had been made the victim of a "frame-up." A king gambler named "Policy Bill" Smith had hired a detective agency to put the Cincinnati *Post* out of business. Wellman was attacking the enormously wealthy Smith on his policy activities, and also the police, for permitting the swindling to continue.

The Wellmans were all for settlement. They wanted to close the paper, quit, and leave the city. Walter had been promised immunity from further prosecution if he would do so. I told the men they had no power in the matter, and employed an attorney to take care of the case. Since I had control of the paper, I was able to prevent the publication of any confession or apology.

My lawyer told me that this offense of blackmail was not extraditable. I told the Wellmans that I would buy out their stock and pay them $3,000 for it. Then they could slip across the river into Kentucky, and by staying out of Ohio, avoid danger. They accepted my proposal, with the result that the Scripps interests now owned all the stock of the Cincinnati *Post*. I forget what proportion of the Wellman stock I took—probably all or most of it.

At my brother's instigation, I put in as business manager of the *Post* an old fellow named Charles A. Worthington, who was very honest and very wooden-headed. He had been a serviceable employee in the business office of the Detroit *Evening News*. As editor I installed Robert B. Ross, whom I have mentioned already.

These two were in charge of the *Post* when I left in 1881 to go to Europe. When I visited Cincinnati on my return from Europe in 1883, I found business conditions terrible. The paper had an income of about $1,000 a month and expenses of about $2,500. However, for a man looking for work, it had several advantages over the other Scripps papers in Detroit, Cleveland, Buffalo and St. Louis. While Ross was absolutely worthless as an editor, he was a genius as a writer, and was a fighter from start to finish. His own work on the Cincinnati *Post* had made the paper, little as it was, a power in the city. Another advantage the *Post* had over the other Scripps papers was that its competitor—the Cincinnati *Times-Star*—was then a weak sister. While I was looking for work—and hard work—I was not looking, just then, for an impossible task. It seemed to me that the size of the job presented in Cincinnati was big enough for me, and not too big.

I found that Ross had been sick for some months, and was confined to his room. A cub reporter named Ridenour was acting as editor. Ross was discouraged on account of his health. Worthington was very depressed by the economic situation, and considered the case hopeless. The paper was in debt for around $10,000. The original $10,000 advanced by the Scrippses had vanished long before my return. Worthington had, by the death of an uncle, come into an inheritance of about $30,000. He calculated that his share of the losses of the *Post* would more than eat up what interest he would get from his inheritance. Besides, he was much put out by his share of the debt represented by the stock. He offered me his stock for one dollar, provided I would take over the debt liability of the stock. A few weeks later I bought Ross's stock, paying him about $2,000 for it. I also assumed his debt. Then I bought Sweeney's stock. Thus I gained possession of fifty-five per cent of the whole stock. The other stockholders, after this, were my sister Ellen, five per cent; James E. Scripps, twenty per cent and George A., twenty per cent. For the first time in my life, I owned the controlling stock in a newspaper. I realized well enough at the time that I had bought only a prospect hole; but, as I have said, I was not looking for anything else but a chance for hard work.

The Cincinnati *Morning Enquirer* was the most influential and prosperous of the daily newspapers. It was owned and edited by John R. McLean. The Cincinnati *Commercial* was edited by a man famous in his day as a journalist, Murat Halstead. The *Commercial* and the *Enquirer* were both morning papers. The *Times-Star* was an old evening newspaper owned by a very rich but vulgar and base-minded man named David Sinton. His only daughter married Charles P. Taft, brother of W. H. Taft, who later was President of the United States.

The *Commercial Gazette* was an extremely high-class paper, with fine editorials. As a newspaper it was not even third class. The main function of the *Times-Star* seemed to be to support the business interests of David Sinton, who had large holdings in the gas company, local street railway, and other similar interests. There was no paper in Cincinnati representing the common people. Such matters as religion and morality were ignored entirely, except that the *Enquirer* made much of sex immorality.

I Hire Some Christians

On the *Post* I found a strange and highly moral crew. Ridenour, the acting editor, had graduated from a small Ohio college a few years before. He had vacillated in his choice of a profession between the medical and ministerial fields, and had been a male nurse in a hospital. He was a zealous Christian Presbyterian.

One of the cub reporters on the *Post* was a man named Lemuel T. Atwood. He was about thirty, and was working to support a wife and two children, at a seven-dollar weekly wage rate. He was a graduate of Michigan State University Law School, and for several years had attempted the practice of law, and failed. He was, I found out, a devout Swedenborgian. He later showed me that he was indeed one "in whom there was no guile."

I had been in Cincinnati only a few weeks when a wild-looking man came to me looking for a job. His name was Delos R. Baker, and he had been employed as a special writer for the *Enquirer* for some time, was married, and had a family of several children.

I told him I had no use for *Enquirer* men on the *Post*. He told me it was because my paper was so different from the Sinton paper that he wanted the job. I found that he was a graduate of a Methodist college, that he had a brilliant career in the pulpit for several years, until he was excommunicated from the church for heresy. I told him I wanted no "unfrocked priests." He stated that his excommunication was no reflection on his character, since he had only lost caste and his license to preach because he rejected one of the church's dogmas.

I asked him what he had been drawing from the *Enquirer*. He replied thirty dollars a week. I told him the *Post* could not afford so costly a man at that time. He replied that he knew, and that he would take one-half his former salary to work on the *Post*. I told him I wanted no such fool on the staff of the *Post*. Baker retorted that he was no fool. He said he expected to get his full wage of thirty dollars—one-half from me, and the other half from the Lord, his God. He stated that in prayer he had submitted the whole question to God and that he knew he would be doing God's will by coming to work on the *Post.* I saw that, while he was very eccentric, he was very learned, very eloquent, and, in fact, an all-round brilliant character. I took him on.

It was with such men as I have above described that I undertook a very peculiar experiment in journalism. While I reckoned myself entirely devoid of religious sentiment or beliefs, I had, at that time, one thing in common with all of these three men: a great moral zeal. I had, only a few months before, resolved on a complete moral reform and on devoting the remainder of my life to the service of men.

I had many an inward chuckle, surveying the situation. There was myself, with a long past though young in years, and these other three men, only one of them my junior, all of them zealous Christians, and as pure and honorable men as I have ever known in all my life.

Mr. Atwood so attracted me by the nobility of his character that within a few days my sympathy for him was such as to cause me actual pain. Here was a man of thirty, not only a college graduate, but a scholar, with so much intellectual development and such intellectual potentiality that he shamed me, taking on a new profession with a wife and two children dependent on him, and for a pittance of seven dollars weekly. He did not know the ABC's of journalism; his copy was crude; he wrote a newspaper item as he would a lawyer's brief. Such was his style of writing that condensing it without rewriting it was impossible.

I called Atwood in one evening and urged him to give up the job, telling him that he could not, in justice to his family, work for such a wage, and at the same time I told him that, in justice to the newspaper, I could pay him no more.

He said he could do nothing else.

I told him he could earn better wages working on the street as a laborer.

He replied that God had given him a mind and a capacity to do his Maker a greater service than employing himself in manual labor. During our interview Atwood was chewing tobacco all the time. He had no meat on his bones, the skin of his face had an unhealthy color. In fact, he looked like a starved man, and I believe in those days that he actually was starving, and that he overcame the cravings of his stomach by the use of tobacco in order that he might use all of his wage in feeding his wife and children.

Of one thing I was certain about these three men: not one of them would, for any financial consideration, be dishonest to me or dishonest to the public they were employed to serve. I knew that not one of them would write a line for the paper, even on peril of discharge on the one hand or a great reward on the other, that they did not believe would be of service to humanity and in honor of their God.

The accident of finding myself at the head of a small staff of newspapermen dominated by three such characters was the cause of the future growth and character of the Cincinnati *Post*. When I took charge of the paper, it had about 13,000 daily circulation. Of this 7,000 was handled by carriers and newsboys, and about 6,000 was in the neighboring towns. I decided that, with the small means at hand, I could not afford to make a general circulation both in the country and the city, so I cut off the country circulation and made the *Post* exclusively a local paper.

Mr. Worthington, the business manager, had been a bachelor until a few weeks before coming to the *Post*. He was about forty-five when he married, and the marriage brought no children. Even in the office of the Detroit *News* it had been noted that Worthington was a great friend of the little newsboys, and that he was a sort of daddy to them all. In going to Cincinnati, he carried with him his love for children. All the newsboys of the *Post* were little fellows ranging between the ages of six and ten years. The relation between these boys and Worthington was that of adoring children and a loving father. Worthington was playing no business game when he was gaining the affection of these boys—he simply loved them and they loved him. Every day when the little fellows gathered in the office to get their papers, Worthington would have his pockets filled with peanuts, licorice, cheap broken candy, or something of the kind. Each little fellow got something. Every Saturday afternoon he had a special treat for them. When watermelons were cheap, he would buy two or three and cut them up for the children. When he could buy oranges for ten cents a dozen, as sometimes happened, there was an orange for each boy. No matter what season of the year it was, there was always a Saturday afternoon treat. It was always inexpensive, of necessity, for Worthington paid for it out of his own pocket. In the summer he often gave the boys cheap excursions on some river steamboat. He would find some kindhearted captain or owner who would charge little or nothing for the excursion. The boys were restricted to some part of the boat while the rest was filled with ordinary excursionists.

Worthington was such another Christian, just such another man of morality, as were the three men on the editorial staff.

I was maneuvering and planning how to make the best possible use of the material I had found in my editorial room and my business office, when an event occurred that solved the whole problem for me.

There came to town a youngster named Harrison, known as "The Boy Evangelist." He was not a favorite of the churches and clergymen of the city. He was perhaps too common a fellow, too vulgar. He began preaching the gospel in some out-of-the-way corner lot. He got a large tent, then a larger one and soon was drawing thousands and tens of thousands to hear him.

It was Baker's idea to write up this revival as a great news story, but not from the standpoint of the ordinary critical and sensational journalist. He described his plan to me this way:

If we were to have a great Republican Party rally, the reporters of the Republican papers would attend the meeting and write it up with full sympathy, showing any amount of partisan bias. If there were to be a Democratic Party rally, the reporters of the Democratic papers would attend the meeting and write it up in the same partisan spirit.

"Now," he said, "we belong to the Lord's party, and the partisans of the Lord are having a great rally down here in Cincinnati, so why not deal with it in the same way?"

Ridenour as acting editor thoroughly approved of the idea. I saw the novelty of the enterprise, and I had long ago learned that men could do those things which they most approved of, and especially could they do those things best which they themselves originated.

Then the work began. Column after column and page after page was devoted day after day to this great religious revival. This boy preacher and the little *Penny Post* were vying with each other and co-operating with each other in saving souls. I have never heard of, and do not believe that ever before or since had there been such a thing in the newspaper business. From the first Murat Halstead and other leading citizens began to josh me and joke with me about turning my paper into what they called "a Sunday-school advocate of daily issue."

Some of the editorials of the *Post* were prayers; some were sermons. But the effect on the circulation was remarkable. It grew rapidly; doubled, trebled and quadrupled. Nor was this effect on the circulation a mere passing incident. The boy preacher's revival meetings finally closed, but the *Post's* efforts in this direction were continued for years. In the news columns and editorials too, great space was given to religious and church matters, Protestant and Catholic alike. They were not treated in the ordinary way, just as items of interest to small classes of society, but as matters of universal importance.

The rise of Atwood from the humble place where I found him to the editorship of the *Post*, and later to the position of my personal representative in all business matters, was remarkable and due solely to one characteristic—his absolute reliability.

I have often said that, if at any moment I should tell Atwood to set fire to and burn down my office, he would do it without questioning or remonstrating. There was no order I ever gave him that was not instantly obeyed.

Once, in the later part of Atwood's life, I asked him how he could consistently do this. He replied that, during his early experiences with me, he had often questioned himself about the righteousness of submitting himself so completely to the orders of a man whose reputation had been such as mine was, and who was avowedly an atheist. He said he had determined then, if ever he got an order that his conscience told him was wrong, he would not only refuse to obey it, but would resign his position regardless of consequences. He said however, that as time went on, he began to understand me better, and to know what my underlying motive was in regard to the *Post*. He added that, as he had never received an order from me that caused his conscience to rebel, he finally arrived at such a condition of reliance on me and confidence in me that there seemed never to be any occasion to question the righteousness of any act that I commanded him to perform.

I told him then that perhaps he was more responsible even than I was for the character of all my dealings with him, because I knew that he was incapable of doing wrong things. I had never ordered him to do anything that a most conscientious man could not do.

The history of the *Post*, editorially, was for many years that of a newspaper that existed solely for the purpose of serving its community without regard to business consequences. In its later life, it lapsed from this course for several years, and fed from the swill trough of corrupt politics, not openly and fearlessly, but covertly. It tried to keep the favor of the masses, the good will of the really good people, and still accept favors from a class of men who were public enemies. The paper served these men, if not by commission, at least by omission.

This happened at a time when I was too deeply absorbed in other work, and suffering too much with my own bodily ailments, to give the *Post* close attention. When I finally discovered what was being done to the *Post,* I waked up to the seriousness of the situation. I took a firm hold, and completely reversed its later policy and put it back on its old line.

The direct result of this was great increase in circulation, but an enormously decreased volume of advertising business. For about a decade following this switch in policy, the *Post* was more or less boycotted by the large business interests of Cincinnati. But, during all this time, so enormous was its circulation that it never failed to make some profit. It never failed to exercise tremendous influence in the social and political field, not only in Cincinnati, but throughout the state of Ohio and several adjoining states.

Just before my reform of the *Post,* the paper was in a very prosperous condition. I had appraised it at not a penny less than two million dollars. It was my custom annually to appraise the value of all my newspaper properties. At the next annual appraisement, following the reform, the profits had fallen to such an extent that I was compelled to knock off a full million dollars from the value of the *Post.*

XV

Marriage Is Work

I WAS REFORMED, more or less, but still I wasn't married. When I found that getting on the water-wagon was no easy matter, I decided to put that off until I should begin the performance of my resolve to be a good father and husband.

Now I had no particular person in mind when I decided to marry. I had left behind me several old flames. In fact I had been nearly engaged to marry five different times, but had had the good fortune to evade, in an honorable way, all of these obligations. Some of the girls had been married before I returned to the States. Some of them were too near my own age for me to mate with them now. Still, there were several, and so, drawing up a list, I numbered them according to my preference, No. 1, No. 2, No. 3, etc. There wasn't a particle of romance in any of my plans. I did agree with myself that I would make no false pretenses to any woman who might choose to accept me. Of course, this prevented any love-making. I went to see No. 1 and made my proposal, candidly stating I wanted to marry because I wanted the job of taking care of a family. I was turned down. My second trial was no better. My third journey resulted in the discovery that this choice had become a faddist, with a fad that was extremely repulsive to me. I made no proposal.

In the meantime I was on the lookout for some young woman other than those I had known. I made several acquaintances, two of which resulted in embarrassing complications from which some good fortune and some tactful management on my part relieved me.

Colonel Charles A. Gano, a member of one of the oldest and best families of Cincinnati, had a small farm and a large house beautifully situated in the Mill Creek Valley north of the city. The colonel was somewhat broken in fortune, and I began to board in his home when working on the *Post*. I proposed to settle down to a quiet life in the country, go on reading, take plenty of physical exercise and entirely eschew the society of men and women.

I had not been at the Gano home more than a week or ten days when Mrs. Gano asked me to go with her to a church fete given by the Cumberland Presbyterian Church of Sharon. The pastor of the church was the Reverend Samuel K. Holtsinger.

Almost the first person Mrs. Gano introduced me to was a young girl she called Miss Nackie. She appeared so young that I would have hardly thought she was yet in her teens. This was partly due to her dress, which was a simple white frock, quite short—the kind of thing a young girl would wear. I regarded her at the time as only a child, but a very beautiful child. She was diffident and reticent, but still she had a certain poise and demureness that attracted me. Instead of going on with Mrs. Gano and meeting others, I chose to entertain this little girl. We got along famously.

I learned she was the daughter of the Reverend Holtsinger, and sang in the church choir. I had not attended church for a number of years, but on the following Sunday evening I took my walk up Westchester way and went into the Holtsinger church. Seeing my little girl dressed up in sober church clothes, and with a long dress on, it dawned on me that she was not such a child at all. The next day I called at the parsonage, and thereafter I was at the parsonage every day that I was at home. Miss Nackie was not yet nineteen, and I lacked a few weeks of being thirty-one.

Although I had started out to hunt for a wife in the most cold-blooded, unromantic way possible, I felt as desperately and insanely in love with this girl, after my first meeting with her, as any youngster in the puppy-love stage. I felt positively ashamed of myself, and worse still, I felt that to court and win this girl, if I could win her, would be an outrage. There is no fool like an old fool, and at the age of thirty-one I was in many ways much older than most men are at fifty-one.

I abused myself roundly for my infatuation. I reminded myself of my old-time resolution to marry only someone nearly my own age. I recognized the impossibility of ever telling this young girl just what sort of a man I had been—and still was, for that matter. I saw also that, even if some brute should tell her, she would be utterly unable to understand. I found later, as I have related, that it was just as impossible for me to make any confession to her father.

I made up my mind to quit and leave my ideal country home. I would run away from one place of temptation to another, and would only find myself still more sorely tempted than ever before. I reviewed mentally a number of ladies with whom I was sufficiently well-acquainted, and who knew enough of me, to make it extremely likely that at least some of them would accept a proposal of marriage, even if it were accompanied with a frank avowal on my part that I was only looking for a wife in a practical way.

But I married Miss Nackie. I would, if necessary, have resorted to lies and false pretenses to get her. We were married on October 7, 1885, within four months of our meeting. Our marriage took place in my wife's home. The only witnesses were Colonel and Mrs. Gano, and my wife's father and mother. My wife's trousseau consisted of only one little brown dress, so short that the bottom came well above her shoe tops, and a little turban to match. I had not announced my engagement to anyone, not even to members of my family.

I failed bitterly in my second resolution—keeping away from alcohol. The best I could do was to switch from spirits to wine. I have told how I eventually broke the habit. It is my opinion that any girl who marries a drinking man in the expectation of reforming him is doomed to disappointment.

The fact of the matter is that I had never been married, and had no idea of the ordeal that a young married man has to endure for several years. The young woman who becomes a wife seldom has knowledge of the real nature of a man needed to manage herself and her household in a way to help her husband in this matter of drink. It is more likely than not that the trials of early married life might drive an ordinarily sober man to drink.

When I completely licked the alcohol habit, there came a considerable change in my disposition. I wanted to work more. I wanted to read more. I wanted to adventure more than I ever had before. I became less amiable in my disposition, less thoughtful and attentive in my duties as *paterfamilias*. Of course, my wife is far too conventional and too well-regulated in the properties ever to admit the fact that the sober husband was not nearly so nice a companion as the one who was never entirely sober and never drunk. But before I undertook teetotalism, my wife had borne me seven children, and was past middle age, while I had reached the state when I had frequently heard myself referred to as the "old gentleman."

It was hardly ten months after I married before I had my first child.

For ten months, several of which I had spent in the sickbed, I was in a state of mental confusion. I didn't understand my job of being a husband. At the same time I was a thoroughgoing egoist in all essentials. I did my duty I believe, completely. I was in love with my wife, and there was no sacrifice that I would not make for her greatly and gladly. But still, I was an egoist.

For a full fourteen hours I was at my wife's bedside when she was suffering from the pains of her first childbirth. It was shortly after sunrise that our child, a boy, was born on July 19, 1886. A few minutes after the birth the child cried. Then a startling thing happened, something that I had never dreamed of as a possibility. I instantly ceased being a complete egoist. My child was, as it were, me, and I felt I was living for him and had always lived for him. Within sixteen years seven children were born to me and I worked always for these instead of for myself, as I had formerly. Each newcomer brought a renewal or extension of what I might call "nonegoism."

I was not only doing business now for pleasure, but as an obligation. I was always planning for the future of my offspring. One of my children, a third son, died when he was six years of age. That was another startling shock and one I have never recovered from. Seventeen years later my second son died, and four years later still my first-born died. I have only one son left of the five that were born to me. Still I can say now that I have never regretted that I married and that I married the wife I did marry. I think someone said that living is only a process of feeling. The childless man is not only not half a man, but he is only a small part of a man and if he lives—no matter how long or how successfully—he will die not having lived wholly and fully. Even the grief that comes from marriage, I think, is a kind of joy. It is part of the great adventure of living.

Between the date of my marriage and the birth of my first child, I had hardly become acquainted with my wife. I am sure she had not become acquainted with me, at least as a husband. Ours was a brief courtship. Only fourteen months elapsed from the time when I first saw the woman who became my wife till the birth of my first child.

Well, what happened? I knew what the effect was on me. I am sure the effect upon my child's mother was greater even than it was on me. From the moment when she first nursed him until the day he died, this son of mine took first place in his mother's affections. Then came the other children, each one crowding me farther and farther out into the extreme periphery of the family circle. My position was more than unusually unfortunate because in one respect my wife's attitude toward me was remarkable. She regarded me as a superman. She believed I was almost omnipotent. As a result, I was held largely blameworthy for all of our joint misfortunes. Her position was not a reasoned one. It was, one might say, instinctive. As she believed that I could do anything that I wanted to do, then everything that wasn't done that she wanted done was solely because I chose not to do it.

XVI

Letter to a Young Editor

A YOUNG EDITOR of a new Scripps paper came to Miramar in 1911 to ask some advice of me as to his future conduct. I told him:

You have come to me to learn something of my general policies and fundamental principles of journalism as well as to seek particular advice on the subject of this enterprise.

From what you tell me there is to be a comparatively large number of stockholders. I think that this division of ownership with the large number of stockholders, each one having his own peculiar aims and opinions, is a handicap.

No one person has so large an interest in the new paper as to offer exceedingly great reward for success or to make final failure unendurably painful.

Such of the stockholders as are named are of two classes: One class—those who have money—can afford to lose their "prorata" in case of failure; those of the other class have nothing to lose except their time. I presume you are the only one in this latter class.

Of course, while you have little or nothing to lose by failure, you have a tremendous amount to gain by success. If you are to succeed, and make your ten per cent of the stock worth anything, you must make it worth from ten to twenty thousand dollars. The great advantage to you of this would be that it would be a first and very substantial step on the road to financial independence, and to a certain extent will make you a capitalist. It will remove you from the ranks of the great majority of newspapermen who have no other status than that of wage earners.

However, the greatest advantage you can gain will be—in case of the success of the newspaper—that you have demonstrated that you are one of the very, very few men who have real ability as an editor. Of all the vast army of journalists in this country perhaps only a small fraction of one per cent of them have ever proved (perhaps by reason of lack of opportunity) that they are really fit for any other position than that of hired men.

You are twenty-nine years old now. In one year—if you are a man of the first order—you might have a successful paper, but if in two years, or even in three years, you succeed in establishing your paper as a profit-paying concern, and gaining the confidence and respect of the community and establishing yourself as a worthy member of the newspaper association to which you belong, you may well enough expect to go far in becoming an important influence in the country and a man of considerable personal wealth.

My advice to you is that you shall consider all of your fellow stockholders, and especially those who are strong enough actually to control the newspaper, both in its editorial and business policy. It will not be safe or wise for you to follow my individual advice unless the same is fully sanctioned by the controlling element in your association. I warn you that you must consider the real character of these men. While you might in the beginning obtain their consent to any line of policy, and while you might be allowed for a considerable length of time to pursue such line of policy, you must always hold in mind that the condition of the minds of these men and their attitude will be radically changed at some future point of time—at the time when your nonsuccess, or apparent nonsuccess, will show up strongly or at the time when your success will be such that the stockholders of this paper will regard it as being a valuable property. Your associates may be very willing to let you go on finding your own way, playing your own game with this paper so long as it is purely experimental, and so long as it has not determined any real intrinsic value. But when the property becomes a property and is valued as such by its stockholders, every man among you will make it his business to protect his own interest by maintaining or increasing its value. Young journalists and young journalistic institutions are naturally honest and fearless. It is only when they are far advanced and have a more or less considerable capital stake that mind-corrupting influences begin their work.

My advice to you is to start right and to keep going on right, and to make your greatest effort to avoid temptation. In other words, so conduct your paper that never at any time will you be tempted to color in the least possible particular your editorial policy for the purpose of maintaining the patronage of advertisers. I have found it infinitely more easy to resist the temptation to do cowardly work for the purpose of getting a new patron than it is to resist the temptation of doing the same thing for the purpose of maintaining patronage that I have already got.

Therefore I would advise you to consider the majority of the advertisers that you have a prospect of getting as being your enemies. Right from the start deal with the advertiser as an individual and with the whole class of advertisers in such a way that you will never get any of their patronage as a result of his or their individual or collective good will. The only kind of advertising that your paper can afford to receive or that any young paper can afford to receive is that which results from the commercial instinct and the selfish promptings of the customer. You want no man's advertising who can, as a purely business proposition, refrain from patronage.

I warn you against allowing your advertising business to grow too rapidly.

I have told you that while many of the new papers that have been added to our concern, by foundation or purchase, since the early days of my career, have, in respect to volume of business—that is to say, cash receipts—grown more rapidly than did those papers that were founded in the early days and were more or less directly under my personal and daily supervision and oversight; not one of these papers in their early days has grown in circulation and in influence even half as rapidly as did the Detroit *News*, Cleveland *Press*, and Cincinnati *Post*.

I believe the reason for this has been that the young men who have been engaged in the founding and building up of these new papers have regarded them as purely business institutions—as commercial ventures.

For myself, both in those early days and even up to the present time, I have never regarded a newspaper in any such light. It is true that I sought for increasing revenue eagerly enough and that I have also been determined always to make my papers profitable, that is to say, independent and self-sustaining. But my purpose in doing this has been solely that of seeking means for making my papers largely read and hence influential.

One thing, and only one thing have I ever considered as of very great importance in a business way and that was the growth of my newspapers in circulation, the development of their character as influential organs of public opinion being proved by this growth.

Naturally as I concentrated all my efforts on the one object of obtaining circulation and dissipated no part of my energy in acquiring revenue from advertisers, I had to be, and was, successful in rapidly building up circulation.

While there have been other reasons for my always desiring a small newspaper, my chief reason has been that there is a large profit in the small newspapers, while there is small profit or no profit, or actual loss, in the sale of large sheets. Therefore both as editor and as owner I had the inducement to sell as many papers as possible, and my business managers, because they must of necessity be commercially-minded, have themselves been anxious to increase the circulation because there was a profit in such increase.

Given a large paper, whether there was little or no profit or actual loss in the sale of the paper, the business office and even the editor himself is compelled to look to the development of the advertising business to secure funds not only to pay a profit, but to meet running expenses. In fact the smaller the circulation—providing the advertising public could be kept in ignorance—the larger the profit would be. Therefore on large papers the whole effort of the counting room has been to obtain advertising, and even when they have made an effort to obtain circulation it has been only for the purpose of extending its billboard space or increasing the price to be charged for the same. Necessarily the editors have been compelled to take a similar view and act accordingly.

As I said, you want to avoid temptation. I consider a small paper as one of the very best guards and guarantees against temptation to any evil practices of commission or omission.

I would advise that you use your influence to get your associates, in the beginning at least, to abstain from all expenditure on account of advertising. I would even advise against putting in any advertising type to start with, and I would not have an advertising solicitor or permit any man to solicit advertising in the beginning.

The most that I would do would be to make an announcement in your paper (perhaps keeping it standing) that whenever you had a circulation that would warrant your demanding an advertising rate of say thirty cents per inch you would open your columns to advertisers and solicit business, but that before that time you would prefer to receive no advertising patronage whatever.

I would advise you to use your influence to have the paper started as though there was no desire or expectation of ever taking advertising at all. Have your office organized, to begin with, strictly for the purpose of making a newspaper that the people want to read and getting it well circulated.

The economies that would result from this course would, I believe, during the first year of your existence fully equal all the possible income from advertising during the same period of time, so that the first cost of founding your paper would be no greater as the result of your spending nothing and getting nothing on account of advertising.

Then before the time should have come for you to solicit advertising you would have created a personality for your paper and established all of its principles. Every advertiser whose patronage you would thereafter obtain would come to you with his business well knowing that you were independent and resourceful and that he would have no possible reason for hoping or expecting to influence your editorial course by his patronage.

You must remember that that particular class of men that make up the advertisers are men of extremely sordid minds. Their lives are given up to dollar getting. They presume that every man is equally sordid. They presume—and they have a perfect right in this country to presume—that newspaper publishers are venal and that they have but one object in view and that is to obtain advertising patronage and make a profit. Every new newspaper is regarded with suspicion by the business public. No really intelligent advertiser would waste much money in patronizing a newspaper venture that may—and probably will—eventually fail. The vast majority of newspapers founded do fail and go out of business.

The principal cause for patronage of a new newspaper I have found by past experience is that while the advertisers regard any new newspaper as a venture that will probably fail, they also recognize the possibility of such a newspaper's being a success. Thus some of them more crafty than the others are prone to cast an anchor to leeward by patronizing (using the word in the most contemptible sense) a new newspaper in order that in case of its future success such early patronage may put them in a position to demand special favors and consideration on account of their presumed friendly acts during the trying days of the beginning of the new paper.

I really do not know what your own personal views are on many subjects. You tell me that as a whole you like and admire the policies of the Scripps papers. As the principal owner of these papers I am going to tell you that there is much in the management and conduct of our papers that is contemptible in the extreme. While they are to a certain extent independent, it is noticeable that their independent dealing with public questions is in direct proportion to the amount of business interests involved. They are often very independent in dealing with questions when advertisers will not resent their actions in so doing. Where the advertisers are either indifferent or divided in their opinions they can be, and are, very radical.

I would advise you to begin your course as editor of this paper with one object and only one object in view, and that is to serve that class of people and only that class of people from whom you cannot even hope to derive any other income than the one cent a day they pay you for your paper. Be honest and fearless with them, always without regard to the good will or the ill will of the so-called business community.

As a man of experience in these affairs, and one having perhaps many times more experience than any other man has ever had, I will tell you that it is absolutely certain in the end that you will get far more patronage and far better patronage from the advertisers by taking this course than you can possibly hope to get by any exhibition of flunkyism. It is the weak man who really admires the great athlete. It is the rascal who has the highest opinion of the gentleman. It is the sordid, money-making businessman who courts and fawns on the man with a newspaper that appears to be or that actually is influenced by higher motives.

In time, if you succeed in getting a circulation, advertising patronage will come to your paper. When it does, remember that in all Scripps papers the editor, and the editor alone, is responsible for every line of matter in the paper—advertising as well as news and editorial matter. He, and he alone, therefore, can shape the business policy of the paper. The advertising patronage of any Scripps newspaper is that, and only that, which the editor of the paper chooses it to be.

When you come to dealing with the advertisers, as a matter of business policy I advise you never to accept from any one advertiser so large an amount of custom that, if he should withdraw his patronage, it would materially affect your receipts or even your profits. The advertiser is the enemy. The big advertiser is the mortal foe of honest journalism. I would rather go through a dark alley with a thug than to couple up, in a business way as a young newspaperman, with a big advertising patron.

It is customary and imbecile for the general newspaper business manager to seek to get the patronage of large advertisers, that is to say, of advertisers who use a large amount of space; and it is no less imbecile, of course, that lower rates per inch are given for a large amount of space than for small amounts. Ten dollars a month received from ten advertisers is a far better asset to a newspaper than the patronage of one man that gives you twenty dollars a month. Hence the smaller the advertiser the more desirable his business and the lower his rate should be.

Remember another thing: the big men of the future are the small businessmen of today, and the big businessmen of today are generally approaching the end of their careers. As a young man and as a young newspaper you and your paper should keep your eyes continually on the future. The men whose patronage is going to be of great worth to your paper in the future are the so-called little fellows in business today, and the men who have but small amounts of money to spend for advertising.

But as editor of the paper it would perhaps be better that you should almost ignore even the existence of an advertiser except as a necessary and disagreeable intruder into your columns.

I would advise you especially during the period of time when you will be engaged in building up the circulation of your paper that you should not even think of the future when the advertising patronage of your paper will be an element in your business.

Speak your mind—or rather write it—freely on every and any subject. What is good, praise. What is evil, condemn.

I do not here advise you to set yourself up as a universal judge and arbiter of affairs in your city. That would be foolish. This is a democracy: we are bound, both of us, to accept the rule of the majority. As an editor you must keep your ear to the ground.

You must know what the majority of your people think is right, and if you disagree with the majority it is not your province to take a club to them; it is your business rather to persuade them to your way of thinking if you can, always evincing a willingness and even a desire to voice public opinion. This is pure demagoguery, but I want to tell you that pure demagoguery is pure democracy, and that you need suffer no shame on account of either.

While you are a poor man, and have been a poor and struggling boy, you must not forget that all your training and association has been by and with the aristocrats, intellectual or financial.

As the editor of this paper you must, in order to succeed, strip yourself of all the vanities of your class and be not only able but glad to be one in the ranks of the vulgar masses.

You cannot deliver a message to the masses from an elevated pulpit or dais: it is only by standing on the same level with these men that you can appreciate their sufferings and aid them in their efforts.

You may be, and probably are something of a coward—most men are; at least you are very timid, but whether you are frightened or not you must act the part of a courageous man. It takes courage to found a paper. It takes more courage than most men have got. Sometimes I think that courage is even more necessary than is either intelligence or honesty in conducting a newspaper.

A drunken bully with a pistol in his hand may terrorize a whole community of which the main portion may have more real courage than the bully himself. But the man with the gun who gives evidence that he is ready to kill any man that opposes him is the man that the community fears.

A fearless editor has in his paper a more powerful weapon than any pistol. If he has courage as well as a good conscience he can safely defy any man or any combination of men in any community.

Be diplomatic, but don't be too damned diplomatic. Most men fear to speak the truth, the bald, whole truth, to any man or community because they fear that the man or the community is not prepared to endure such frankness. I think this is a mistake. It is rare indeed when the circumstances are such that a conscientious man can lose anything by fearless, frank speech and writing.

XVII

The High Cost of Ignorance

WHILE I was amusing myself in ranching in California, I had occasion to learn something about horses. My ranch was a large one, and on it were several hundred head of horses and cattle. The stock was not fed, but grazed. The pasturage was good enough so that most of the stock was in fairly fine condition.

My wife was from time to time purchasing and turning out on the ranch highly bred breed mares—saddle stock. I noticed that most of these mares gathered around in the vicinity of the ranch house and barns, instead of remaining on the pastures. They became thin and starved-looking, and finally one of them died, as I was told afterward and led to believe, of starvation.

After that, these high-bred mares were driven back into the pasture land for part of the day and given one ration of hay each day.

Along with these high-bred mares were a number of standard-bred brood mares intended for breeding work horses. There were also a dozen or more broncos. While the high-bred mares were starving to death, and the standard mares keeping in only fair condition, the broncos were always plump and sleek.

The fine mares had evidently, from their colt days, been stable-fed, and perhaps made little other use of their paddocks than for exercise grounds. The middle-class mares had been partly stable-fed and partly allowed to maintain themselves on farmers' ranches. The broncos probably had hardly ever eaten out of a stable manger, and had always rustled for a living as had their ancestors in the days of the Spanish conquistadores.

American workingmen today are like that thoroughbred of my wife's on my California ranch, excepting that they are not starving to death, but only suffering from poverty because they do not know how to "rustle." They will only go on suffering the pangs of poverty—greater or less pangs—until they die sooner than they have to die, having enjoyed less than they might have enjoyed, and having suffered much more than they would have needed to suffer.

Almost every American workingman and businessman and capitalist is getting too little for his work and is paying too much.

If he were better informed and more given to thinking than he usually is, any American could, with less effort, get much more of the good things in life than he does get.

Yet the greatest part of our community is now suffering because of the high cost of living. I think the real reason why people are not getting a good enough living for the work they do is that they are not working in the way, and at the jobs and for the things that will produce the greatest benefit to them. Far, far too many men and women are working at jobs for wages or for salaries which are insufficient; and the reason why they are working for such low wages is that for their employers they are producing things which are not sufficiently in demand to make possible a great increase of wages or salaries without the destruction of profits or even without causing losses.

The high cost of living is mainly the high cost of food, clothing, homes and fuels. Food is produced from the land. There are millions and millions of acres of land in the United States that are not used at all for food production or for the production of material for clothing, housing and fuel. There are other millions on millions of acres of land that are not half so productive as they might be with more human labor. If city workmen would work on the land, there would be more food for themselves and for the other city workmen left in the city who could not produce food, and food would be cheaper. There would be more wool grown, more cotton and other fibers, and these things would be cheaper and hence clothing would be cheaper. There would be more and better forestry, and hence cheaper house-building material.

There are few men who would not be benefitted in many ways by leaving the thickly crowded cities and having their homes in the surrounding country from whence they could go to their city work. These homes, including comparatively large lots of land, would be far less expensive, either to rent or to own. Each such home, with from one to three acres of land, could in itself be a little farm on which most of the food consumed by the workingman's family could be raised. The work on this land would be beneficial to the health of the adult owner, his wife and his children.

I am not here suggesting the idea, you see, of more farms. I am only suggesting the idea that every mechanic, clerk and even day laborer might, if he chose, produce a large part of his family's provisions without cost and without any sacrifice.

But no one would heed such a suggestion. These workingmen, impressed as they are with small wages and salaries, have their habits and customs. They know no way of living except the way they have always lived. They know no way of improving their living conditions except by getting their wages increased.

I am very, very far from contending that the wage scale in America is large enough. In fact, it has been, and is, my contention that the wage scale on the average could be doubled, and ought to be doubled.

So far as I am able to interpret the statistics of the U.S. Census Bureau, and the reports of many national, and state, and private investigations, it appears to me that the annual per capita product of wealth (including increment) is not less than $500 per annum. This should give each family of five an income of $2,500 per year if all gains were equally distributed.

Under such conditions, it would appear to me that a minimum wage of $1,000 a year, or even $1,200 a year would not be overgenerous to the workingmen and working women of the country. (Editor's Note: This was written in 1917.)

I have even the idea that certain results would follow from the increase of the wage scale and the decrease of the number of hours of work. Among other results would be that workingmen and working women would be so much more efficient that their employers would gain instead of lose by increase and decrease. I believe also that wage earners, having more money to handle and more leisure, would more quickly learn how to spend their money wisely, and hence, how to be thrifty.

Still, I am conscientiously convinced that of the two possible cures of poverty in this country—one, increase of wages, and two, a more intelligent use by wage earners of their wages—the latter is by far the more important. In order that the workingman should be secure against poverty, his income should be larger than enough to meet the cost of the necessities of himself and his family. But no matter how large the income of any man might be, an unwise expenditure of it must produce a condition of poverty.

Marx's cry was: "Workingmen of the world, unite." I would repeat this cry and add the words—"to increase your efforts in producing."

Almost every American workingman knows that by increased political effort and by increasing the thought given to his work and by being more loyal and helpful to his employer, he can produce twenty-five, fifty, one hundred or even a greater per cent more than the amount he now does.

The first step that every workingman must take in the direction of increasing his wages must be in the direction of increasing his product. The second step is to exact, by force if need be, from his employer a fair and just proportion of this increased production in the way of wages and salary.

"You cannot squeeze blood from a turnip." You cannot obtain from your average employer more wages until after you have produced for him more value. Strong a partisan as I have been all my life for the system represented by labor unions, I have never failed to observe and condemn the fallacy of many labor unionists in openly advocating and covertly practicing the system of keeping down production. The idea of reducing hours of labor, while the workmen individually and purposely keep down production in order to give other workmen a chance to work, is a foolish one.

If reduction of hours of labor is only for the purpose of reducing the per capita output of production, then this reduction is of little benefit, and perhaps much harm to the workingmen themselves. It is because I know that a man can produce more in eight hours than in a greater number of hours that I advocate the short-hour day as a benefit to workmen and employer alike.

The wage fund which all workmen must be paid is limited by the value of the product. The smaller the product, the smaller the value, the smaller the wage fund and hence the necessity of the smaller wage. The greater the product in its value, the greater the wage fund will be, and the more certain will the wage earner be of an increase in wages by reasonable demand or by violence and strike. The more profits the employer is making the less inclined he will be to allow his business to be disorganized by strikes and ill will from his employees. The smaller the profits of the employer are, the less he will be concerned in the contemplation of strike or lockout.

But workingmen united in their unions and forcing up their wages and securing for themselves many other advantages are serving their employers quite as much as and I think even more than they are serving themselves.

So I would exhort the workingmen of America: Unite to work as hard as you can to use your minds to the utmost to increase the actual wealth and the daily and annual income from business, and then keep united for the purpose of compelling your employers to give you a fair share of the increase of your product.

I am myself a man of means and a large employer of labor. Naturally enough my associates have been largely other capitalists and employers. Often enough I have been held by my associates to be entirely inconsistent and foolishly blind to my own interests when I have advocated high wages, short hours, the closed shop and the cause of labor in general.

It is useless, I have found, to attempt to discuss these things with these men on moral grounds or even from a very large and general view of the subject. However, there is one argument that I generally use which often nonpluses my contestant in an argument on this subject.

These men usually regard a common workingman as a fool, incapable of knowing what his own best interest is, or gaining any real advantage from either large wages or assured employment. They will always admit readily enough that the workingmen gain little or nothing at all from a big wage because no matter how large the workingman's wage is he will squander it.

Having come to this agreement I then say: What difference does it make to us, employers, capitalists, and businessmen, as a class, what wage we give our men so long as all of us give the same and no one of us has the advantage over the other by paying a lower wage? If we do this, I continue, we only lend for a day or two or a week, or a month at most, to our workingmen the money we are supposed to give them as wages. The workingmen no sooner get their wages than they come back to some of us and give us their wages in return for commodities or services which we sell at a large profit. We as a class get all our money back again anyway. We know this must be so because as a rule while the rich are growing richer very rapidly, only a few of the poor are becoming comparatively less poor. If the wage worker got and kept his money, then only could the moral question arise as to whether the union laboring man through the closed shop got more than his share of the joint production of capital and labor. But we cannot admit this so long as we hold to our major premise, viz: that the wage earner is such a fool that he will not keep his wage when he gets it.

In fact every businessman will admit that civilization and society advance in direct proportion to the mobility of wealth, and if he admits that money moves more rapidly through the hands of workingmen and wage earners than through any other hands, then he should admit that any system which permits the laboring man to increase his wages is a good thing for society at large.

To me there is a prima facie case established that the prosperity of a nation at large and of the employer and employee classes is in direct proportion to the wage scale. If then we consider it proved that organized labor, the main principle of which is the closed shop, results in increased wages, it is at least possible to consider that the employing class and the capitalistic class benefit as much as if not more than the laboring class, as a result of organized labor.

I believe that the union labor principle is a step as far in advance of the open shop system as wage slavery is in advance of chattel slavery. The union system, so far as economics is concerned, delivers the workingman from the bondage of the employer and puts his case—the right to employment and wages—to a very large extent in a court composed of his peers—that is, his fellow workingmen.

History and present observation prove that the open shop is an impossible condition, if the end sought for is the liberation of the workingmen from entire dependence upon an individual for employment. Even if the open shop principle were adopted by good men who had no ulterior motive or intention of making a closed shop against the unions, it still would be an impassable bar across that road to justice which workingmen are seeking to pursue, across the road that leads to where the workingmen's case would be submitted to a court composed of his peers.

Personally I am not seeking for a plan to increase the wages of workingmen only. I am seeking to bring about those conditions which will make it impossible for me and others of my class to control the means of existence and hence, the right to live, of our employees.

(Editor's Note: Most of the material in this chapter was written in 1916-17.)

XVIII

I Break with Jim Scripps

TWO YEARS after my marriage in 1885 my brother James fell ill from gallstones, and departed for Carlsbad on the advice of physicians who told him his life was in grave danger. His illness came at an embarrassing time. Since my departure from the *News* in 1878, the paper had had its ups and downs; but about the worst period of downs came in 1887. Circulation was down due to the then unpopular editorial policies. With circulation down, advertising business was falling off, and the steady profits of the enterprise were endangered.

James sent for me, told me of his condition, consulted with me about the *News*, and finally suggested that, in addition to my duties on the Cleveland *Press*, the Cincinnati *Post*, and the St. Louis *Chronicle*, I should take over duties as president of the Evening News Corporation. Despite our many disagreements, my brother James and I had a very great degree of mutual respect.

Some time before James left for Europe, his eldest daughter married George E. Booth, a young man who had never been in a newspaper office. I knew that, whether my brother lived or died, he and I would need a very dependable man in the *News* office. I undertook to initiate George Booth into the mysteries of our office. He was a wonderfully apt pupil. He studied me and my methods. He studied the business. He was deferential and resourceful. I knew him very soon for a young man of marked ability.

My brother James began to recover very quickly, and I foresaw that my days as chief of the *Evening News* were numbered. I informed Booth of this. He protested. I am sure that Booth meant just what he said. Yet I had so well read his character, and even admired his ambition, that I told him and his wife that, as Peter had been told by Jesus that before the cock crowed twice he would deny Him thrice, so would Booth, before very long, covet and secure my position.

When James returned two years later he found all his old methods of business abandoned. A revolution had taken place. While still good profits were made, the actual money expended during the previous twelve months had been greater than the total receipts for any one year during the whole period of my brother's management. The paper had been enlarged in size; a lot more presses and other material had been purchased and installed. I think my brother James was really frightened at the conditions he found. He said that he recognized I had built him up a large business, but that he was sure I had so transformed the business that he would be unable to manage it successfully.

I was a dictator. It was true that I had a "big head." I was autocratic and arbitrary. I had a staff of men who were thoroughly disciplined and dependable; but there was not a man in the office who had not been often made to suffer in his feelings. As part of Booth's training, I had disciplined him more than anyone else.

My brother was very keen to get back to work, now that his health was recovered. He was very, very suspicious of me. He felt that I had so organized the business that sooner or later I would insist on ruling it or ruining it.

I may as well confess that it was part of my intention to make such a demonstration of my ability and my activity (I spent more time with the *News* than I did with my own papers) that both my brothers would thereafter make me the actual head of the whole concern. I felt they would be satisfied with growing profits and the possession of great influence over me.

Almost from the first day of my brother's return, disagreements rose between us. I told my brother of Booth's efficiency, but he was able to discern that for himself. In the meantime, my brother's second daughter had married a man named Edgar Whitcomb, who had already earned a reputation as a shrewd businessman. It occurred to James to make his son-in-law Booth manager of the *News*, and his son-in-law Whitcomb manager of the Cleveland *Press*.

While my brother George had been, in the main, loyal to me, he had resented my new enterprises and what he called my very reckless expenditures. At this time he was very ill; and when he was not apathetic, he was inclined to be antagonistic. Once before James's return I got sick of things, and tried to fix up some sort of organization for the *News* with George as *de facto* head, and myself as adviser. George wanted to have me remain, so we had a conference. As a result I agreed to remain with the *News* until James came home, and to do certain things in a business way, on condition that George would turn over to me the absolute control of all of his stock in the Cleveland *Press*. He was to turn this, and perhaps some stock in the Detroit *News*, over to me on my demand, for certain considerations that I felt I was able to undertake. I also secured from him an irrevocable power of attorney to vote all of his stock. These documents were drawn up in legal form, and were as binding as such documents can be—which is not saying much.

After a few weeks, the explosion occurred. I was fired not only as president of the Detroit News Association, but as president of the Scripps Publishing Company, the company that published the Cleveland *Press.* I was furious. My rage was great. However, I never lost control of myself so far as to make any attempt to retaliate or to make any use of the great power I had to demoralize either of the papers from which I had been ousted.

I think that nothing has occurred in my life that I am more ashamed of than the feelings and thoughts that I had during a period of one, two or more years after leaving the presidency of the *Evening News.* During a great deal of the time I was nursing a grudge. I was silly enough to so far overestimate my achievements in training Booth and Whitcomb and in building up a powerful organization that I felt they would be unable to long endure in the absence of their creator. Time showed that, not only had I done my work well, but that my brothers were both even more efficient businessmen than I had ever given them credit for. The Detroit *News* began a career of enormous prosperity, and the Cleveland *Press* continued to do well.

At the time of the rupture between James and myself, I went to George and demanded, on pain of using the power that he had given me, that he co-operate with me. His only reply was that he was then too sick. He added that, far from being afraid of my threat, he only hoped I would carry it out. I talked with him about the possible legality and the binding character of his obligations to me. I intimated that he was probably depending on the legal loophole. He assured me that, lawful or not lawful, he would not contend with me, but would submit, and be glad of the chance. He said he was sick and tired of life, and the newspaper business, and everything else, and wanted to go off and play with some mining properties he had acquired.

I ended the interview by stating that I had no intention of testing the validity of his contracts with me, and that what I wanted was his friendly and loyal support as a brother. I added that if he was not inclined to give me that, I wanted nothing more to do with him.

I left Detroit immediately after this interview. When I arrived in

Cincinnati, I took from my safe deposit box the two documents relating to George's case, and sent them to him by post, together with a letter, perhaps as harshly worded as any letter I have ever written. I must admit that I had lurking in my mind the very strong hope that my action in this matter would have some effect upon George, and cause him to relent and seek reconciliation.

I know that my action did very strongly affect George. I learned later he had a number of interviews with James, some of them quite violent, in which he protested not only against the way I had been treated, but against the bad business judgment that actuated that treatment.

My immediate hopes for action from George were, however, disappointed. Then, miserable creature that I was, burning with resentment which at times became strong enough to be called a spirit of revenge, I continued to wait for events. I did not need to be told that my two brothers were quarreling. Under the conditions, they had to quarrel.

It was not possible for me, however, to long harbor feelings of deep resentment or bitterness toward George. In a way, he was a very hopeless sort of man. He had always to depend upon somebody, not so much to do his thinking, but to do his deciding. He had for so many years relied on me in emergencies that our parting in anger could not fail seriously to affect him.

There wasn't an ounce of sympathy between himself and his brother James.

Before the first year of our difference had gone by George had become reconciled to a certain extent to me. I forget at just what time George joined me in opposing James's control of the Cleveland *Press,* and favored the view that it should be turned over to me. I have an idea I was never out of absolute control of the *Press* for over one year from the time of my return from abroad in the spring or summer of 1883.

I Break with Jim Scripps

The rupture between my brother James and myself happened late in the fall of 1889, and friendly relations had been almost completely severed before the next year began. I was in a condition of mind bordering on disgust with everything in the world, except my wife and babies. I took stock of my personal business affairs. While they were not in the best condition, because I had given so much attention to the *News* and the *Press*, which no longer were managed by me, they were still in a good enough condition. I figured that I could have had a tolerably free income of from thirty to fifty thousand dollars annually.

During my long absence from Detroit and Cleveland, Mr. McRae had managed the Cincinnati *Post* and the St. Louis *Chronicle* with a fair degree of success, while under my direction. So it was that, in the beginning of 1890, when I was only thirty-six years of age, I determined to retire from actual business. It was just at that time that I was founding Miramar Ranch, near San Diego.

One of the things that made San Diego so attractive to me was that it was off in the extreme corner of the United States—a busted, broken-down boom town. It was probably more difficult of access than any other spot in the whole country.

My own business interests were mainly far in the East. San Diego was about three thousand miles away from the people who bothered me about my newspapers and about their own political or business ambitions.

I first came to California in 1890 to see my sister Annie, who was very ill in Alameda, on San Francisco Bay. She was not expected to live, but improved a little. When it appeared that I would have to remain in California for several weeks more, I decided to make a boat trip to San Diego. I got there early in December and was greatly attracted by the country. I spent a number of days driving around the city and the back country. The climate seemed identical with that of North Africa, especially Algeria. Trees and plants growing about the houses of the San Diegans were the same I had seen in Algeria. As I had always suffered from colds in the East, and had been free from them in Algeria, Mexico, Egypt and Syria, it occurred to me that I should have a winter home near San Diego.

I bought four hundred acres about sixteen miles outside San Diego, where the Miramar Ranch now stands, for five thousand dollars cash. I sent my brother Fred out to take charge of it and do some clearing. I had two objects in view in establishing Miramar Ranch: first, I wanted a winter home; second, I wanted to join my sister Ellen in establishing a ranch business for my brother Fred. It was my brother's wish to set up a lemon ranch. For several years he devoted his whole attention to clearing, planting and cultivating about one hundred acres of lemon and orange orchards. Ellen and I put a good deal of money into this project.

A drought came a few years after the ranch was founded. For many years the rainfall was so small that only occasionally was any water at all impounded. One period of drought lasted seven years, so that not a drop of water was caught in any of our reservoirs or any other reservoir in southern California.

Our lemon ranch was a failure. My brother Fred soon gave up in disgust. Ellen and I then asked out brother W. A. Scripps, who was then out of employment and out of funds, to come to Miramar and act as manager. W. A. Scripps spent ten years at Miramar. He loved bookkeeping, but was not a successful executive. He was retained as manager while my brother Fred acted as foreman. The whole ranch was kept up more for the purpose of giving our brothers something to do than for any other reason.

I made up my mind around 1895 that if Miramar Ranch was doomed as a business undertaking, it should at least be one of the pleasantest of southern California homes. I began planting the land immediately around the house with trees and shrubbery. I began building roads. I proposed to make a large park. I increased the acreage until it amounted to 2,100 acres all told.

My outdoor work in making Miramar a beautiful home place was a great boon to me in maintaining my health. I built the house without the help of landscape gardeners. Natural conditions—the lack of water, the very poorest possible quality of soil, and the absence of roads—made the undertaking to the last degree difficult. I was the laughingstock of all my friends and acquaintances, not only those in San Diego, but those who visited me from other parts of the country, because of my attempt to overcome the perfectly apparent natural conditions. But I knew then as I know now that my chief interest in the undertaking was due to the obstacles that had to be overcome. Had the task been an ordinary and easy one, I would have turned it over to some employee. But the conditions were so difficult that it seemed impossible for anyone but myself to do anything successful. These conditions kept me out of doors a large time, on foot or on horseback. My employments as a rancher, at times, distracted my thoughts from business and books, and this was good for me.

With Miramar well founded, I turned my attention to building roads, other than those on my own property. Miramar was situated out in the wilderness, almost a desert. There was only a sagebrush trail between Miramar and San Diego. The seashore at La Jolla was fifteen miles away, and was only approachable by going to the city and then doubling back—making a total distance of thirty miles.

I first built a good road to the city. I followed this up with another road to La Jolla. I built a road north to connect with the Escondido Road, and one east to connect with El Cajon Valley. Later I built a new and better road called the Murphy Canyon Road. I had become acquainted with the Torrey Pines country and La Jolla by visiting these sections on horseback with Mrs. Scripps. Until I built my first road into the Torrey Pines, there were perhaps not twenty people in the city of San Diego who were familiar with that wonderfully beautiful natural park. I also built the road connecting Del Mar with La Jolla, largely at my own expense and partly at the expense of H.E. Huntington. This road is now the main traveled highway between San Diego and all northern points including Los Angeles.

I like road building, and I particularly like road building in southern California. I like it because of the obstacles, sometimes real and sometimes only apparent, that have to be overcome. I always liked to play in the dirt, and with water. By building reservoirs and roads I was only continuing a propensity of ordinary childhood.

After a time public attention was attracted to my roads. The people of the city and county decided it would be a good thing to extend a system of just such fairly good, economically built roads, all over the county. A bond issue of $1,250,000 was voted. As foreman of the highway commission in charge of building these roads, I served for the first and only time as a public official. I succeeded eventually in changing the reputation of San Diego county of being the worst county in the state for roads, to that of being one of the counties best provided with rural roads.

Despite my avowed retirement from business, Miramar soon enough became not only my business headquarters, but the gathering point of the several score of lieutenants who were serving me in my different newspaper offices. It was rare indeed that one or more of these men were not at Miramar, and at times there must have been between thirty and forty of them in the house at one time, for special conferences. My home was also used by many other people, such as politicians and political reformers, who came to consult me or influence me.

Annually, for many years, I made a tour through the entire country, visiting all of my offices. So scattered were the properties that it took a journey of over ten thousand miles to visit all of them. With one or two secretaries, I kept in touch with every one of my business ventures, by mail and wire. From all of them, I received at least full and complete weekly statements. From some of them I got daily statements. During long periods of time I kept my business so well in hand that not a dollar's worth of material was purchased, or a man employed or discharged, without a requisition bearing my signature made by my own hand.

I called this sort of thing "long-range management." I had accustomed myself to it even when I was in the same city where my business was. Even when I was in the same office as the newspaper, I did all of my business through representatives. Very rarely indeed did I meet anybody but one of my employees. After a while, I rarely met anyone connected with any of the papers excepting the editor-in-chief and the business manager. I became very expert in this way of working. I was thoroughly acquainted with every detail of every business. By glancing through one of my papers and spending a few minutes on one of the statements from such a paper, I could tell the exact condition of affairs, both business and editorial, and even the menial details of work done in the editorial rooms.

While probably ninety-nine out of a hundred of my employees never clapped eyes on me, there wasn't a man in any office who knew all the details of that office, business and editorial, as well as I did.

XIX

I Buck the A. P.

I HAVE A high opinion of my journalistic work as public service. I believe the most valuable service I have rendered to my country has been that of thwarting the plans of greater, abler and richer men than myself to establish a monopoly of news in the United States, and hence a dominating influence over all the newspapers of the country.

When, if ever, an accounting is made of my life's work, especially my financial contributions to public service, I would require, in fairness to me, that account should be taken not only of the huge effort, but the great outlay of money that I have made personally to secure freedom of the press in this country.

I am talking about the foundation of the United Press in competition with the Associated Press.

Around 1895 a warfare broke out between the two press associations of the country. These were the old Western Associated Press (later known as the Associated Press) and the old United Press. The old U. P. was the lineal descendant of a series of weak efforts to establish a press association to oppose the old Western Associated Press.

The United Press, under Walter Philipps, was then at the zenith of its power. It included in its membership the leading New York City newspapers of the time—the *Herald, Tribune, World* and *Sun.* Its principal financial backer and controlling spirit was John P. Walsh, the owner of the Chicago *Chronicle,* and a Napoleon of finance who ended his days in the state prison. All the Scripps papers were then included in the United Press as clients or members or stockholders.

At this time the idea occurred to such men as Bennett of the New York *Herald,* Whitelaw Reid of the New York *Tribune,* Laffan of the New York *Sun,* and some others, to create a great news monopoly out of the United Press. This organization, it was felt, was sweeping everything before it, while the Western Press Association was constantly losing clients and members. The United Press, as it existed then, threatened even the existence of a free press in this country.

To match this development a number of newspapermen, headed by Victor Lawson of the Chicago *News,* my brother James, Frank Noyes, then editor of a Washington paper, and some others, undertook to reorganize the Western Press Association with the aim of making it a great monopoly. In the early days of the reorganization of the Associated Press, when it was proposed to make it a regular stock company rather than the mutual company it later became, I was waited upon by a representative of the reorganizers. He offered me twenty-five per cent of the stock of the proposed new association, jointly with James E. Scripps, if we would take all our papers out of the United Press and join the new association.

I declined on the grounds that the new Associated Press proposed to have exclusive contracts; that is to say, if any one or more newspapers in any city should join the new association, these papers would have the right to keep any new paper in their city from receiving the news report of the A. P. In other words, the plan was to establish a monopoly pure and simple.

Both the Western Associated Press and the United Press were

overwhelmingly controlled by the publishers of morning newspapers. The result was that evening newspapers all over the country were slighted. It was the custom of the news associations to hold back important news developments that occurred in time for publication in afternoon papers, in order that they might be used in the morning papers of the following day. This gave the morning paper a monopoly of important news.

The Scripps papers were afternoon papers. Because of this condition in the press associations, I set up a sort of mutual press association for the Scripps papers when I became president of them all in James's absence. This association, later known as the Scripps-McRae Press Association, had representatives in New York, Washington, all of the Scripps newspaper cities, and at other points. These men sent us special telegrams of important events. By this means I greatly increased the news value of our several papers. To keep costs down, I succeeded in making contracts with both the Western Union Telegraph Company and the old Baltimore & Ohio Telegraph Company. I got practically Associated Press transmission rates.

The Associated Press, a magnificently reformed organization, won a great victory over the United Press and seduced away from it all of the big New York newspapers except the *Sun*. This move was followed by a countrywide stampede of United Press clients to the Associated Press.

Although the A. P. was still solicitous to get my papers (by this time James E. had again taken over control of the *Evening News*), it was no longer offering me stock as a special inducement. They were now warning me that I was in danger of being left out in the cold, and threatening me with destruction if I did not join them.

I was irritated to the highest pitch of anger by the insolence and arrogance of those who had once so humbly petitioned me. My brother George had a very pugnacious disposition so long as he had someone to lead him in a fight. Partner McRae, however, was panic-stricken, and begged and pleaded and implored George and me to get on the ark before the deluge came.

The U. P. by now was on the rocks. Its treasury was not only empty, but as a concern it was largely in debt.

The A. P., in a new move, set a date after which no newspaper that was not then a member could ever get the Associated Press reports. The fateful final meeting at which new members would be accepted into the A. P. was, I believe, held in the summer of 1897 in Chicago.

Early in the morning of that day McRae made haste to see Melville Stone, Victor Lawson, Charles Knapp, and others of the inner circle. They all assured him that, even though we presented ourselves at the eleventh hour, we would be cordially welcomed. McRae returned to us, his face beaming, saying he had no doubt we could get into the association on a full plane of equality with the best of all the other papers represented.

I knew better. I knew better because I had other channels of communication to the A. P. directorate, and had taken pains to have them hear reports of our internal dissensions and weaknesses. I had, in fact, paved the way to have any petition we made turned down so hard and with so much insolence and arrogance as to rearouse my brother George's fighting instinct. (I might as well confess that I had in my mind, all of the time, the memory of that other occasion on which George had failed me.)

At the last hour, and almost the last minute, Mr. McRae carried our application, in written form, to be admitted to the Associated Press not as clients but as first-class voting members of the association. Much to his chagrin, his proposal was met—as I had expected it would be—with ridicule, and laughter and contempt. That was what I desired and expected. I wanted him to be fighting mad. I wanted to stir up the pugnacious Scotch blood in him. I knew that if I could get McRae fully aroused I could depend on him to do more than half of the fighting that was sure to result.

McRae returned to us with face red and eyes shining with resentment and anger. Our telegrams to the different newspapers were all written out, together with our prospectus. We said the firm of Scripps-McRae was going to start a press association and finance it, and that we would, on the instant of application, serve all would-be clients with the evening report. Our organization was actually so complete that it was sending out a news report even while McRae was making his application, although the report was only going to our own papers.

I do not recall the figures, but I imagine that in founding the new United Press, the Scripps papers actually paid out several hundred thousand dollars more than they would have paid out had they been members of the Associated Press. Notwithstanding these comparatively large payments, I felt that the investment, bad as it was financially in one way, was a good one, since it secured for the Scripps papers and all the other papers in the country, freedom from the temptation of one huge news monopoly. (Not a small part of our own gain was that we were able to found evening newspapers in any city that we chose.)

As our corporation was not a mutual one, but a stock company for the purpose of profit, we were governed by the same laws that govern common carriers. We could not legally refuse a report to any newspaper that wanted it, even if we desired to do so. We could not refuse an applicant which might come in direct competition with our own newspapers and cause them to suffer seriously. In one case I think my own paper has never been profitable for the simple reason that a rival paper, taking the United Press, was founded. It was being conducted, furthermore, not only to compete with my paper but to ruin it.

In 1905 a young man named John Vandercook, who had worked for the Cleveland *Press* and the Scripps-McRae Association in New York and Europe, demanded a promotion of me. His approach impressed me. I got him named editor of the Cincinnati *Post*, where he demonstrated great ability. He then demanded a greater field of operations. He proposed that we buy the East Coast Publishers Press Association, consolidate it with our two others—the Scripps News Association and the Scripps-McRae Press Association—and form a large united institution.

We had discovered before this negotiation began that corrupt influences were working on the Publishers Press, so that important news from Washington and New York and other places was being colored or suppressed for the purpose of affecting the stock market. Even false reports came over the wire. During Vandercook's negotiations, a flagrant incident of this kind occurred. I felt that this incident, and its predecessors, absolved me from all moral obligation toward the Publishers Press Association. Meantime, the term of the contract for exchange and co-operation between the two associations had expired.

On the basis of their flagrant abuse of their power over a news association for their personal gain, I sent Mr. McRae to deliver an ultimatum to the officers of the Publishers Press Association. This stated that unless they sold their whole business to us at a figure which Mr. McRae would fix within our maximum, we would discontinue the exchange of news and all co-operation, and enter their field as competitors.

McRae had furnished himself with information that a stock broker of the New York Exchange, of a very questionable reputation, was a large creditor and stockholder of the Association, and was using it to further his stock-manipulating enterprises. With this information Mr. McRae concluded the purchase of the association, free of debt, for $150,000.

When I acquired ownership of the Publishers Press I united all three press associations on June 21, 1907, giving the name of the United Press Association to the consolidated institution.

The original United Press corporation issued $300,000 of preferred six per cent stock, and, I think, $100,000 common stock. I personally endorsed and guaranteed the $300,000 preferred stock, and then distributed it to the owners of record of the three associations. I had fifty-one per cent of the stock of Scripps-McRae Press Association, fifty-one per cent of the Scripps Press Association, and of course, one hundred per cent of the Publishers Press Association. Therefore, my own share of preferred stock was practically $202,000. The preferred stock I received I used to pay off certain personal debts; so that in the end, I had no interest in the United Press Association excepting fifty-one per cent of its common stock. I apportioned the other forty-nine per cent to young men I put in charge of the management of the institution. As there was practically not a dollar paid in by the common stockholders, the new institution, the United Press Association, started its existence in 1907 with $300,000 of liability, and what might be termed "a bag of wind."

At the time I was organizing the U. P. in its present form, I told my associates we were embarking in a business that would either have to be a flat failure or a property worth many millions, not less than $3,000,000. This kind of business, I said, must be large in order to exist.

Now the United Press has been in existence ten years [written in 1917] and it is worth not less than $1,000,000. I assumed the risk of guaranteeing the preferred stock; beyond this, I have paid no money into the concern. I have put no labor into it that would be recognized as labor. I have practically done no more for the institution than exercise my judgment, based on a knowledge and skill I had acquired in other business fields.

During the past ten years, I have received as my share of dividends perhaps $200,000, an average of $20,000 a year. Beyond that, I am the owner of a block of stock worth $500,000. This has grown from what might be considered nothing at all. As a matter of fact, the preferred stock that I had guaranteed was considered by me, as I have said, a liability.

Divide the $500,000 worth of property by the number of years involved—viz. ten—and we have $50,000 as a net annual gain for myself. Add $20,000 a year, or the average dividend, and it would appear that I have received $70,000 a year for my services in founding this institution. U. P. General Manager Roy Howard's estimate of the 1917 value of the concern as being $2,500,000 is, at least, possibly correct. My share of this being one-half would amount to $1,250,000, which would be equivalent to an average salary for ten years of $125,000. Add to this $20,000 average annual dividends, and it would appear that my annual earnings on account of the U. P. have been so far $145,000.

Now, is the United Press Association a property at all? If it is a property, what does the property consist of? Owing to the very nature of the business, there are practically no capital goods in it, and none are required. A few office desks, a safe, typewriters, chairs and filing cases, and such things, represent the total of its tangible possessions. I am sure that the cost of this material has never been $10,000.

Does value lie in organization of men? I know that with but one exception, there is not a person employed in an important position by the United Press that was employed ten years ago.

The value of the United Press Association, then, consists in what? Get right down to bedrock, to brass tacks, and it will be found the whole value of this property consists largely in the mental attitude of some six hundred or seven hundred men. These men are the owners or conductors of newspapers, clients of the U. P. These men, rightly or wrongly, are convinced that a report sent out daily by something which calls itself the United Press is worth to each of them a certain number of dollars more per day, per week, or per year, than it costs the manager of the U. P. to get and transmit to him the report.

Have I earned the comparatively speaking vast annual income that I have received from the U. P. during the past ten years? Am I entitled to it, morally as well as legally? What have I done in the way of actual labor, intellectual or other, that has entitled me to this money, this amount of property?

As I said, I regard my life's greatest service to the people of this country to be the creation of the U. P. I have secured to every man in this country who desires to found or purchase a newspaper, something that he must have in order to found or own a newspaper. I have given him something that nobody else has been able to give, or willing to give. It is quite possible that I am the only man in this country who could have performed this service. I doubt if there was a single newspaperman in the United States, other than those in my employ, who at the time I made the decision to do this, believed I would be successful.

Has this money, which I have received in the way of dividends, and this property which I have become possessed of, been in any sense a property income? Will my future income from this institution ever be other than a service income? What did I do to earn my money? Did I really do anything? Were these dividends, these so-called stock values, any other thing than a condition that was co-existent with my own existence? Because I was what I was, this condition, called the U. P., came into existence.

"Yes," it might be said, "you did create something. The United Press Association was a thing you manufactured. But so soon as it was created and manufactured it became a property; and therefore, all, or a large part of your derivings from it is a property income." Now this disposition of the case does not satisfy me at all. I wish it did.

It would be mighty satisfactory for me to know that the United Press, or any other so-called property that I am possessed of, actually exists as a property, something entirely different from, and detached from myself, something that can be transferred from my ownership to the ownership of another, something that a child of mine can receive as a gift or an inheritance.

It is impossible for me, or for anyone else, to know just what would happen to the U. P. if I were to die, or to transfer it to someone else. One thing I am sure of, and that is: if it should be transferred in any way to some one person who had a public fame and reputation of a certain sort, the U. P. as an institution would dissolve into thin air and become nonexistent.

I do not know, and it is impossible for anyone to know, to just what extent the existence, and the actual daily management and conduct of the U. P., is affected by the mere fact that I am alive, and have it in my power as controlling stockholder, to take any action I choose. I exist, and my existence and my personality are known of by every important personage connected with the U. P. So long as I exist, and it is known that I can control this institution, certain men will do certain things that they would not do if I were dead, or if I did not own the controlling stock. And these things which are done, or which are left undone, may be the very things on which the life and prosperity of the institution depends.

Many times I have contended in my disquisitions, and in my talks with other men, that the most substantial thing, the thing which is very, very long enduring, is the thing which has no substance at all, has no tangible, seeable, smellable, tastable quality. It is the thing that no one can be made aware of by the use of any of his five senses.

This thing is the stream of thought, habit, custom, convention, tradition, faith—all of these things, or one of them, which is the same thing. This thing flows through what we call the minds of men; through the existence of one man's life into and through the existence of other men, living or to be born. It is something that spreads through a small group of minds, or through larger, and still larger groups.

The value of the U. P. depends not upon any patent right, or anything the possession of which can be defended in a court of law. It does not depend upon any secret processes or knowledge. Its value is, first, the mental attitudes of a few hundred people. Secondarily, and more largely, its value depends on the mental attitudes of many millions of people, who value certain newspapers because of the value that they themselves assert is existing in certain words that are published by the U. P., or are supposed to be published by the U. P.

Among other motives in founding the U. P. was the altruistic one. I do not believe in monopolies. I believe that monopolists suffer more than their victims in the long run. I did not believe it would be good for journalism in this country if there should be one big news trust such as the founders of the Associated Press fully expected to build up. It was their idea to set up a monopoly that would make it impossible for any new paper to be started in any of the cities where there were A. P. members. I recognized that this was valuable to an established newspaper manager like myself, but I was just then feeling very cocky. I considered myself a sort of man-of-destiny. I had ambitions for planting a score or more of new papers. I pointed out to my associates that under the proposed conditions no one else could start new newspapers in our town, but, on the other hand, we would never be able to start another new newspaper.

I not only wanted to start a new paper if I chose, but I wanted to make it possible for any other man to found a newspaper in any city in the union. Were it not for the U. P., I am convinced that the men who hold a controlling interest in the present A. P. and Mr. Hearst would inevitably combine into a trust.

Perhaps my greatest reason, however, for refusing to join the A. P. at the critical juncture was that I knew that at least ninety per cent of my fellows in American journalism were capitalistic and conservative. I knew at the time at least that unless I came into the field with a new service, it would be impossible for the people of the United States to get correct news through the medium of the Associated Press. I determined to be as free in gathering telegraph news and printing what I wanted to print as I was in gathering local news and printing what I wanted to print. In those my youthful days of pride I swelled up with vanity at the thought that I was to be the savior of the free press in America. Of course, I have learned now that it needs more than one man to guarantee such freedom.

I believe I have done more good indirectly with the U. P. than I have done with it directly, since I have made it impossible for the men who control the A. P. to suppress the truth or successfully disseminate falsehood. The mere fact that the U. P. can be depended upon to disseminate news that is of value to the public and that is against the interest of the plutocrat band makes it not only worth while for the A. P. to put out such information, but positively dangerous for them to try to withhold any such information. If a U. P. paper in Cleveland gets a piece of news that the A. P. client there doesn't get, there is a kick from the A. P. paper to the management. If the A. P. should attempt to give real news only to its client papers in towns where there were U. P. papers, then A. P. papers in other towns would kick because they didn't get as full service as did those A. P. papers in the U. P. towns.

XX

I Buck the Advertisers

IN 1911, in the city of Chicago, I undertook an interesting experiment in journalism: the publication of a newspaper that would never accept advertising.

I wanted to show the feasibility of publishing a daily journal in magazine form and also wanted to show that such a journal could be published at a profit with no other receipts than money derived from selling it at wholesale prices. I called the project the "Ad-less Newspaper."

Later, when I sent Negley Cochran, then editor of the Toledo *News-Bee,* to Chicago actually to start the paper, it became known as the *Day Book.* Under this title it continued publication every day until 1917, when, for various reasons, I saw fit to discontinue it.

There was one great principle at stake in the *Day Book,* and only one, and that was the founding of a newspaper to be successfully supported by the reading public, as distinguished from the advertising public. This being the case, the sole and only aim of its editors and writers was to make a paper that would have the largest possible number of buyers.

I thought that we ought to prove the possibility of the existence of such a paper. Later, certain editorial policies might be pursued for other purposes than purely financial gain. A sufficient amount of propaganda might be tacked on to such a newspaper. But it should not have to carry too great a burden of propaganda. (Personally, I have no use for martyrs. I maintain that a live fox is more worth while than a dead lion.)

There is no room in any democracy for what might be called an endowed or subsidized press, I felt.

I also wanted to show the practicability of founding a newspaper on such small capital as most any man would be able to secure.

I thought that newspapers are made by men and not by money; by brains and not by capital, and that everything else being equal, every dollar that is spent over and above the minimum amount required to meet fixed expenses and keep body and soul together (of the would-be founder of the newspaper) is not only wasteful, but is real poison forced into the system of the new organization.

It was my idea that Cochran and I should learn to publish a paper that the public would demand, the maximum cost of production of which would not much exceed $2,500 per month over and above the cost of newsprint.

I did not propose to attempt the vain effort of bolstering up inefficient men or an inefficient organization by use of money. I proposed to find the men and produce the organization which in themselves would be so efficient as to secure a living and growing institution. It was my intention rather to create hardships in a financial way than to bridge over such hardships with money.

Neither did I propose to increase the monthly expenses of this ad-less paper, except for newsprint, until the receipts of the paper were not only equal to the beginning expense, but until they were great enough to permit a fair living profit over and above any increase of expenses that might have been made.

When Cochran and I were discussing the new paper we were gloating over the prospect of having such freedom from commercialism as would permit us to publish whatever we wanted to without regard to the enmity or favor of certain classes.

Of course we were thinking of the editorials that we could publish and the articles we could print which would be of benefit to the masses. In fact, we had our heads up so high that they were bumping the stars.

Now there is another kind of freedom that I wanted. I wanted to be absolutely indifferent to the contempt of all classes. I did not want to impress on the common people that we were their worthy advisers and leaders, nor did I want to impress upon the classes that we are what they call demagogues.

What I wanted the newspaper to be was the common vulgar friend and companion of the common vulgar crowd, of which, if I am not a member, I would like to be.

Such a paper as I proposed would not give us much space for preachments and lectures. There is a class of literature in the old-fashioned yellow-backed dime novels, and in such a paper as the *Police Gazette* once was, which came nearer to what I was thinking of than anything then to be found in the average journal of the most democratic proclivities, whether daily or weekly.

In fact, I told Cochran, it would be difficult to find among journalists of any class, men who have not been trained into what would be called snobs by our readers. For too many years, I said, we have lived too far above this level to be able to do much more than sympathize—looking downward from on high.

Our one great business, I felt, was to get an audience. Whatever else it was, our paper must be excessively interesting, not to the good, wise men and the pure in spirit, but to the great masses of sordid, squalid humanity. Humanity was vulgar; so we must be vulgar. It was coarse; so we must not be refined. It was passionate; therefore the blood that ran in our veins and in our newspaper must be warm.

We were not going to preach at all, and even the lessons we taught must be from ABC to the First Primer.

We wanted to organize democracy and could not do this if we assumed the attitude—which had to be aristocratic—of leadership and control.

We would have to say—for a time at least—farewell to our friends who think they know political economy, and who wear the fine clothes of literature and philosophy. We must be content to be as despised by our gentlemen and lady friends as the ex-hoodlum is despised by his, when wearing the Salvation Army uniform, he talks to the crowd in the streets in the slum quarter.

I doubted if beneath the veneering, which is not a hundredth of an inch thick, that Cochran and I wore on our surface we were a bit less vulgar, a bit less passionate, selfish and sordid than the mass of the people whose servants we desired to be.

Regarded purely as a business institution, the only kind of circulation that is highly valuable is that which owes its existence to the paper's being an entertainment rather than an instructive document. When any man takes a newspaper just to help a good cause along, he is a doubtful asset, but when a man takes a newspaper for the same reason that he takes a cigar or glass of beer, or goes to a moving picture show, he becomes a thoroughgoing asset that can be calculated in dollars and cents.

I told Cochran that the world of journalism, unlike that of fiction, was almost wholly composed of matter that made men and women think, or think that they ought to think. That task of public enlightenment is so thoroughly prosecuted that our labors in this field are not as necessities cried for by the people.

Let us amuse our folks first, let us gather around us a great audience first, and then we can slip into their minds, entirely unsuspected by them, some bits of information, some pages on which thoughts will hang, some things which will help them to help themselves and help their country. Let us quit teaching and lecturing and instructing as the main part of our business, or as any more than the thirty-second part of our occupation, and devote the rest of ourselves to just being common, plain, everyday, interesting, good-natured, laugh-provoking fellows.

In starting all my new papers, especially the very earliest of them, I have always suffered a great deal of embarrassment and I believe a great deal of loss both directly and indirectly as a result of confusion of mind and uncertainty of action because of the overhaste and impatience of my young men to get under way.

I had the idea always and it has been confirmed by experience, that the development of a newspaper business should be something like that of the founding of a medical or legal practice. Hang out your shingle and do thoroughly every day such work as you can get to do and patiently wait for public favor, confidence and good will to grow up around you and in you and with you and for you. Forcing things does no good, and more often than not it does harm, since it arouses in the first place suspicion and latterly antagonism.

To me the history of the San Francisco *News*—the paper I founded shortly before the 1906 earthquake—had been a most illuminating one. So long as that paper had little money to spend, and so long as its managers devoted themselves to the one essential of a newspaper, and hadn't the money to follow and imitate newspaper contemporaries, the *News* won its way with remarkable rapidity.

It was only after advertising money coming in permitted its management to do in some fashion what other newspaper managers were doing, that growth stopped.

I proposed, in the ad-less paper, to adopt a scheme very similar to that adopted in the starting of the San Francisco *News.*

If the editor could not get along on $2,500 per month, excluding white paper bills, I would consider the whole scheme unworkable.

So many of my young papers have gone to smash, I reasoned, because of the men trying to depend on money instead of brains and work to build them up, that I had no inclination to try any more such experiments.

I was going to furnish all the money myself and take all the risk myself, and so far as concerns business methods and investment, I was going to have absolutely my own way. I wanted no one connected with the paper who was not willing to carry out my ideas, and who did not also fully and completely believe in my method so that he would do the same thing that I wanted done even if he were furnishing all the money.

Up to the time when the paper would pay its own expenses, I would absolutely control it, generally and in detail. From the time it began to pay its expenses I would continue to control it in two ways: First, the paper would receive absolutely no income from any source excepting from the sale of newspapers. Second: it would always be the organ, the mouthpiece and the friend of small wage-earners and of that class who were not working for wages but still maintained themselves by daily labor of the humblest sort. Our paper was to be the poor man's advocate and friend whether the poor man be right or wrong.

On the day I finally saw that little paper in print, I felt I was a perfectly free man for the first time in my life.

(Editor's Note: The United States got into World War I in April, 1917. E. W. Scripps went to Washington to resume control of his entire newspaper institution, to aid in the winning of the war. For this purpose he "drafted" Mr. Cochran into his Washington group of advisers. As neither he nor Mr. Cochran could direct the *Day Book*, it was suspended. Six months later, Scripps's health broke and his illness and convalescence sent him into retirement. He never gave up the idea of again starting such a venture, and when he died in 1926, he was planning another ad-less daily newspaper. In fact, he was even dreaming of a chain of twenty of them, if he were to live long enough.

(The average monthly deficit of the *Day Book* for the years 1912 to 1916 was:

1912	$ 2,690
1913	1,826
1914	1,515
1915	1,352
1916	1,270

Newsprint prices were soaring but, even so, the newspaper was showing a slight profit when it was suspended.)

XXI

The Case of Roy W. Howard

OFTEN, IN retrospective mood, my thoughts center about some man, or group of men—youngsters whose lives I have more or less molded—molded in part for my own business purposes, and perhaps even in a larger part, experimentally. A very large portion of my life's enjoyment, in fact, has come from the curious and inquiring attention I have given to the development of my young helpers. I am inclined to dispute the truth of the saying that you can't make a silk purse out of a sow's ear. I put very little reliance on the equally vulgar and often sneering comment, Blood will tell.

It was around 1885 that I went to live in the country house of Colonel Gano of the U. S. Army, about sixteen miles outside Cincinnati, on the old turnpike leading from Cincinnati to Dayton. On this little turnpike, not a hundred yards from my host's home, was a tiny cottage occupied by the keeper of the tollgate. The tollgate keeper had a family of several children, sons and daughters. Now it is easy enough for anyone to form an opinion of the general characteristics of a tollgate keeper and his family. Certainly, tollgate keeping is anything but the occupation of an industrious, ambitious and enterprising man.

I kept a saddle horse at that time for exercise purposes. It was provoking to me always to have to stop my ride and call the tollgate keeper, to wait for the tollgate to be raised when I paid my little fee. Actually, I seldom submitted to this indignity. Sometimes I would make my horse jump the tollgate, and sometimes the hedge fence at the side of the road. I would jump into the adjoining field, passing around the tollgate, in order to bring the horse back again into the pike.

The reason I had to encounter this tollgate was that it extended straight across the road that led from my lodging place to the door of the young lady who afterward became my wife.

I never made the acquaintance of the tollgate keeper, or any member of his family. Being a newcomer to the neighborhood, I knew nothing of the past of the family. It was not until many years afterward that I learned that there was a man in the employ of one of my newspapers who was a son of one of the daughters of this family. The occasion of my learning the origin of Roy Howard, and of my subsequent interest in him, was my mother-in-law's writing my wife, informing her that a son of my wife's old schoolmate, the daughter of the tollgate keeper, had become a reporter on one of my papers. Something about the association of young Howard and a very important incident in my life caused me to be especially interested in him. I am inclined to believe that Roy Howard's whole career has been greatly influenced by this interest I felt in him.

What could be expected of a tollgate keeper's grandson? Had I not known so much about his origin, I would have had no more curiosity about or interest in him, than I would have had in any of the other hundreds of my employees. Although I did not see young Howard until several years after I heard of him, my interest in him certainly had its effect in opening opportunities for him.

I do not recall having seen Howard until he had made considerable headway in the way of promotion. When I finally met him for the first time, I think it was at Miramar. He was a striking individual, very small of stature, with a large head and speaking countenance, and eyes that appeared to be windows for a rather unusual intellect. His manner was forceful, and the reverse from modest. Gall was written all over his face. It was in every tone and every word he voiced. There was ambition, self-respect and forcefulness oozing out of every pore of his body.

Since those days Howard has learned to affect some degree of deference in his speech and manner in my presence; but in my first interview with him, he did not reveal, and I do not believe he experienced, the least feeling of awe. However, so completely and exuberantly frank was he that it was impossible for me to feel any resentment on account of his cheek.

He passed from his reportership on the paper to a subordinate position in the United Press, which I had just launched. When he went with the U. P. he may have been twenty-one years of age. Of course he was only an employee. I do not suppose he, or anyone else, ever thought he would be anything else. He demonstrated his ability to be a good assistant to the general manager while the institution was still in almost an embryo state. Then, fortunately for him, its first manager, John Vandercook, died as the result of a surgical operation. Learning of this, I immediately gave attention to the appointment of a successor. I had no idea of appointing Howard. If my remembrance is correct I had not seen Howard, even then.

I suggested to my associates several men, any one of whom I would have been willing to name as Vandercook's successor, had the other man who worked on the association agreed. I was surprised at being urged to let Howard be tried out for a time, at least, on the job.

Certainly, at this critical point in Howard's career, he owed everything to the fact that he was the tollgate keeper's grandson. My fancy was tickled with the idea. My propensity for experiment demonstrated itself again. I recall that I was much amused, and that I told my wife what I had done. However, Howard made good.

Owing to the growth of the U. P. and to the fact that the important news of these times has been connected with the European war, it has been necessary for the manager of the U. P. to go to Europe frequently.

The statesmen of Europe deem it extremely important that the American people should be kept well informed in all the controversies going on between the belligerent nations. They are, therefore, bound to give much attention to the representatives of the American press. The United Press is, next to the Associated Press, the largest medium for the dissemination of news in the United States. Consequently, Mr. Howard has not only had no difficulty in coming in contact with both the political and military leaders of the countries he has visited, but has been warmly welcomed by them.

Owing a great deal to his peculiar personality, Howard seems to have gained some personal favors among these men. He has had interviews with premiers, foreign secretaries, generals, and civilians of the higher grade. Lord Northcliffe, the giant journalist of English, has been particularly intimate with Howard. Owing to Northcliffe's relations to the powers-that-be in England, Howard of the U. P. is favored above all other American journalists and journalistic institutions. So far, Howard has not come into contact with royalty itself, though I have very little doubt that he is yet to stand before kings.

The other day Howard called on me at Miramar and spent an hour or two talking to me. While he occupied the seat at the end of the table, where I usually place my favored guests, I could not restrain myself from looking him over, up and down, and laughing uproariously, as I kept comparing in my mind that little old tollgate house with this friend and intimate of a belted earl, great statesmen and famous generals.

It is characteristic of Howard that, when I told him the cause of my mirth, he indicated neither confusion nor resentment. He seemed to have his own fancy tickled by it. I do not believe that in this respect Howard will ever change. Of course he is an upstart, and a very innocent upstart. He wasn't to blame for his origin, and in fact there was nothing blameworthy in it. I do not think he would ever be ashamed of his origin. I do not think either that his success in life, or his position in life, will add anything to his vanity, or his self-respect.

As I indicated in some part of the foregoing, Howard's self-respect and self-confidence, right from the start, were so great as to make it impossible for them to increase. Doubtless to himself his present situation in life, his successes and his prosperity, all seem perfectly natural, and no more and no less than he expected, if he ever wasted his time in forecasting. Of which, I have very much doubt.

XXII

Is Honest Journalism Possible?

IS HONEST journalism possible?

Perhaps I can best answer this question by discussing some of the most commonly held opinions concerning the press.

The usual critic dwells particularly upon the fact that newspapers are owned by men who do not edit them. For the newspaper writer's shortcomings, he offers the excuse that he writes for a living, writes under orders, and writes what his employer wants him to write, and not what he, the writer, thinks.

This critic also has a very commonly held opinion that newspaper owners are part and parcel of the plutocratic clique, and that by choice they suppress some news and distort other news happenings, and generally try to create a public opinion that is favorable to plutocracy.

This critic is also a victim of a very common delusion, a delusion so common as to be practically universal. This delusion is that a newspaper can only be founded at great expense of capital, and hence, that it is impossible for one of the nonplutocratic classes in these days to found or purchase a newspaper property.

There are tricks in all trades, especially in our trade. I am a newspaper owner. Newspaper owners do not like competition. They want as few newspapers in existence as possible. It is but natural (even if to be natural is to be dishonest) for newspaper owners to desire to create the impression that it required tremendous sums of money to found a newspaper, and that even when founded, a newspaper is not a very profitable property.

Yet I cannot say that I know of a single great and successful and influential American newspaper, the first cost of the founding of which has been equal to the cost of founding any third- or fourth-rate business in the locality where the newspaper was founded. That is, granted that both were founded at the same time. As a matter of fact, no great newspaper has ever been founded by the aid of large capital. As a matter of fact, no more substantial obstacle to success can be presented to the founder of any newspaper than the possession of abundant capital.

It has been said that there has been more money lost in journalism in America than has ever been made out of it. That's possibly true. But the losses have all been made as a result of an attempt to found newspapers by means of capital, or the attempt to own and conduct newspapers by the sheer force of capital. In journalism, money does not make money. In journalism, money makes for failure.

I am frequently accused of being paradoxical when I utter opinions about those subjects on which I am most accurately informed. If I were governed by the principle of Machiavelli—that is, always to dissimulate I would know no better means to do this than by always speaking truthfully about my own business and my own profession. No one, especially the laity, ever believes a word I say about journalism.

Now here is a proposition I have frequently made, and in making it, have been both sincere and truthful:

Given one man, or two men, or a collective staff of men, of a certain ability; and it being proposed that this man, or these men should form a newspaper; and it being further proposed that they should be endowed with no more capital than enough to purchase old, almost worn-out, second-hand office equipment, together with a cash capital sufficient barely to feed and clothe and house the man or men for a period of two or three years, on a standard of living expenses not superior to that of ordinary day laborers—given these circumstances, what would be my judgment as to their chances of success, as against their chances if they had large capital to expend?

I would say that the newspaper founded on large capital would not have one chance of success, where a paper founded on the smallest possible capital would have a hundred or perhaps a thousand chances. In fact, my conviction is that there would be no chance at all for the success of a newspaper founded by men who intended to use relatively large capital in the foundation of their newspaper.

I have been interested in a proprietary way in between thirty and forty daily newspapers. Some of my newspapers have been remarkably successful, some of them have been absolute and complete failures, some of them have succeeded moderately, and some of them have been founded and conducted at so little expense as to be considered small failures. On the average, however, whether coincidences played a great part or not, my newspaper successes have always been in inverse proportion to the amount of original capital accessible or employed. The most pronounced failures that I have had experience with have been those in which either large capital was available, or in which there were managers who supposed that large capital would be put eventually at their disposal.

Therefore I would say that journalistic honesty does not necessarily suffer because of any original natural dishonesty of men who eventually become capitalists. Young newspapers, papers that have not yet become so profitable as to corrupt the morals of their owners, are, for the most part, the most honest newspapers. The young and struggling newspaper has to establish itself, and the first thing that an intelligent young owner of a newspaper, or owner of a young newspaper learns, is that it pays to be honest. His older, more successful and more profitable rivals in the journalistic field, having become corrupted by wealth, no longer depending entirely for existence, for their daily bread, on continued and growing public confidence, may be dishonest, and hence cannot compete with a poor young publication for the public favor on the grounds of absolute honesty.

If, then, it requires but a small capital to found a newspaper, and if honesty is a good business policy, my critic will ask: Why is it that the daily press of the United States is almost exclusively owned by capitalists, and why are its practices almost invariably plutocratic or dishonest?

I can answer this question very easily.

There is no more valuable and substantial property in the world than a successful newspaper. In every community the property value of the most successful newspaper in that community is greater, perhaps, than the property value of any other single business institution in the locality. If it is not greater, it is at least as great as any but a very, very few local business institutions.

It is impossible to have a very successful newspaper in a town of 50,000 population, whose capital value is not equal to $200,000. It is impossible to have a successful daily newspaper in a town of 100,000 population which is not worth $500,000. It is impossible to have a very successful newspaper in a town of 500,000 people that is not worth more than $1,000,000.

One can see, then, why the great and successful newspapers in the United States are owned by millionaires. One cannot own a newspaper that is worth several millions without owning many more million dollars worth of property. A newspaper cannot be a very great and successful newspaper without being worth several millions of dollars. The publisher who has succeeded, then, is necessarily a capitalist.

Now, then, to a second critical question: Why should great and successful publishers, that is to say, newspaper owners, be dishonest?

The usual newspaper critic, in common with the vast mass of humanity, consciously or unconsciously holds the belief so tersely expressed by some eighteenth-century French philosophers—"Property is theft." A thief, of course, is dishonest. If property is the result of theft, or dishonesty, then the man who owns property is dishonest. A man who owns a little property may be considered a little dishonest, while the man who owns a great property must be considered very dishonest. A man cannot own a great and successful newspaper who does not own a great property and, hence, the owner of such a great and successful property must be very dishonest.

I do not think that the usual newspaper critics would confess to the charge that they believed property is theft.

It is a fact, however, that the mere possession of wealth by one man and the lack of such possession by another man, results in the two men having distinct and often diametrically opposite points of view on very many subjects called "moral." The rich man and the poor man are almost never in agreement on any subject of property rights. This is markedly the case when they are considering the subject of dividing and appropriating the respective shares of the profits of the joint efforts of labor and capital.

The writers who are employees of newspaper owners have, necessarily, points of view that differ from those of their employers. The owner of the newspaper, the employer, requires his employees to write those things which the employer either believes or wants his readers to believe. As he is human, he will not allow his newspaper to be used to controvert his own opinions. Nor will he pay to the writer wages to produce matter which he does not want to appear in his paper.

As an editor originally, and a newspaper owner latterly, I have always been in a quandary on this subject. Whatever the opinion others may have of me, I have thought I was honest. I have felt it my duty to express my own honest convictions through my newspapers. But a newspaper is a large institution. The amount of space in it devoted to reading matter is many times larger than that which I or anyone else can fill. I, the owner, or the editor of a newspaper, must employ many assistants.

I not only want to be honest, but I want my editors and my writers to be honest. By a careful selection of my staff, I have been able always to have around me a set of men who agreed with me on many, many important matters connected with our calling. But it is impossible for any two men to agree on every subject. It is impossible, or nearly so, to find a newspaper staff of men numbering from twenty to one hundred or more who will agree on any one subject. But a newspaper is a single entity, an individual. It, as a rule, is compelled to have only one opinion on any one subject. Now what has happened when I have discovered daily differences of opinion between myself and some one or more of the writers who were subordinate to me? If I waived my opinion in favor of that of my subordinate, I, who was responsible for the utterances made in my paper, would have been insincere and permitted my paper to express opinions contrary to my own. Would I not have been dishonest? Of course, I have never done this. I have required my subordinates, the writers of a given article, to express my opinion, which in many a given case was contrary to his own. In doing this, have I compelled the writer to be dishonest?

To resume my arguments. I will concede that the usual criticism of the press is a just one, that the press is plutocratic, and that it is unfair in its dealings with the public, that it shows partiality in its dealings with the wealthy, and a far too great amount of indifference to the rights and welfare of the masses.

The possessor of great wealth may be, and frequently is, corrupted. No matter how good and moral a man may be, the possession of great wealth must have a certain amount of corrupting influence upon him. The possession of great wealth isolates a man to a great extent from his fellows. This isolation results in a constantly diminishing sympathy for humankind. The duties connected with the administration of a large property are so absorbing and so strenuous as to permit a man who is the possessor of wealth no time to think of even his own misfortunes, much less of the misfortunes of others. Only very rich men, perhaps, fully appreciate that the most unhappy men are those who are farthest from the center of the general average. The very rich and the very poor are, if not equally unhappy in their situation, at least far more unhappily situated than the great mass of men who occupy the intermediate space between wealth and poverty.

There are other reasons than that of mere personal absorption in business affairs which tend to make wealthy men unsympathetic with the masses. Birds of a feather flock together not merely because they want to, but because they have to. Save in rare instances, there can be no close congenial intimacy, mutual affection and confidence, between a very rich man and a very poor man. The mere possession of wealth so modifies a man's personal character that it is impossible for him to find congenial company except with men whose characters have been modified in a similar way.

There is not only a community of interest, but a community of social feeling between the capitalists of any locality, section or country. The successful journalist, that is to say, when he owns his own newspaper, is a wealthy man, a capitalist by necessity. His associates are necessarily other capitalists. The greater his association with capitalists is, the more completely does it minister to and give satisfaction to, the natural, normal, human instincts. A social capitalistic class quickly crystallizes and solidifies into a social caste, and the journalist who has become a capitalist is inevitably estranged from the larger community.

Hundreds of thousands of American citizens are condemning the American press because it is unfair to the poorer class and is a false witness in every case being tried at the bar of public opinion, between capital and labor. This criticism may be as just as the condition is necessary.

What would one think of a poor man who had a case in court against a rich man and allowed his rich antagonist to employ the lawyers on both sides—who would allow his rich antagonist to employ and pay his, the poor man's, lawyer fees? Yet this is just what the poorer people of the United States do in every case that is tried between capital and labor, before the bar of public opinion. A modern great newspaper is published in the form of a great and bulky document. The white paper used by the publisher in many cases costs at the paper mills more money than the reader pays for it. This being the case, all the other expenses—the employment of great staffs of writing journalists, of printers, of other mechanics, the cost of rent, machinery, and the wear and tear on the same, the telegraph tolls, and all the profit of the business of making a great newspaper—are borne, not by the readers of a newspaper, but by the advertisers, men in business, men who are capitalists.

When a man attempts to get something for nothing, or anything at less than cost, he is certainly fooled, and, I think, deservedly fooled. The readers of newspapers can only surely secure reliable advocates and, to them, friendly newspapers, by employing and paying their own journalistic servants, and not accepting gratuities from the capitalistic and advertising class. If the public would insist on paying the publishers of the daily and weekly and monthly journals the full cost of producing the same, plus a profit, so that a would-be honest publisher would not be compelled to depend for his existence upon the good will and patronage of the advertiser, there would be a chance at least of our having a less dishonest press.

I want to see established all over the country a number of papers, the selling price of which is so much larger than the cost of white paper that there will be a fair degree of profit in the newspaper publishing business without the assistance of advertising. There is a large amount of legitimate advertising business to be done, and all such advertisements are beneficial to both the public newspaper and to the public at large. All advertisements, however, that are published at a rate lower than the profit line, or that are obtained for any other consideration than the advertiser's desire of publicity, and all advertisements that are not clearly beneficial to the public at large, should be excluded from these papers.

XXIII

Highbrow Scientists and the Ignorant Public

IT'S USELESS to think of making the world safe for democracy without thinking of making democracy safe for itself. And the only possible way of making democracy thus safe is to make it more intelligent. But since to be intelligent is utterly impossible without having much of the knowledge, the method and the spirit of science, the only way to make democracy safe is to make it more scientific.

Now the scientists in this country are doing some wonderful work. They are telling about it in books. But they are writing their books at each other, and using such big words and such technical language that the average man, even if he attempts to read their books, can't understand what they say or what it is all about. They need an interpreter who can translate their language into plain United States that the people can understand.

Many of these scientists might be likened to a lot of silly owls roosting high up inside of some hollow trunk of a dead tree expressing their disgust because all, or nearly all, the rest of the birds and beasts are living out in the sunshine.

They are so blamed wise and so packed full of knowledge and so much the creatures of reason rather than instinct, that they cannot comprehend why God has made nearly all the rest of mankind so infernally stupid.

It was General Booth, I think, who said when he was adopting music for his Salvation Army songs that the devil should not have all the good music, and so he stole his tunes from music halls.

It was in an attempt to bridge the gap between the scientists and the ordinary readers that I caused to be formed, in 1919, the American Society for the Dissemination of Science. Later this organization came to be known as Science Service.

The Science Service was founded for the purpose of giving the American people a better opportunity to know the aims and achievements of modern science. Its charter is a wide one, authorizing the service to employ newspapers, books, lectures, conferences, motion pictures and any similar educational agencies in the distribution of scientific information.

We know that a very small portion of the great human story that is being unfolded daily by the scientific institutions, government and industrial research bureaus, and by individual pioneers the world over, finds its way into the American press.

There has always been, and particularly since the war gave new impetus to scientific research in America, pressing need for some agency that could and would make its major interest the intelligent application of American journalistic methods to the mounting fund of scientific knowledge.

The scientist has full appreciation of the romance of his work. Yet the tales of his adventures into the unknown, dramatic as they are, seldom find their way into print because he so infrequently has the time or the training to tell them in the language of everyday men.

All the best writing by men of exceptional ability on all scientific subjects appears only in publications and books which are absolutely unknown to the public and rarely indeed studied by the journalists of this country who have the ability to, and actually do, mold public opinion. Every thorough scientific man who is in the habit of reading the daily newspapers is constantly reminded that there is a vast quantity of misinformation being constantly spread abroad by our newspapers.

The first aim of Science Service should be just the reverse of what is called propaganda. Its objects should never be to furnish argument or facts for the purpose of producing partisans for some cause. Its sole object should be to present facts in readable and interesting form—facts upon which the reader could and probably would base his opinion on a subject of politics or sociology or concerning his duty to himself and his fellows.

No matter what protests are made or what contempt may be expressed for the condition, it is a fact that the government of this nation and of our states and of our cities is such as results from the opinion-making activities of the daily press.

It is only through the press—mainly the daily press—of the country that the vast majority of the people of this country receive any information or education at all. It is therefore only through the press that the public can be quickly and well instructed on matters of its greatest interest.

The object of this institution, Science Service, should be to make the greatest use possible of the press in disseminating that knowledge which is the result of painstaking research carried on by a few hundred or at most by a few thousand well-trained men equipped with great mental capacity.

It is not intended that Science Service should be run for profit to anyone. It is only intended that fair compensation should be paid to those who take an active part in making the institution an instrument of great public service.

But no one—least of all the editor or publisher of a paper—values anything that costs nothing. Further than this, it should be the aim of the association to increase greatly the income of the association for the purpose of increasing the number of active members and especially to employ special research workers.

All journalistic clients of the service should be assessed for the services rendered by it, according to the client's ability to pay and, further, according to the value of the service to various publications.

My aim in building Science Service was not to build a monument for myself or anyone else. I had in view just one objective, namely, the founding of an institution with a very modest endowment—an institution so organized that it would, by the mere process of its functioning, develop and grow into something of great national value to a future generation or to future generations.

One of the foundation principles of this institution I wish to be the avoidance of both of the two greatest economic sins, getting something for nothing and giving something for nothing.

The modest endowment that I propose I considered merely the seed from which the plant would develop.

On one of my ranches I have a considerable forest, every tree of which sprang from seeds which I planted myself. The primary cost of this forest was insignificant. Had I planted older trees the growth to maturity might not have taken so long a time. I will not live to see this forest ripen and become ready to harvest. I did not expect, desire or hope that Science Service would in my lifetime or that of any of my associates grow to be of sufficient importance to attract public attention and hence contribute to gratifying the vanity of any of us by adding to our fame.

I have often used the phrase "hard wood grows slowly."

The laborer in this field of science dissemination is worthy of his hire—that is to say, sufficient compensation to enable him to afford to work for a future generation of people who would not even know of his labors. My own commercial experiences had convinced me that such an institution as I proposed might easily be so managed as to make it in a comparatively few years a valuable and largely profit-paying institution if those who first undertook to cultivate this young plant and care for it were not too much inclined to desire a large commercial success.

There are objections on the part of some of my associates to receiving any sort of financial compensation for their work on behalf of the institution. While I respect the motives of these gentlemen I cannot overlook the fact that they are the very ones who are now inclining the twig so that it will grow away from the line I first proposed—from the line which I believe will be the only one that should be pursued if ultimate success is to be attained. These gentlemen are proposing to "give something for nothing." They are contributing to the original endowment, which has already proved that it was quite large enough to bring the infant to life and to maintain it in healthy condition.

The future of Science Service does not depend on its original endowment except to a very small extent. Its future does depend upon the good will, the faith and the good work performed by the fifteen members of the association—or some of them.

Personally I would feel greatly mortified if I thought that at some time in the future I, to whom the least of credit should be due for the foundation, should have anything but an inferior position in any public recognition—an inferior position relative to those men of science who have really contributed far more than have I, the general manager, and the whole of the general manager's staff.

It is my opinion that all or any of those of the association who perform valuable service should be bound to receive some actual money compensation for their labor.

In considering the degree of success that may accompany our

efforts, I strongly urge that only secondary consideration be given to money income. In this institution success should only be reckoned by the growth of our audience coupled with the development throughout the country of other independent "sowers of the seed of knowledge."

As our purpose is only to secure in every way possible the spread of science, we should rather congratulate ourselves when we find others doing better than we do, as well as we do, or even partly as well as we do.

Our sole aim I think should be to labor to increase or cause to be increased the amount of general knowledge possessed by the general public—not only the general public of today, in this generation, but the general public that will exist in future generations.

I am not sure that I would, if I could, try to inspire any of my associates to greater efforts. It is only those among us who bring into our group their own enthusiasm, their own vision, and their own will to make our people wiser and possessed of greater knowledge, who can do well the work that lies to their hands.

XXIV

Plain Talk from an Old Journalist

HERE'S SOME talk from an aged penman to youngsters who want to get into the newspaper business:

First and foremost I want to tell you that a college is about the last place in the world where a man should go to learn journalism.

A good many years ago I was in Paris traveling with a friend who was also a newspaperman. He came to my hotel room to tell me of an adventure. He happened to see in the lobby of the hotel a great American newspaperman, the owner of one of the leading papers in this country. He had never met him before but he recognized him from the numerous portraits he had seen in American newspapers and magazines. This man was well along in years. My friend, who had a trait pretty well in common with all young newspapermen, namely cheek, went up and introduced himself to the great man and told him that he himself was in the newspaper game.

The old fellow turned his fishy eyes on him and stared for several moments and then—"Working in a newspaper office, eh!!! Whore-house, eh!!! I'm a prostitute, you're a prostitute, we newspapermen are all prostitutes." As to what else he said doesn't matter.

Whatever else you think about newspapers I can frankly tell you that this old publisher and editor is a good deal nearer right than you want to think or than you do think. I believe that a great many of you young fellows would immediately turn your backs on journalism if you knew how great a risk you're going to run of being properly designated as "no gentlemen," if you further pursue the calling that you've elected.

Are there no clean, honest gentlemen engaged in the profession? I'll say "Yes, but not many." There are few opportunities for a man to be both a gentleman and a journalist. There is only one position in the newspaper business which a man can hold that is not only profitable in the long run, but which gives him the choice of whether he is to be a gentleman or not. That position is ownership.

When you go out to seek a position as a reporter and you find one, how are you going to know whether the owner of the paper you are going to work for is a gentleman? How can you know whether the city editor under whom you are to work directly is a gentleman? All you can know is that you are to obey orders, to do as you are told, and if required lie and not question why. If the owner of your paper is a gentleman and your immediate chief is a gentleman, it is probable that you will be working on a newspaper that is to have a short life.

I will not repeat the words of this old gentleman my friend met in the lobby of the hotel in Paris. I will not say that I have been a prostitute, knowingly, willingly, all the time. As you know, I have been successful. I have done many things that I wouldn't want my son to do. I have climbed the ladder from cub reporter to editor and owner, and the only consolation I have now is that I have been less of a rascal than most of my colleagues.

However, let me tell you this one thing. I do not think that as a class we newspapermen are worse than the average run of other men in business. I honestly believe that owing to our peculiar position we are constantly being impressed with the idea of our responsibility, and hence we are constantly straining to be less bad than we would be if we did not have this feeling of responsibility.

Stop and think of it. A paragraph of a half-dozen lines thoughtlessly dashed off without the least bad intention may make a whole family unhappy and drive a wife away from her home, a husband to drink. The power of the press is mighty. But, if it is a power for good, it is a power for evil also.

Praise given to a man who does not deserve it, blame bestowed on a man who does not deserve it, may result in an honest candidate for the judgeship being defeated and a rascal placed on the bench. A paragraph that you contribute to your paper may set afloat an impression that will grow and grow for years until a whole community at some critical time condemns the good man and supports the bad man.

As a reporter you must obey orders or get the sack. As a reporter you are instructed by your chief or by your fellows as to the policy of the newspaper on which you work so that without any direct orders you will comply with that policy, whether you think it right or wrong. You will probably not think about the rightness or wrongness of the item or the article that you write. You will almost certainly think only of its effect on your pay envelope.

Walter Bagehot, journalist, philosopher and historian, in one of his books makes a statement something like this: "I worked on a number of journals in London. These journals all had different policies, some antagonistic to others. When I changed my position from one newspaper to another I'd have no idea of changing my views on politics or any other subject, but I always found that very shortly after I began my work on the journal the environment so affected me that I had thought and written as my fellows on the journal thought and wrote. I had no influence on the journal, it was the journal moulded me."

Personally, I have had a similar experience. I have owned several newspapers. Did these newspapers reflect me and my judgment? Rarely. The community molds its newspapers. I went from one of my newspapers to another fully determined to carry out a certain policy, but although I owned the newspaper I couldn't control the newspaper, but the newspaper controlled me. Oh, I admit that in certain particulars I could and did control the policy of my newspapers, but community feeling, the staff *esprit de corps,* and more than all else the traditions of the newspaper had a greater effect on me than I had on the newspaper itself.

I have been well acquainted not personally but through their newspapers with two great journalists. At one time one of these was the owner of a newspaper that made him considerable wealth. This paper was a blackmailing sheet in the large sense and in the meanest sense too. One day, a very wealthy, a very respectable merchant of the city came into this man's newspaper office and told him that if he didn't sell his paper and leave the city in a week, he would shoot him. The paper was sold and its publisher moved to a different city. He conceived the idea that now he was rich enough to be respectable. So he founded another newspaper, and although its founder and first editor has now long been dead, the paper has been respectable and powerful.

The other man had made a great success in a small western city. He had accumulated enough wealth to buy another paper in a much larger city. This latter paper was on the rocks when he bought it. But he was a very skillful man and soon enough he made a success and became very famous. He continued to own both papers, but even years later anyone reading first one and then the other, would never dream that one man owned both these papers.

The trouble with journalism is its hermaphroditic character. It isn't all a profession; it isn't all a business. Perhaps originally, or to speak more correctly, a few decades ago, journalism was a profession much more than it is now. Men practiced the profession for the love of it or for the love of the little or large influence or power that the calling brought with it. But times have changed. Everywhere, all over the country in the various communities, the owners of newspapers in these communities are among the wealthiest members there.

Out of every dollar expended by newspaper publishers, on the average ninety cents is spent for the purpose of getting advertising revenue, and only ten cents is spent in payment for news, instruction and opinion creating. The poorest paid employees on a newspaper are the men who write. The largest compensation in the way of salaries or commissions is paid to the men who sell advertising space. We publishers of newspapers pay the largest salaries to those men in the editorial department whose writings get us the most readers. That editor is esteemed to be the greatest who procures the largest number of readers for his paper and the largest amount of good will on the part of the advertising customers. I know it to be a fact that most of our great newspapers sell their newspapers at a price less than the cost of the white paper used. The modern American newspaper is little more than a billboard carrying advertising. The more people who take our papers the more we are able to charge for the advertising in same. Why, journalism is "big business" pure and simple.

Dollar chasing is anything but an ennobling pursuit. Well, but what of it? The business is as it is, and it is our business to make the best of the situation that exists. If our publishers seek for and obtain an enormously large number of readers for the purpose of commanding a profitable advertising patronage, that at least incidentally gives to our newspaper writers an enormously large audience to whom we professional journalists can deliver whatever message we have to deliver. Those businessmen engaged in the newspaper work are giving us our opportunities to do good or ill service to the public. We can so teach the ignorant until they become less ignorant. We can to a very large extent mold public opinion to our own views.

In reality journalism is statesmanship. The government of such a democracy as ours is practically a government by newspapers. There are comparatively few readers of books. There are more readers of magazines, but practically everybody reads the newspaper. What the public knows it learns through the newspaper. Whatever the bias of the public mind may be, it is very largely the result of newspaper writers.

Let us call ourselves, if we will, mere parasites sucking subsistence from a big commercial enterprise. Yet we can easily enough recognize that our situation can give us opportunities to render services good or ill to the public. If journalism has fallen from its highest state of being solely employed in directing the public mind for the benefit of the public, and become a mere dependent on capitalism, it may even be safely asserted that it has gained as much as or more than it has lost, because without journalists there could be no newspapers and without newspapers there would not be so many millionaires.

I have often enough been reproached as a newspaperman for not being more patriotic and more loyal to the people, by men and women with perfectly good intentions but very small economic intelligence—men and women whom I can best describe by calling them economic imbeciles. Such people insist that I ought to teach and preach, preach and teach, and they tell me that I am very wrong in furnishing reading matter that will degrade and corrupt the minds and characters of our readers. If you have not already learned the fact, you will eventually learn that men and women do not like being preached at and taught, and that the moment that the average reader finds under his eyes some article intended to instruct and guide his or her opinion he or she will skip that article and read something else. If we do not amuse and entertain our readers we will have few readers or none at all. We will have no audience listening to us.

As patriots and altruists it is our business to improve that public mind in the only way possible. In order to instruct the people we must conceal as far as we can our intention to do so. We must slyly insinuate into the baser sorts of minds lessons that will be valuable to them and facts upon which they will be compelled to base their judgments when they are called upon, by their votes or by that sort of clamor which is called public opinion, to indicate their wishes and their demands to their servants in official positions—executives, legislators and the judiciary. We must keep our audience interested, whatever else we do, and then craftily work upon their minds.

The general public may be considered as a class in a kindergarten who are furnished with playthings and games which are unsuspected by the pupils of teaching them those things which their teacher desires them to learn. The daily press is intended for the great mass of our citizens and not for the highbrows, as we call them.

You and I all think that we are superior people and that, in fact, we belong to the highbrow class. I think we are right in concluding that the more people who read what we write the better it will be for the people as a whole.

A word about writing. I have had great advantage in being able to observe the beginnings, the development and the final accomplishment of many writing journalists. By experience and observation I have learned that those writing journalists who let themselves go, as it were, and wrote as nearly as possible, considering the limitations of the English language, what they thought, using the language and style chosen by themselves and not at all the language and style of any other writer, rose quickest and highest in their profession.

You've all read books; you've all your favorite books and authors. If you have thought about the matter at all you must have become aware that there is but little similarity either in the style or thoughts expressed by any two of the authors that have pleased you most. Think of Kipling and Meredith, of Milton and Browning, of Irvin Cobb and Wodehouse. I think the greatest blemish on the American press today is the likeness of the newspapers, taken as a whole, each to another, and of all the writings in any single publication.

Fifty years ago and more one might read an editorial by Dana or by Halstead, by Henry Watterson or by Joe McCullogh, and without looking at the title page of the paper, he would know whether he was reading the New York *Sun,* the Cincinnati *Commercial,* the Louisville *Courier Journal,* or the St. Louis *Globe Democrat.* Why, forty years ago, in reading any article I would know whether it had appeared in one of my own papers or some other paper, and I would also know, which would be more easy to understand, in which one of my own papers the article had appeared. Today, with very few exceptions, you could read an article in any public paper published in any city from New York to San Francisco, and you would not be able to make a guess as to what paper it appeared in or even in what section the paper was published.

Ben Franklin, who was himself a newspaperman, in *Poor Richard's Almanac* said that "honesty is the best policy." That honesty in journalism is the best policy you might all reasonably doubt. However, I think none of us have reason to doubt that honesty is a good enough policy at times. Because we are all frail human beings, the best that most of us can do is to be as honest as we can afford to be.

(Editor's Note: This chapter was written in 1925.)

XXV

Muscles, Mind and Opportunity

I AM A professional advocate of the "underdog" and my fees have been so large as to make me, if not a conspicuous, at least a very typical member of the class that has no "underdogs" in it. I try to reproach myself for this, but can find no rational justifications for my reproach for my general condition, although I do in innumerable instances give evidence of thoroughgoing human frailty.

For a long time I have been thinking on one aspect of the case.

Are the rich men to blame for the poverty of the poor, or are the poor to blame both for their poverty and the misery that every rich man annexes with his wealth? Have I been doing right all these years in my constant outcry of "stop thief"? Would I not have more usefully employed my energies had I devoted myself to an attempt to teach the people, the poor and ignorant, that they sinned more against society than they were sinned against?

I think it is evident that if two brothers of equal strength and capacity were living on a farm, and if one of these brothers worked hard and produced not only enough food for himself but for another, and the other refused to labor at all, the idler would have no right to live on the product of his brother's toil. The industrious brother would not be duty-bound to feed and care for the idler.

This conclusion might be followed by a question: Is it not the duty of the industrious brother to refuse all sustenance to the idler, thereby compelling his brother to work for himself, and by working to become rich in health and in bodily and intellectual vigor? Really, isn't the industrious brother by very reason of his charitableness in supporting the idler actually doing his brother an injury—actually reducing him to potential slavery? Is not the industrious brother putting temptation in his own way, a temptation eventually to enslave his idle brother and cause him, sooner or later, to labor by compulsion, not for his own, but for his efficient brother's benefit?

Analyzing the whole system of modern society, it seems to me that I find a parallel between the industrious brother and the idler on one side, and the ruling classes and the masses on the other.

However, in order to make the example of the two brothers fit the general case better, I will slightly alter the situation.

Given two brothers of unequal natural capacities but each competent to work on his own account and live, though on different standards, still in such a way that the inferior brother could live as a free man, independent and comfortable. Now, if one of these two brothers should elect to work hard with mind and muscle, and the other should elect to do only physical labor, the result would be that the idle-minded brother would leave to the industrious-minded brother all the mental work and direction, both of their joint and several labors. In such a case, the two brothers in accepting the situation would, one of them, make the other a master, and the other would make his brother a slave. The superior brother would put in his own way the temptation which he would surely submit to: the temptation to become the oppressor of his brother.

Both brothers would be to blame for this condition. Which would be the most to blame? I, and other friends of the "underdogs" unhesitatingly put all or most of the blame on the brother who is industrious in both mind and muscle. We call him a thief, an oppressor and a criminal. We extend sympathy and support to the mental idler. For the latter we have nothing but excuses. We do not blame him for his shortcomings, but we blame his brother, the industrious man, and we blame the whole class of the mentally laborious and industrious men in our community. Without knowing the origin of the present terrible conditions we recognize their evil and we teach that the evil exists purely as the result of the wickedness of mind of one and not at all as the result of the slothfulness of mind of the other.

It is true that the temptations of wealth and power develop in the mind of the industrious and superior class, vices of every form and character, so that the individuals of the class become hateful. Poverty and ignorance develop vices too, but they are such humble vices, such normal human natural vices that, compared with those others, they are considered by us insignificant and easily forgivable.

Esau sold his birthright for a mess of pottage. The Israelites yearned for the fleshpots of Egypt. Men are not conquered into slavery. They voluntarily accept it. They do not even ask the price of a mess of pottage in return for their birthright, freedom. They demand slavery, they demand the right to live without laboring with their minds, and of all labor, thinking is the most grievous, as those who have performed so much of it know to their cost.

I am familiar with American statistics. Owing to the richness of our natural resources and the comparative thinness of our population, it is probable that the joint product of capital, management and labor is large enough to support in comfort every man, woman and child in this country, provided there is an equitable distribution of products per capita. If all of the idlers were as well or nearly as well provided for as the industrious, then all would have enough.

If all the products of England, on the other hand, were equally divided per capita, so huge are the numbers who now live in want of actual necessities, and so large the numbers that exist upon a bare subsistence allowance, that not one Englishman or woman, after the division, would have sufficient to supply more than actual needs. If there was an equal distribution of all the products in the empire of India, the whole people in that land, without any exceptions, would be reduced to a standard of living far humbler than that of the poorest American laborer when employed.

Instead of saying that every man has a right to live if he will work, and that every man has a right to work, I might say that every man should be compelled to work or suffer nature's penalty; and that being a man and possessing a mind, he must work with his best natural tool (that is, his mind) as well as with his muscles.

It is not opportunity that men lack; it is necessity. When the individual has no other existing compulsion to labor, society should enforce the only natural penalty. Christianity or some other form of ethics may dispose of the cases of the inefficient by extending charity to such.

When I admit that there are thousands and perhaps millions who are willing to work with both mind and body and cannot find employment for both sets of functions (actually, no opportunities present themselves to them), then I have to admit also that perhaps there is no spot on earth lacking in opportunity, when the man there is not too blind to see it.

In our family life and in our schools especially we, as a nation, are engaged in blinding our children, or at least so affecting their mental eyesight that they cannot see what is valuable to them and the country. We are blinding them to such an extent that they can see nothing and do nothing that is of value to anyone but the infinitesimal few whose eyesights and minds have been properly developed, either by intelligent parents or the accidental necessities they encounter.

I believe that there is hardly any difference between one man and another at birth other than physiological. Just as any of the eggs of the queen bee may be developed by nurture into another queen bee, so can any infant be developed into a king man or queen woman, with the proper nurture of body and mind.

All men are so much alike that no one of them is naturally inclined to exercise that last gift to the animal kingdom: the power to reason. Every man therefore seeks a master—some other man who will think for him. Perhaps the most unhappy creature among all mankind is that rare man who finds no other man against whom he can lean, and on whom he can depend for direction and support. Such a man is always of necessity a lonely, sad-hearted, overworked individual. He is ostracized by the commonalty and set upon a gilded uncomfortable throne where he must perform in solitude the huge labor of doing the world's thinking and directing.

The world may laugh and jeer at such a proposition. I know something of the pains that such a man has to suffer. Although my own throne is a humble one, it is nevertheless and has been a throne all the same. If such seats as mine are comfortable and easy to occupy, why are so many men yearning to abdicate, and why do many men go so far as I have gone in abdicating?

While it is impossible to cast aside the crown—that is, the intellectual capacity which carries with it real responsibility—the scepter of activity can be and often is not only willingly dropped but impatiently thrown away.

Now, while my whole life's experience has been crowded with nothing else but examples of one kind or another of this tendency, this almost insane determination of men to seek enslavement (a determination no less on their part than that of the moth to die in the candle's flame), I can call your attention to a very homely example—the flight from the country to the city.

I have nine thousand acres of southern California land. Acre for acre its potential productivity is greater than the average lands of Japan. Japanese lands provide sustenance for three people to the acre. My nine thousand acres of land at present are not more than enough to support one person to the hundred acres.

When I first came into this country there were in my neighborhood many cultivated farms. The average yield of each, all things considered, was greater per annum than a family of first-class mechanics in the city could win as salaries. Large as this yield was, it was capable of being increased many fold by the gaining of a little more knowledge and the exercise of a little self-restraint. Yet there are today remaining on these farms not ten per cent of their original occupants. They have all gone to the lately boomed city of San Diego. They have exchanged independence and affluence for dependence, and in such times as these, poverty. Often I have talked to these people and others like them. Always the excuse for desiring to desert the farm for the city has been the lack of social intercourse. Always it has been too apparent that the desire was to escape anxiety. They wanted to avoid that amount of thinking and studying which was necessary to provide for the usual emergencies that arise not only on the farm, but in every position where one is self-dependent and where another cannot be depended upon to do the thinking that will provide a steady flow of wages.

Poverty and slavery are with rare exceptions solely the wages of intellectual indolence. This indolence is generally the willful intellectual indolence of individual men and women. Sometimes, however, poverty and enslavement are the result of similar indolence on the part of a parent, or a community.

One of the cure-alls of this great evil, that I have dwelt on much, is the minimum wage. I have proposed a universal minimum wage of three dollars a day for all adults, and a somewhat smaller, but not much smaller, wage for apprentices. I proposed that none should be allowed to work, except for the state, for a smaller wage. For a generation, untold misery and hardship would follow as the result of such a change. But when no man could accept smaller wages than the minimum, there would be no employment by employers of men and women who did not earn this wage. This condition would compel every man not paid a wage to work on his own account. As agricultural pursuits are just those in which any able-bodied man can produce enough to support in comfort his family, the cities would soon enough grow small, slums and sordid vice would disappear and the countryside everywhere would be peopled by healthy and strong men, women and children. They would be healthy and strong in body, and necessarily well-trained and well-developed in mind, developed broadly and sufficiently all through the mind, and not narrowly and in spots, as minds must be developed in order to accommodate themselves to urban life and occupations.

(Editor's Note: Most of this chapter was written in 1917-18.)

XXVI

Don't Grow Old Gracefully

WE HAVE heard and read enough of this silly prattle of growing old gracefully.

Remarks of this kind are generally made by people who have had no experience in growing old at all—people who draw on their imaginations exclusively for depicting conditions or by people who have had some experience with age, being more or less advanced in years, but who have not reached the period when they are free from foolish, or even childish or adolescent vanity. Older people who speak of such methods are the kind of old people who make fools of themselves by dressing themselves in raiment that is only really becoming to youth and by resorting to masseurs to smooth out their wrinkles and to manicurists to have their fingernails polished.

This kind of people can even be heard to say that one is no older than he feels, and they then proceed to mimic in their walk and in their talk, in their posing and in their employment, younger people in their environment. They are people who are never wise and who are never capable of becoming wise, people congenitally afflicted with the tendency to be continually arrested in development.

Perhaps there are some old people who do grow old gracefully.

That is to say, who grow old naturally just as a child grows to a period of adolescence, to maturity, naturally. But what is commonly understood as growing old gracefully is mimicking to a greater or less extent while aging all sorts of exhibitions made by the young.

Grow old gracefully! One might as well talk of dying gracefully. I saw my mother die gracefully in her eightieth year. She fell asleep and ceased to breathe. There was nothing shocking, nothing terrible in her activities and speech of the last few hours. She seemed to be aware of the fact that she was dying, or at least not at all impressed by the importance to her or to anyone else of her condition. But she was very old, and succumbed to a disease that was painless.

I have seen others die, suffering terribly, and there was nothing graceful presented to my sight. Pain—and terrible pain—distorted the features of the faces and what the dying ones actually said ploughed deep and harrowed into the feelings of the onlookers.

One may grow old without suffering and one observing such a person might say that he or she grew old gracefully. But I saw one who was very near to me in blood growing old from her middle age to extreme old age, suffering always, her hearing gradually diminishing to deafness and her sight gradually diminishing to blindness, and yet she lived well into her ninth decade. Could she grow old gracefully? I have seen the very old suffering from poverty, and the very old possessed of great wealth, not one particle of whose wealth could allay terrible physical and mental anguish.

Resignation! What is the difference between resignation and despair? In either case the only hope is for death to cut short the pain of living.

Perhaps the nearest approach to that which is called growing old gracefully can be defined as growing old sensibly—enduring pain that cannot be avoided, anguish that cannot be appeased.

My own idea of the best way of growing old is to grow old sensibly, recognizing social, physical and mental conditions that change from day to day, from month to month and from year to year, and making the best possible personal adjustment to all of these conditions.

It is my opinion that the best period, at least of every man's life (I will not speak of women) is the time when his children are being born to him and when these little sprouts from himself are fresh and beautiful. Then the father can dream beautiful dreams of the future of these little ones. Then as a rule the father has himself had no experience of old age and is still so strong in body and spirit that he rather delights in than resents his own struggles for his existence and the welfare of those he loves most, wife and children. He has no time to devote to foreboding, nor has he any inclination thereto. How can he dread that which is going to happen to his offspring when he has had to suffer nothing himself—nothing worth while.

I, for myself, having experienced the joy of living in my own children, have never forgotten this experience.

I believe that most fathers have had similar happy experiences or, at least during the period of the infancy of their children, had their sufferings greatly mitigated. Then they suffered less than they had to suffer later on; then they could hope more for their own future than they could have any reason to hope in those later years when their children had grown to manhood and to womanhood. All great accomplishments are really the accomplishments of youth, so that when youth, or at least comparative youth, is past, then there is nothing reasonable in hoping for a future better time for oneself.

Then comes the time when, if the father would grow old reasonably, he should live in the lives of his children. He should appreciate and sympathize with their hopes and aspirations and enjoy for himself those things that only his children can feel and enjoy. But time flies so swiftly. It is so long a distance to travel—that stretching from grandfather to grandchildren—that I more than doubt the commonly expressed view that grandparents enjoy their grandchildren more than they ever enjoyed their children. If there were no other grounds for this doubt, it could be found in the common expression that we, the grandparents, have all the pleasure derivable from the little children and none of the pain and suffering and trouble.

I have lost by death a grandchild. Three of my sons have died. I know that when any one of my children was suffering even from a slight illness, my mind was filled with anxiety to such an extent that I have spent many and many a sleepless night. When my grandchildren have been ill, it is true that I have been anxious about them, but my fears were not nearly so poignant. I wonder if there are any old men, or middle-aged men, or even comparatively young men who have forgotten the thrill and ecstasy of their early youthful love or loves. For all such I feel the greatest pity.

I know there are children who have spent no part of their lives outside of cities, great or small, who have never run barefooted over green fields and through shady forests, and who have never seen more than a streak of blue or green above them for the only sky they have ever known. For these too I have a feeling of pity.

An approaching thunderstorm; the sighing of a breeze through forest trees; the roar and groaning of the leaves and branches in a great woods when the storm was sweeping through it; fleecy clouds floating overhead seen by a boy lying upon his back in some deserted place; the rippling stream and the majestic sweep of some great river; the ever-recurring adventures of the boy of gun and rod, in boat or on horseback—each and all of these things are a rich store of memories of the country-reared child.

If I had the power I would procure these for every living child, that his or her youth should be spent in such a way as to have such a store of memories—the last and finishing touch of which would be the first boy-and-girl love affair; perhaps accompanied by a kiss or an embrace, or perhaps only the desire, such intense desire as to cause the whole frame to tremble, the knees to feel weak.

But I am not to write the beginning of life but the ending. When a man's children are full grown, then is the time when the process of growing old has fairly begun. Just imagine a man stopping at this period to think of growing old gracefully! He is a happier man if not a wiser one if he thinks not at all of growing old. He has enjoyed so much living in his children that he knows, or should know, that there are any number of other young lives in which he can live, and in so living, forget all about himself. There are young men who are only beginning their careers; there are young men who have started on their careers, and there are young men who are rearing their families and little ones and who are enjoying themselves thereby.

The man who has passed through these periods can sympathize joyously or sadly with the triumphs and defeats of these younger ones. If such a man with such experiences has chanced to be of the successful few, his opportunities are great—his opportunities to lend a helping hand to those who have both the strength in mind and body and strong ambitions.

While one's own children generally are few in number, so that all of them pass through adolescence in a comparatively short time, other fathers and mothers are also producing life, so that in any man's immediate environment there is a constant army of youth marching up from whom to select those to whom favors can be given and those who can profit by the aid of elders. No man need ever lack the inspiration, the wholesome urge, of youth around him.

I take it that no man can grow old more sensibly than by making full use of this opportunity of living with and in the lives of those who are young. I have lived long enough to see babies grow into manhood, to see these become fathers, and even a few of them grandfathers. If, perchance, I live many years longer, the distance between myself and even a new grandfather may be far enough to make me enjoy the companionship of these older young men more than I have enjoyed the companionship of men whose children are yet young.

Growing old sensibly consists of doing many things, of eliminating many things that were once pleasurable and taking on new occupations that are still pleasurable, though not so pleasurable. More than half, I think, of all the pleasures and all the pain of human life, are inextricably interwoven, or rather proceed from the laws of action and reaction. But as a man approaches what is called middle life he usually loses the power to enjoy greatly purely physical occupations, such as sports of all kinds. As we get older, the palate becomes less imperative in its demands or else wise physicians advise such things as change of diet.

Then later comes the sad climacteric when a male of the human species can no longer find great joy in intimate contact with his chosen companion of the other sex.

There are some men who are so foolish as to attempt, in all possible ways, to prolong certain pleasures. I do not consider that these men are growing old sensibly. All too frequently—perhaps almost invariably—comes that period in the life of a man when he suffers from many disappointed hopes, if he permits himself so to suffer.

His family has ceased to be his family. His children have families of their own. His mate may have died, or, having himself passed the period of subordination of the sex motive, he discovers that her interests in life have become different from his.

Somewhat synchronizing with this condition of affairs, the man whose life interest has been largely made up of business and professional pursuits, or purely intellectual achievements, finds that his power is so far diminished that he is no longer able to practice successfully in his old occupation or else his interests in the same have become so dessicated that he no longer covets achievement.

For these four great reasons a great majority of men find themselves compelled to live lonely lives, unoccupied or uninterested, instead of growing old sensibly. Such soon perish.

I have known professional men in such periods who abandoned their professions entirely. Some not only abandoned their profession, but abandoned all interest in it. I have known such older men to retire from business, thinking vainly that they would be contented to live on their income. I have even known scientific men to lose all interest in their science and become mentally inert. I take it that none of these men are growing old sensibly.

The man who finds himself aging should accept conditions as they are, pine not at all, and refuse to actually feel the sense of disappointment. This is growing old sensibly.

There are not only always the younger men with whom he can co-operate, but then the whole land is filled with children who are growing up to be men and women and then there are the future generations.

To grow old sensibly, one should always keep one's eyes turned from the past to the future, and continue to strive with all his might to serve those who are coming even more efficiently than those he has served shoulder to shoulder with in the past. There should be no feelings of remorse, no feelings of regret, no feelings of mortification for past failures. If wrong has been done, reparation is impossible. If one feels that he has suffered ingratitude, he has not become sensible as he has become old. Such an attitude of mind is rather evidence of a man's unworthiness, for he who has only served others that he might be served himself in return has really given nothing, and has only bargained for *quid pro quo,* and at best has only made a bad bargain.

If he has lived rightly and righteously and lived truly, he has never even considered the word gratitude. Hence there can be no feeling of disappointment. When one has grown old and life persists in him, and promises to persist so that he must continue to grow older and older still, he has still his occupations, the occupations that he as an old man can excel all the others in performing.

There is nothing that he can learn that he cannot turn to someone else's use. If it cannot be turned to the use of someone immediately near him or dear to him, still some human being may get profit by the knowledge gained by the labor of the most efficient of men, namely: the oldest of men whose minds have not suffered too greatly from senile decay.

The old man who has grown old sensibly is more sensible than any younger man can be—more sensible concerning not only his own needs and requirements, but concerning the services he can render to others. In order that he should grow older and older still sensibly, he must govern his own conduct.

Providing this old man has grown old sensibly, he has performed as well as he can perform all, or nearly all, of his duties to society. He, of all men, may feel himself exempt from all commands addressed to him, all demands made upon him by others. To continue to grow old sensibly, he cannot fail to strive to increase the happiness of others or diminish the sorrow of others to the extent of his powers without ever imitating the folly of youth or overstraining his capacity. Sensibly as a man has lived, sensibly as a man has aged, there can be no guarantee against that man's suffering greatly in spirit and in body before he is finally released.

If this old man is sensible, he will recognize the inevitable and march boldly or totter along feebly to the end, neither thankful nor of complaining spirit.

www.ingramcontent.com/pod-product-compliance
Ingram Content Group UK Ltd.
Pitfield, Milton Keynes, MK11 3LW, UK
UKHW041623031026
15587UKWH00001B/21